ECONOMICS
for Managers

ECONOMICS
for Managers

Geraint Johnes
University of Lancaster

Prentice Hall
New York · London · Toronto · Sydney · Tokyo · Singapore

First published 1990 by
Prentice Hall International (UK) Ltd
66 Wood Lane End, Hemel Hempstead
Hertfordshire HP2 4RG
A division of
Simon & Schuster International Group

© Prentice Hall International (UK) Ltd, 1990

All rights reserved. No part of this publication may be
reproduced, stored in a retrieval system, or transmitted,
in any form, or by any means, electronic, mechanical,
photocopying, recording or otherwise, without prior
permission, in writing, from the publisher.
For permission within the United States of America
contact Prentice Hall Inc., Englewood Cliffs, NJ 07632.

Typeset in 10½ / 12pt Garamond
by Colset Typesetter Ltd, UK

Printed in Great Britain by BPCC Wheatons Ltd, Exeter

Library of Congress Cataloging-in-Publication Data

Johnes, Geraint, 1958–
    Economics for managers / Geraint Johnes.
      p. cm.
    Includes bibliographical references (p.   ).
    ISBN 0-13-224585-X : £15.95 (U.K.)
      1. Managerial economics. 2. Economics. I. Title.
HD30.22.J64   1990   90–6960
338.5'024'658—dc20   CIP

British Library Cataloguing in Publication Data

Johnes, Geraint, *1958–*
    Economics for managers.
    1. Economics
    I. Title
    330

    ISBN 0-13-224585-X

1 2 3 4 5   94 93 92 91 90

To my parents

Contents

Preface xi
Acknowledgements xiii

Chapter 1 **Introduction** 1
Microeconomics, macroeconomics and managerial
economics 3
Economic methodology 4
Structure of the book 7
Prerequisites 8

Chapter 2 **Demand and supply** 10
Demand 10
Supply 15
Market price 18
An algebraic analysis 21
Exercise 23

Chapter 3 **Elasticity of demand** 25
Own price elasticity of demand 26
Other important elasticities 30
Engel curves and cross price demand curves 32
The demand function 33
Exercise 34

Chapter 4 **Empirical demand functions** 36
Statistical analysis of demand 36
Test markets 44
Gabor–Granger tests 46
The trade-off model 47
Exercise 51

viii · CONTENTS

Chapter 5	**Optimization in economics**	53
	The production function	54
	Isoquants	56
	Isocost lines and the optimum	58
	Applications of optimization theory	60
	Application of optimization theory to demand	62
	Exercise	64
Chapter 6	**Mathematical programming in economics**	66
	The method of Lagrange multipliers	67
	Extension to n dimensions and m constraints	71
	Non-linear programming in economics	75
	The general optimizing problem	79
	Linear programming	81
	Concluding comments	85
	Exercise	86
Chapter 7	**Costs**	87
	Fixed and variable costs	92
	Cost curves and product curves	94
	The cost of capital	96
	Exercise	99
Chapter 8	**Optimizing profits**	101
	Market structure	105
	Perfect competition	107
	Perfect competition and welfare economics	112
	Monopoly	113
	Monopoly and price discrimination	116
	Advertising and monopoly	118
	Exercise	120
Chapter 9	**Coping with uncertainty**	122
	Frankel's model of pricing under uncertainty	123
	The theory of games	126
	Statistical decision theory	131
	Example	135
	Exercise	138
Chapter 10	**Individuals and the economy**	139

Chapter 11	**The circular flow of income**	143
	The Kuznets puzzle and Friedman's theory of consumption	155
	Fiscal policy and monetary policy	159
	Exercise	159
Chapter 12	**The money market**	161
	ISLM analysis	167
	Diagrammatic derivation of IS and LM curves	173
	Real and nominal balances	177
	Exercise	178
Chapter 13	**The labour market**	180
	Aggregate demand and aggregate supply	180
	The Phillips curve	186
	Stagflation and expectations	190
	Empirical estimates of the Phillips curve	193
	Tying it all together	195
	Exercise	197
Chapter 14	**Foreign trade**	199
	Spot markets, futures markets and options	200
	The economics of the Dutch disease	202
	The balance of payments	203
	Purchasing power parity	208
	Graphical analysis	209
	Empirical studies	212
	Exercise	215
Chapter 15	**A macroeconomic model and its usefulness to the firm**	216
	The problem	217
	Solution	217
	Summary of results	227
	Conclusion	227
	Summary	230
	Exericise	230
Chapter 16	**Behavioural theories**	231
	Baumol's sales revenue maximization model	231
	The behavioural theory of the firm	237
	Exercise	243

Chapter 17	**Concluding comments**	244
Appendix 1	**Elementary methods of differential calculus**	247
Appendix 2	**Elementary methods of matrix algebra**	251
Appendix 3	**Ordinary least squares regression**	255
Appendix 4	**Profit maximization under monopoly in a two-period model**	258
References		261
Index		265

Preface

This book concerns the economics of management, but differs from other texts in this field in one important respect. While others concentrate on microeconomics applied in the business context, the present book emphasizes also the importance to the businessperson of a thorough grounding in macroeconomics. Only thus can a manager understand the economic environment within which the firm operates. This understanding is crucial for making correct pricing and marketing decisions as well as for planning future resource needs.

The book is generally oriented towards applied economics. Tools of analysis in widespread use – such as linear and non-linear programming, investment appraisal, demand estimation, decision theory and advertising analysis – are all discussed. The necessary theory is illustrated, where appropriate, by case studies and other references to empirical work. Each chapter is followed by exercises which use real world data. Hence the student will be able to estimate demand functions and cost functions, calculate profit maximizing prices under various market conditions (including uncertainty), and forecast values of key macroeconomic variables. I hope that this will convey to the student a sense of excitement and discovery as well as an appreciation of the power of economic techniques.

The book will appeal to students on a wide variety of courses; these include Master and Bachelor-level courses in Business Analysis (MBA or BBA), and second and third year undergraduate courses in managerial economics. It will also interest students on management development courses, refresher courses and conversion courses aimed at those who have entered management via an unrelated discipline. While accessible to students meeting economics for the first time, the approach differs from that typically adopted on introductory economics courses, so the book will also be suitable for readers who have some experience of elementary economics. The text assumes that the reader is familiar with the simple rules of differential calculus, as students will typically encounter these on other courses. Nevertheless, a straightforward introduction is provided in Appendix 1 for those who remain unhappy with the use of such techniques. The mathematics in the book should therefore be accessible to all students; it is there only to illuminate and illustrate.

The structure of the book is as follows. Chapters 1 to 10 concern the microeconomic issues which concern the firm. These include demand analysis, the study of costs and the structure of markets. Macroeconomic topics are then covered in Chapters 11 to 14. The material of earlier chapters is synthesized in Chapter 15, which examines the optimal response of the firm to predicted changes in the macroeconomic environment. Some alternative theories of managerial behaviour are studied in Chapter 16.

While I, of course, remain solely responsible for the shortcomings of the book, many others have influenced its contents. My colleagues at Lancaster have been generous in their advice and assistance. Some of them – including V. N. Balasubramanyam, Paul Ferguson, Jill Johnes and Jim Taylor – read all or parts of the book in draft form, and provided comments which led to considerable improvement in both exposition and substance. One could not wish for a better group of people to work with. The text has also benefited greatly from the superb comments made by its (anonymous) reviewers. Cathy Peck and her colleagues at Prentice Hall have been marvellous.

The help and support of my parents has also been an invaluable input into the production process of which this book is an output; the book is dedicated to them. My wife, Jill, is a constant source of encouragement both in work and at home, and deserves much more thanks than space permits here. To all these people I am deeply indebted.

If you have had the patience to read this far, I wish you luck on your course. I hope the study of economics gives you as much fun as it gives me. I have tried to make the book as lively and as clear as possible. If you have any questions or comments, please get in touch.

Geraint Johnes
University of Lancaster

Acknowledgements

I am grateful to Basil Blackwell Ltd for permission to reproduce material from the article by Sinclair and Sutcliffe (1982) *Oxford Bulletin of Economics and Statistics* pp. 321-38; to the Department of Agricultural Economics, University of Minnesota for permission to reproduce material from the article by Wetmore (1959) *University of Minnesota Technical Bulletin 231* p. 71; to *The Economist* newspaper for permission to reproduce material from the 1 March 1975 issue, p. 64; to the Department of Applied Economics, Cambridge for permission to reproduce material from *Cambridge Economic Policy Review* (1982) 8 2; to the HMSO for permission to reproduce material from the *Report of the National Food Survey Committee*; to Oxford University Press for permission to reproduce material from Wallis (1985) *Models of the UK Economy* 2nd edn; and to the South-Western Publishing Co. for permission to reproduce material from Halter and Dean (1971) *Decisions under Uncertainty*.

Chapter 1
Introduction

Economics is the study of choice. In particular it is the study of how individuals and groups decide to employ their productive capabilities, and how they decide to allocate between themselves the commodities thus produced. The problem, then, is one of allocating limited resources among unlimited wants.

Although economics is conventionally thought of as the study of choices which involve money – what should I buy? which worker should we hire? what will the levels of inflation and unemployment be if the authorities choose to raise the money supply by 5 per cent in the next year? – many of the tools of economic analysis are more generally applicable. For instance, the methodology of economics can be (and indeed has been) used to study why couples choose to marry when they do (Becker, 1976), and the behaviour of rats (Kagel *et al.*, 1975). The main concern of this book, however, will be the choices made by those involved in the management of a firm.

Any time a choice is made, one option is preferred to all others. A crucial component of any rational act of choice is the criterion (or set of criteria) by which preferences are ranked. For example, if I say that I prefer to sit at a concert rather than stand, my criterion of preference may be comfort. On the other hand, your criterion may be atmosphere and so you prefer to stand. Similarly, two otherwise identical firms may arrive at different pricing decisions because their order of priorities differ; one may wish to maximize its sales revenue while another may wish to maximize its share of the market. It is thus imperative that the criterion (or criteria) used by any decision-maker in ranking preferences is clearly defined; otherwise it would be impossible to prescribe the best choice in any situation. In the language of mathematical programming, there must exist an objective function, the properties of which are known.

For the economist to have any prescriptive power, something must be known about the firm's objective function (or criterion of preference). Since this is likely to vary from firm to firm one might be tempted to give up at this early stage and conclude that economics has little to offer. This would be an unjust and incorrect conclusion, however. Empirical observations suggest that the majority of firms act *as if* they try to maximize their profits, subject to a number of constraints on their behaviour. Shipley (1981) found that in 1979 profits were very important or of overriding importance in 77 per cent of the 728 United Kingdom manufacturing firms in his sample. Although this does not of course mean that all firms set profits as their sole objective, it does suggest that models in which firms try to maximize their profits are likely to provide good first approximations to real world behaviour. Intuitively, also, this seems a reasonable goal for firms to pursue. As an illustration of the way in which economic theory works we shall therefore be assuming profits to be the firm's objective function for much of this book. It cannot be overemphasized, though, that this is only an illustration; the techniques to be described in the remaining chapters are easily adaptable to firms whose criterion of preference is different. Indeed, some advanced theories of the firm in which profits are of little importance are discussed in Chapter 16.

For all its (assumed) concern about its own profits, no firm can afford to be an island, however. Firms in almost every industry face competition from other firms, both at home and abroad, each of which hopes to capture the same market. In certain industries, known as oligopolies, a few large firms constantly try to outwit each other by making frequent changes in their pricing and marketing policies aimed at attracting additional demand for their own brands. Industries in which many firms produce a certain product are also characterized by intense competition; firms which operate in industries which approximate such (so-called) 'perfect' competition, and which fail to adapt rapidly to new technologies, are quickly competed out of business. Awareness of the pricing policy of one's rivals is therefore a fundamental requirement for the survival and fitness of the modern firm. Whatever the objective function of the firm, optimal performance can only be achieved consistently given an awareness of its business environment.

Business environment is not confined to the actions of firms in one industry, though. The business environment of an automobile producer, for example, depends not only on the behaviour of rival motor firms. On the one hand, activity in the steel and other metal industries, the rubber and chemical goods industries will affect the costs of producing cars. The rate of general price inflation will influence the wage demands of workers in the automobile industry and so this, too, will be reflected in the firm's costs. On the other hand, the ease with which the firm's output can be sold in the market, that is, the level of demand, is likely to vary not only with rivals' pricing and advertising strategies, but also with the overall buoyancy of the economy; demand for new cars is higher during boom periods than during times of recession. The behaviour of a firm determined to optimize some objective function therefore depends critically on a whole host of factors, many of which lie outside the control of any one firm or group of firms in a particular industry.

For this reason a thorough acquaintance with the economics of aggregates such as national income, the general price level or unemployment rate is important for the business executive, just as a knowledge of economics 'in the small' is important. Optimal pricing, output and marketing strategies are determined equally by both those variables over which the company has some degree of control and factors that are totally beyond its influence. It is therefore necessary to be aware of the nature of all economic relationships which affect the firm. This includes the likely effect on the firm of government policies to curb inflation and/or unemployment, be these effects direct or indirect; there should also be an awareness of the effects of exchange rate fluctuations, of changes in the price of oil, of variations over time in business confidence, and so on. It is a difficult but exciting problem to be solved: like a player in an everlasting game of three-dimensional chess, the executive must react to each new development in the environment as it occurs, taking the best offensive or defensive action as the game unfolds.

Microeconomics, macroeconomics and managerial economics

It is conventional to divide the study of economics into two major parts – microeconomics (economics in the small) and macroeconomics (economics in the large). Though frequently studied separately, the two are closely related, macroeconomic aggregates being merely the sum of many microeconomic decisions which are in turn heavily influenced by macroeconomic factors. For instance, the national output is the sum of the net output of each individual producer in the economy; the net output of each firm will depend largely on the costs of raw materials, capital and labour services, which in turn depend on macroeconomic variables such as inflation and the interest rate. It simplifies matters very considerably, however, if micro- and macroeconomics are initially given separate treatment and then brought together at a later stage.

Managerial economics involves the application of both micro- and macroeconomic theories and methods to the decision-making problems faced by the management of firms. It might therefore be regarded as a study of mainstream economics with an emphasis on those parts of greatest interest to the firm, namely the theory of the firm, price theory, optimization, competition, oligopolistic interdependence, the macroeconomic environment, government policy and forecasting. Aspects of economics which are of less direct interest to the firm (such as social welfare, general equilibrium or public economics) are given correspondingly less attention. In this book somewhat more emphasis is given to macroeconomics than is usual in managerial economics texts. This reflects the author's belief that a firm can benefit considerably from an ability to predict the buoyancy of its market, and that this buoyancy is largely dependent on macro variables. That this is indeed the case has been amply illustrated in recent times by the 1987 stock-market crash.

Share prices depend in part on speculation and in part on the health of the economy as a whole. Once the underlying weakness of the American economy was appreciated by the buyers and sellers on the international stock exchanges, the speculative 'bubble' was sure to burst. This has not only reduced the value of individual firms in the market-place; the policy responses of governments to the crash have a direct impact on the future prospects of most firms. In Britain, the policy response came in the form of a reflationary budget in 1988. This, in turn, led to inflation and (later) high interest rates, and so raised the costs of production faced by many companies. So an understanding of macroeconomics can be of vital importance to the firm; its relevance is given further emphasis in the chapters which follow.

Economic methodology

In addition to providing a thorough grounding in economics, this text aims to give the reader a working knowledge of the tools of applied economics. It is important for the firm to know what pattern of demand it faces, how much of each of its products it can sell at any given price and at any given time. For this it would not be sufficient to talk in the general terms which are useful in theoretical discussions; precise numerical values must be obtained. That is, a firm must be able to estimate accurately the number of thingumajigs it can sell on 31 June 1990 if the price of each thingumajig is £1. To do this, statistical analyses of demand must be performed which might involve the extrapolation of future trends from past behaviour. Admittedly, a firm will never be able always to estimate the demand for its products with complete precision since the economic environment is subject to frequent but unpredictable disturbances (or 'noise'). But the more educated the firm's guesses are, the better. Statistical techniques commonly used to help solve this problem will be described later.

Another problem frequently faced by firms is that of how it should combine the available resources – both physical and human – optimally to produce its output. Suppose a firm wanted to produce 50 million thingumajigs a year. Some of the processes involved in the production of a thingumajig can be produced either by labour or capital; for instance, it can be painted by humans or by robots, it can be packaged by man or machines. The firm must choose which method of production – which combination of factors of production at its disposal – it will use. In general, the cheaper a given factor of production is in relation to other inputs into the production process, the more of that factor will be used.

If the cost of employing each of the factors of production remains fairly constant, and the effectiveness or productivity of each factor remains unchanged, and at the same time the firm's output stays the same, the problem is not very interesting – the same combination of factors is employed period after period. When the relative price of factors is changing, however, as in the 1980s, the problem of the optimal combination of inputs becomes much more important to the firm. Thus if the cost of labour is constant at £15,000 per annum per worker and capital costs are falling from £20,000 per annum per machine in 1980 to £15,000 per annum per machine in 1990, the tendency will be to substitute machines for workers (apart from the extreme case, considered later, where capital is a 'Giffen' good). But by how much? In order to answer this question the decision-maker must first know the precise relationship between the inputs into the firm and the output it produces; the 'black box' of production, in which all the components of the finished product – including labour, energy, machine time, thought and factory space – are mixed together is commonly represented by an algebraic equation known as a production function. The production function for a particular firm can be estimated using the statistical and econometric techniques of regression analysis. Once the decision-maker knows what the firm's production function looks like, then mathematical programming techniques can be used to solve the optimization problem, subject to whatever constraints might be in operation. These constraints might include the firm's borrowing capability, limits on the changes in labour and capital employment which take place in any given period, legal restrictions and union resistance.

A third area of the firm's activity on which the tools of applied economics can throw light is that of the firm's reactions to risk and uncertainty. No firm can predict the future with certainty, least of all those operating in oligopolistic markets. Oligopoly being the commonest form of market structure in advanced present-day economies, techniques which enable the firm to cope with risk and uncertainty might justifiably be regarded as particularly important tools in the modern manager's kit bag. Such techniques, based on the theory of games and statistical decision theory, cannot, of course, guarantee that a firm faced by an uncertain demand will never lose out because of that uncertainty; they will, however, if used properly, minimize the chances of such loss occurring.

These three areas of economic methodology applied to the firm are all at once important and exciting. All involve a battle of wills against rival firms seeking to capture the market. All involve the unravelling of a complex set of relationships between economic variables which themselves are not easily quantifiable. All involve day-to-day decisions. The use of such techniques is becoming increasingly common and has become particularly widespread in recent years since the sharp decrease in the price of computing time.

An equally important aspect of economic methodology, but one which does not concern the inter-firm conflict represented by micro models, involves the ability of the firm to predict changes in the macroeconomy. The demand for a firm's products is likely to be heavily dependent on such macroeconomic variables as the national income, the rate of interest and inflation. The firm's investment decisions are likely to depend on macroeconomic growth and interest rates. The better the predictions a firm makes about its environment, the better equipped it will be to handle future events. Fortunately, though, the firm need not do all the spadework itself; numerous empirical models of the macroeconomy now exist in the United Kingdom, each consisting of hundreds of equations describing various economic relationships. When solved simultaneously these systems of equations provide predictions about the future paths of national income, consumption, prices, employment and any other macroeconomic variables of interest. Some of the better known models are the Cambridge model, London Business School model, Treasury model and the Liverpool model. Not all the models make the same predictions, however. This is because the internal structures of the models are different. It is possible, therefore, for one model to predict better than another during times of recession, but for the second model to be better during a time of recovery. In order to exploit these macroeconometric models to best advantage, therefore, the manager should know something about how they work. For this reason we shall be looking at large scale econometric models and their relevance for the individual firm. Again this is an exciting field in which many well-publicized macroeconomic controversies are fought.

The applied economics of running a firm successfully certainly represent an interesting challenge. But before diving head first into a sea of empiricism it is necessary to have a secure grounding in theory. Just as an engineer must plan a bridge before it is built, if it is to be a stable structure, the economist must plan and test a model before it is put into practice. Otherwise there is no guarantee of its robustness. Theory is the tool by which the economist's plans are made. Many economic controversies are discussed in theoretical terms, and the theory is often every bit as vital and stimulating to the economist as is applied work; business executives, however, will not in general be practitioners of theory, since they have their hands full with the applied everyday problems of their firm. They should none the less keep abreast of major theoretical developments both because they will affect the ways in which applied models are set up and because they are interesting in their own right.

Throughout this book, the reader should continue to bear in mind the fact that economics is not an exact science. Moreover, modern firms are complex structures, typically consisting of many disparate groups of individuals whose goals are often in conflict. Consequently, managers cannot and should not be mindless slaves of economic analysis. Discretion and the ability to compromise, together with a sympathy for the organizational culture of the firm, are important requisites of a good manager. Nevertheless, as the above discussion indicates, the potential benefits to a firm of granting economic methods a central role in its decision-making process are considerable.

Structure of the book

As indicated above a good grounding in theory is a prerequisite for the successful application of techniques. The structure of this book reflects that. Chapters 2 to 9 concern microeconomic theory and tools of applied analysis. The next five chapters concern macroeconomics. In these chapters a model of the whole economy is constructed piece by piece. A full macroeconometric forecasting model is presented in Chapter 15, together with an analysis of the implications of its forecasts for the individual firm. Finally, some alternative models of business behaviour are considered.

The schematic diagram shown in Figure 1.1. may help explain the structure of the book more clearly. Each of the major macroeconomic markets we shall study influences and is influenced by the decisions of individual households and firms concerning job search, saving and the everyday buying and selling of goods and services. Furthermore, the optimal behaviour of firms depends also on the choices made by households and by other firms which compete in the same market. It is the mutual interdependence of many economic relationships, indicated in the diagram by the double-headed arrows, which makes the study of economics interesting, but also sometimes necessarily difficult.

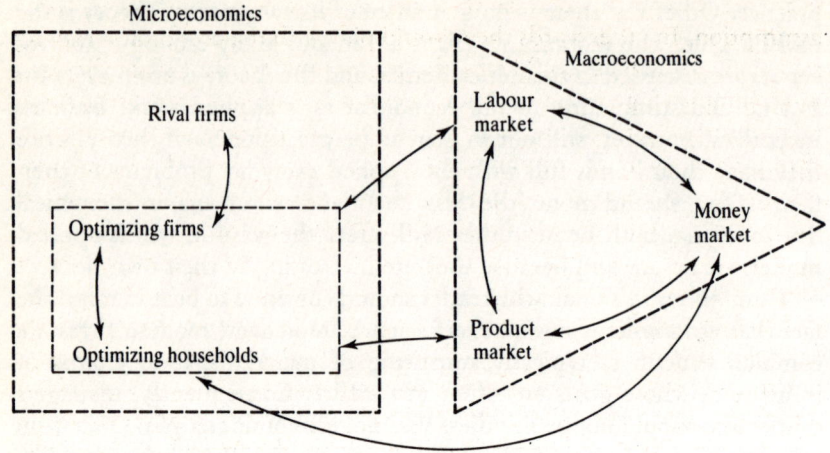

Figure 1.1 Basic approach to managerial economics

Prerequisites

While those who have studied economics before will have a natural advantage in approaching this book, it is intended to be of equal value to students coming to the subject for the first time and those who have already undertaken an introductory course. The emphasis on methodology requires some aptitude for mathematics. In the text a familiarity with simple differential calculus and matrix algebra is assumed. For the student who has not encountered these ideas before, they are described in Appendices 1 and 2 at the end of the book, where references to more detailed expositions are also given. Throughout the book, knowledge of simple algebra is taken for granted.

Having outlined these prerequisites, it should be added that no reader should despair of the mathematics in the book. They are there to aid precision, to clarify and illuminate the economics. The economics can be understood without mathematical equations, and computer software which facilitates the use of mathematical techniques described in the chapters which follow is now commonly available. For the most part, then, the mathematics are not an indispensible part of the exposition. None the less, any serious student who hopes to use economics in practical applications can and should master them fully.

Students should approach their reading actively. That is, they should be prepared to argue with the text and to follow their arguments through carefully and fully. If the derivation of a result is puzzling they should work it out for themselves. When a diagram appears they should ask how it would change in response to a change in some parameter or some assumption. In other words they should play with the economics. Having said that, students should resist the temptation to run before they can walk. Simplifying assumptions are essential if economic arguments are to be understood, and these assumptions often seem to beg relaxation; but if too many such assumptions are dropped simultaneously the analysis often gets very lengthy and untidy. Mistakes and total confusion all too easily result. So the general message is: experiment with the models, but always keep the experiments simple, changing only one parameter or assumption at a time.

Finally, students should always be on the lookout in the media for examples and counterexamples of the working in practice of the theories described here. If an event appears to contradict what theory would lead one to expect, they should ask themselves why. The potential rewards to the manager of a sound knowledge of economic theory and methodology are great. The study of economics is challenging and, if approached actively, can itself be both very enjoyable and rewarding.

Chapter 2
Demand and supply

Microeconomics is the study of decisions made by individual economic agents such as a household or a firm. It involves the manner in which consumers decide what goods they should buy with their income and also the way in which firms make decisions on labour employment, advertising, pricing and output levels. Prices of goods and the quantities a firm produces and sells are determined by the interaction of decisions made by firms and their customers. In setting its price, a firm must consider not only what it costs to produce a commodity but also how much of the product it can sell. No firm can operate without some knowledge about the behaviour of its customers. The starting point of our analysis will therefore be the way in which firms and households interact to determine prices and quantities.

A market is defined as a communications link between buyers and sellers. It is often a very direct link like a meeting at a particular geographical location such as a shop. Sometimes, however, the market may be a telephone line (for example, when I book tickets for the theatre) or a postal service (for instance, when I buy Manx kippers by mail order). Any communication between buyers and sellers concerning the purchase and sale of a product takes place in the market for that product. The buyer is said to be on the demand side of the market and the seller is on the supply side. Each is interested in maximizing their own utility or satisfaction. Consider first the demand side.

Demand

A buyer demands a product if he or she is able and willing to purchase it at the existing price, given his or her income levels and the prices of all other goods. In this chapter we shall concentrate on the demand for final goods by consumers, that is demand generated directly by households.

Consumers wish to maximize their utility – that is, they wish to derive as much satisfaction as possible from the goods and services they consume – subject to the constraint that their resources or funds are finite. They will therefore wish to consume additional units of any good so long as these extra units add to their utility more than they subtract from their funds. In other words, they will continue to buy units of the good in question up to the point where they no longer get as much satisfaction from consuming one unit extra of that good as they would by spending their funds on an alternative use.

Let the total utility a consumer derives from the consumption of a given amount of a commodity, say beans, be defined as a measure of the satisfaction gained from the consumption of beans. The total utility of a typical commodity will rise as the quantity consumed rises above zero; beyond a certain level of consumption, however, the consumer will find that additional amounts of that particular commodity add nothing to satisfaction and may eventually even detract from utility. Thus the total utility curve of Figure 2.1 is derived; it initially rises steeply, but tails off at higher quantities where the consumer derives little benefit from the consumption of more of the good. Such a curve is said to be concave to the origin.

The slope, or gradient, of the total utility curve at any quantity level represents the change in the consumer's utility which occurs if one extra unit of the good is consumed. The economic term for this rate of change is the *marginal utility*. In general, the marginal unit is defined as the last unit added to a variable. Analysis at the margin is extremely important in economics – in practice it is the point at which all decisions are made (do I buy three beers or two?) and in theory it enables the use of powerful mathematical tools (such as the differential and integral calculus). The

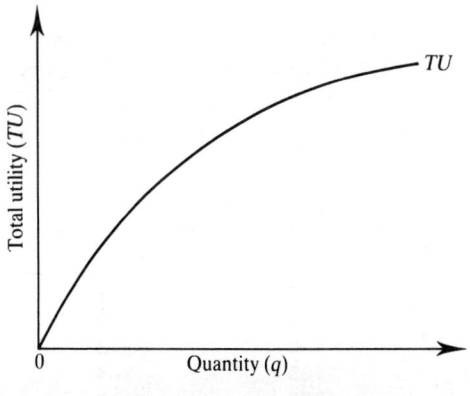

Figure 2.1 Total utility

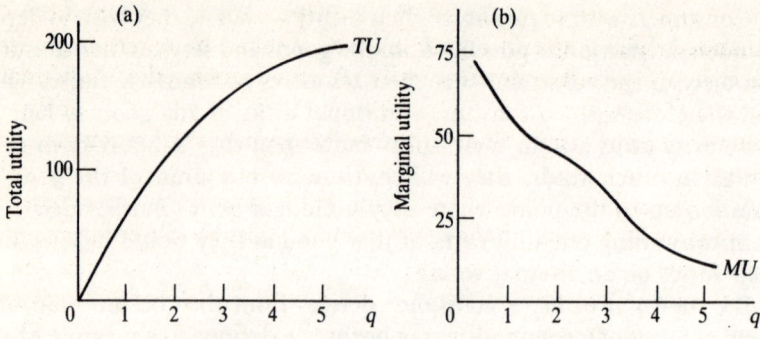

Figure 2.2 Derivation of marginal utility

marginal utility, then, is the increase in total utility enjoyed if one more unit is consumed. The way in which the marginal utility curve is derived from the total utility schedule is illustrated in Figure 2.2 using figures given in Table 2.1, for the case of an individual making consumption decisions about leather shoes.

The downward slope of the marginal utility curve results from the preference of consumers who already enjoy a large amount of the good in question to transfer their consumption to alternative uses. The underlying behavioural pattern is referred to as the law of diminishing marginal utility. Put simply, the law of diminishing marginal utility states that as increasing amounts of a good are consumed, the contribution made to total utility by the last unit consumed gets smaller. As is generally the case with economic 'laws', the law of diminishing marginal utility does not necessarily hold in all circumstances and at all times. It explains the rule but not the exception.

The marginal utility curve constructed in Figure 2.2 has a more concrete interpretation than our discussion up till now would suggest. Suppose the price of leather shoes was £45 per pair. How many pairs would our consumer be willing and able to buy? Clearly, two pairs would be demanded, since a third would not yield sufficient utility to compensate for the outlay of cash involved in buying it. For a similar

Table 2.1 The utility function of leather shoes

Number of leather shoes	Total utility (£)	Change in number	Marginal utility (£)
1	70	0–1	70
2	120	1–2	50
3	160	2–3	40
4	185	3–4	25
5	200	4–5	15

reason, if the price of each pair of shoes was £20, four pairs would be demanded. The graph in Figure 2.2 which shows marginal utility as a function of quantity therefore tells us much about the individual's demand for leather shoes. (This assumes that the marginal utility of money is constant, since otherwise money cannot be used as a measure of utility.)

A *demand curve* shows the quantity of a product which will be demanded over a specified time period at each possible price. In general it slopes downwards from left to right so that less of the good is demanded as the price rises. It is drawn subject to the constancy of income, tastes and the prices of all other goods.

What would be the effect on demand if the condition on the constancy of income is violated? Suppose income increases. The utility sacrificed by the consumer as a result of spending money on leather shoes rather than on other goods will be reduced at each and every quantity level. Thus the total utility curve pivots up, and the marginal utility curve shifts out away from the origin (see Figure 2.3). A rise in income therefore leads to an outward shift in the demand curve. Conversely, if income falls, the demand curve will shift in towards the origin.

There are exceptions to this general rule. The demand for certain goods, known as *inferior goods*, falls as income rises, so that the demand curve shifts to the left in response to a rise in incomes. This is because as

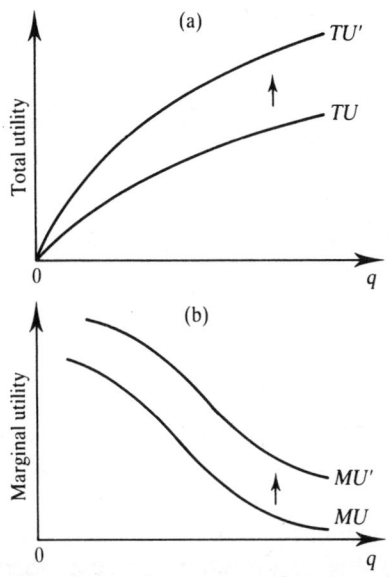

Figure 2.3 Shifting the utility functions

the consumer's budget increases more options become available. Consequently, the demand for goods which have close (but more expensive) substitutes sometimes varies inversely with income. Examples of such goods are offal, tobacco or coal. It should be noted that the term 'inferior good' is a piece of economist's terminology which has a precise mathematical meaning – namely, that demand for the good varies negatively with respect to income. It does *not* imply that a good is nutritionally or technically inferior to any other product; neither does it imply that the economist is making an adverse value judgement about a product's intrinsic worth.

Now suppose that, whenever leather shoes are purchased, the consumer also buys a pair of rubber soles which are to be glued to the shoes. A substantial rise in the price of soles would significantly raise the total price of the footwear (even if the price of the shoes themselves does not change) and so the demand for shoes would fall. Shoes and rubber soles are examples of complementary goods – they are usually consumed together. If the price of shoes made of synthetic materials were to fall, the demand for leather shoes would be adversely affected, because the utility given by footwear can now be bought more cheaply elsewhere. Leather shoes and shoes made of man-made materials are known as substitute goods.

A further factor which can affect the position of the demand curve is a change in the consumer's tastes. A new fashion in leather shoes would, other things being equal, shift the demand curve for such shoes out away from the origin to the right. A new fashion in shoes made of man-made products would shift the demand curve for leather shoes in and to the left. (A vivid example of the influence of tastes on the position of the demand curve was provided in 1989 by the food-health scare. At that time the demand for eggs plummeted as a result of public concern over salmonella, and concern over listeria reduced the demand for certain types of cheese.)

It is convenient at this stage to assume incomes, tastes and prices of all other goods constant, so that the relationship between quantity demanded and the price of a product can be examined in greater detail. Later we shall analyse demand where all its determinants are changing at the same time, but we must first discuss the simple case in which only price variations are considered.

Hitherto we have considered the demand curve of a single consumer only. This is of limited interest to the firm; of considerably greater interest is the market demand curve, which shows how many units of a commodity the firm can expect to sell in the market at any given price during any given time period. The market demand curve is the horizontal summation of all individual consumers' demand curves. If the demand curve of every individual is downward sloping, then so must be the market demand curve. Of course, the market demand curve is also drawn

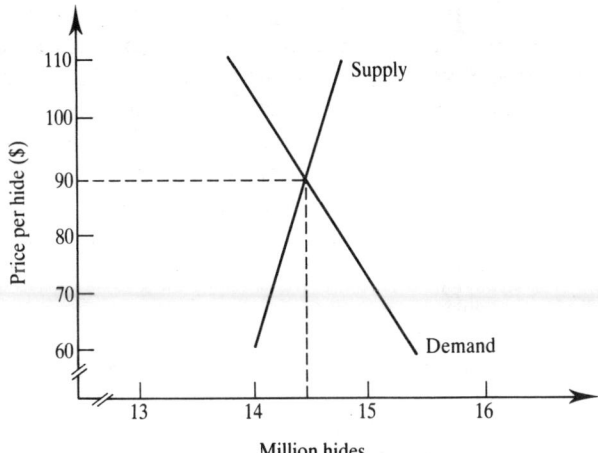

Figure 2.4 Demand and supply

subject to the constancy of incomes, tastes and the prices of all other goods.

Figure 2.4 shows the market demand curve for net American exports of cattle hide in 1969. (This has been calculated from the ordinary least squares regression results reported by Farris (1971). The price is measured in 1958 dollars, and the quantity variable represents millions of hides.) It is easily observed that the market demand curve for hide exports is downward sloping and is fairly steep. This indicates that quite large changes in the price of the hides would – all else being equal – result only in fairly minor changes in the quantity demanded. This is likely to be because many consumers still regard leather as a commodity for which there are no close substitutes. A further observation made by Farris is that a 10 per cent increase in the supply of cattle hide by non-United States producers would in 1969 have led to a fall of 1.3 million in the quantity demanded at each price. As we shall see later, this would have led to a quite dramatic fall in the market price of hides from $90 to around $50 per hide.

Supply

Having introduced the theory of demand, we can now turn to investigate the supply side of the market. Just as a demand curve is constructed for the consumer, a supply curve can be constructed which illustrates the quantities of a product which a firm is able and willing to sell at various

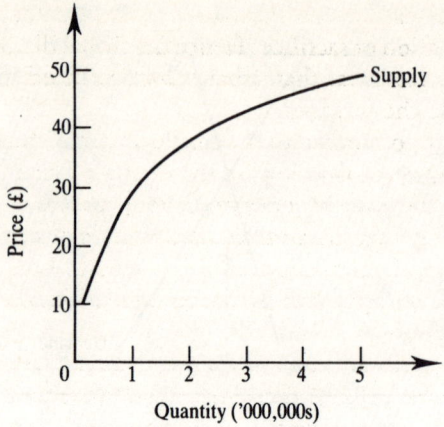

Figure 2.5 The supply curve

prices. The interests of firms conflict with those of individual consumers, however, in that the firm's objective function will generally be maximized if greater quantities are sold as the price increases. For instance, if the firm wishes to maximize its profits or its sales revenue optimal output will rise with price. Consider a tobacco manufacturer; as the price of cigars goes up (all other prices remaining constant) the manufacturer will, where possible, take production lines out of cigarette production and use them to produce cigars. A typical supply schedule for a firm is shown in Figure 2.5 with the values given in Table 2.2.

On what, then, does supply depend? A major determinant of supply is the opportunity cost to the firm of producing the goods in question. The term 'opportunity cost' means the value of the best alternative which has been sacrificed. This is an extremely important concept in economics, and its value is best demonstrated by way of an example. The (opportunity) cost to a student of three years of study does not simply consist of course fees; it includes also the potential earnings which the student has sacrificed by withdrawing from the labour market during the period of

Table 2.2 The variation of supply with price

Price (£)	Number of shoes supplied
10	15 000
20	50 000
30	100 000
40	250 000
50	500 000

studies. It is thus easily seen that the true measure of costs inevitably includes an evaluation of sacrifice. Hence the firm will not (ordinarily) sell its output for a price lower than what it has sacrificed in order to manufacture or provide the product.

It is an easy step to proceed to the conclusion that the supply curve will not usually exist at very low prices. In the example given in Figure 2.5, the firm supplies 15,000 pairs of shoes when the price is £10. It is at this level of output that the firm maximizes its objective function, given price. Suppose the costs of production fall. The firm is now able to produce 15,000 units more cheaply than before and (unless it is the sole supplier of the good) it must pass on at least part of this saving to the consumer in the form of reduced prices; otherwise other firms in the same industry will be able to undercut the price of the company in question thereby attracting consumers away from that firm. Consequently a fall in costs results in a downward shift of the supply curve.

In addition to the overall level of costs, further factors will influence the shape of the supply curve. First, the supply curve will rise more steeply the rarer the commodity being produced. For example, the works of a dead artist exist in limited numbers only, and the supply curve for such items would tend towards the vertical as the upper quantity limit is approached. Secondly, the greater the role of capital (such as plant and machinery) in the productive process, relative to labour, the steeper will be the supply curve. This is because labour input is relatively easy to vary over short periods of time – overtime can be worked, new workers can be hired – but adjustments (particularly upward adjustments) in the firm's stocks of machinery take much longer. The firm may have to order a new machine months in advance of the time it comes into operation. If machines are not easily substitutable by labour, therefore, the scope for varying output over short periods will be very limited, and this will result in a steep supply curve in the short run. A closely-related determinant of the shape of the supply curve is the time period under consideration. The longer the time period, the greater the scope for making changes in the capital stock and so the flatter will be the supply curve.

Just as it was useful to define the market demand curve as the sum of demands of all consumers in the market, so it is useful for us to define a market supply curve. The market supply curve is the horizontal summation of all individual sellers' supply curves. It will be flatter than the supply curve of a typical firm currently in existence; this is because at higher prices new firms will be attracted into the market thus further augmenting market supply.

The market supply curve for net US exports of cattle hides in 1969 is illustrated in Figure 2.4. The data from which this curve was constructed appear in Table 2.3. As theory predicts, the curve is upward sloping

18 · ECONOMICS FOR MANAGERS

Table 2.3 Demand and supply of cattle hide exports, United States, 1969

Price per hide ($)	Quantity demanded (mill)	Quantity supplied (mill)
60	15.4	14.0
70	15.1	14.2
80	14.8	14.3
90	14.5	14.5
100	14.2	14.7
110	13.8	14.8

from left to right. It slopes quite steeply, thus reflecting the fact that cattle take time to grow. So substantial variations in the supply of hide cannot be achieved within a short space of time, regardless of the price.

Market price

We have now arrived at a crucial stage in the determination of prices and quantities. Market demand and supply curves have been defined; as is seen in Figure 2.4, the market demand curve slopes downwards from left to right while the market supply curve slopes in the opposite direction. At only one point are buyers able and willing to purchase exactly the same quantity of goods as sellers want to produce and take to the market: this is the point of intersection of the two curves. In our example, this is where 14.5 million hides are sold at a price of $90 each. When the price is $90, therefore, demand equals supply and the wants of buyers coincide with the wants of sellers. In other words, the market clears – no resources are wasted in the production of unwanted goods and there are no unsatisfied demands.

But nothing said so far can guarantee that the market will settle at this point. Is there a mechanism which guarantees that the market will converge on this price? The answer turns out to be 'yes'.

Suppose the price is fixed at $110. Some 13.8 million hides are demanded at this price, but producers will want to sell 14.8 million. If firms actually produce 14.8 million hides, they would soon see their inventories (or stocks) of finished products rising; they would not want their stocks to increase *ad infinitum* and so they would be forced to reduce their price in order to sell off undesired inventories. If, on the other hand, the firms produce only 13.8 million hides, there would be no inventory accumulation, but the firms would be operating inefficiently – they are not maximizing their objective functions, subject to the constraints imposed by the demand side of the market, unless they are operating on their supply curves. In order to promote the optimization of their goals, therefore, the firms must again reduce their price. In this way they can sell more hides at the lower price.

Suppose now that the price is fixed at $60. The demand exists for 15.4 million hides, but firms are willing to supply only 14 million. Consumers are thus rationed. Firms realize that they would be able to sell more hides at a higher price, and so the price is pushed upwards.

To sum up, then, if the price is above the price which equates supply and demand, a situation of *excess supply* (or surplus) exists and downward pressure is exerted on price; conversely if the price is below the price which equates supply and demand, a situation of *excess demand* (or shortage) exists and upward pressure is exerted on price. The price of a product will therefore tend to the level at which supply equals demand; in our example this is $90. At this level there is no tendency for the price to change in either direction (unless supply or demand curves shift) and so it is called the *equilibrium* price. (An equilibrium is a state of rest in which there is no in-built tendency to change.) It is also referred to as the *market price*.

So far, nothing has been said about how strong the tendency towards equilibrium is in practice. It is generally the case that markets in perishable goods such as fresh fruit and vegetables, dairy products or meat, and markets in fad goods such as skateboards, home computers and certain types of clothes must adjust fairly quickly to equilibrium (i.e. within days or, at most, months). Firms cannot allow stocks to accumulate for long since they would either rot or become dated. In many service industries the accumulation of stocks is impossible and so convergence to equilibrium will be very rapid. If the goods in question are durable and not subject to rapid changes in tastes, however, prices may be held above or below equilibrium over a fairly long period if the firms want to adjust their stock levels. Even so, price cannot be held out of equilibrium indefinitely, since the warehousing costs attached to high levels of inventory preclude this.

A second influence on price which distorts the simple supply and demand analysis is the existence of government taxes and subsidies. Taxes like VAT (value added tax) shift the supply curve up, while subsidies may shift the supply curve down, as was (until recently) the case in the coal and steel industries. In many cases, though, subsidies work by distorting the shape of the demand curve. The Common Agricultural Policy of the European Community (EC) provides an example of this. Farmers are quoted a guaranteed price for a product, say butter, by the authorities. This guaranteed price may be higher than the market price, in which case the authorities themselves buy the entire excess supply of butter. This distorts the demand curve faced by farmers so that it has a discontinuity at

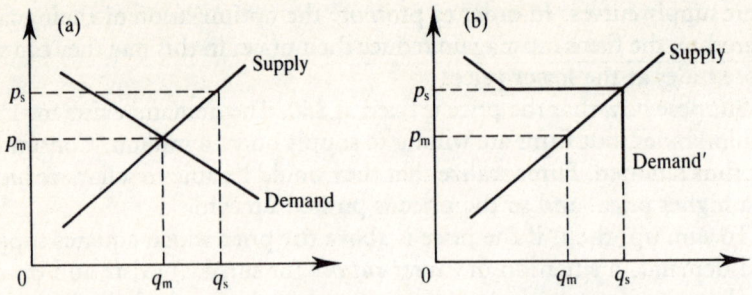

Figure 2.6 Agricultural subsidies (a) Without subsidy (b) With subsidy

the guaranteed price. This is shown in Figure 2.6a, where P_s represents the guaranteed price and P_m is the market (equilibrium) price in the absence of the subsidy. The equilibrium price after the subsidy is illustrated in Figure 2.6b, where the effect of the subsidy on the demand curve is clear. If the market price does not rise before the butter which has been bought and stockpiled by the authorities perishes, it is usually sold to non-EC countries at a lower price.

A third reason why market demand does not always equal market supply is that the firms setting prices do not have perfect information about the market. That is, they may want to let the market clear, but simply do not know what price would guarantee no shortages or surpluses. While they experiment in order to find the market clearing price, the market will be in disequilibrium.

Fourthly, certain markets are characterized by small but frequent shifts in the supply or demand schedules of individual firms. For instance, the price of copper varies very rapidly, and this affects the costs of the manufacturers of copper wire. However, the price of copper wire does not vary so frequently. This is because the costs of changing the price of copper wire frequently would exceed the benefits of doing so; copper wire manufacturers simply do not want the expense and inconvenience of recalculating their profit or revenue or market share maximizing strategy every time they buy more copper – the expense of doing so would likely outweigh the returns.

Finally, external effects can distort the simple picture of market equilibrium. Occasionally we can observe instances of a phenomenon known as market failure; one such example is given here. Suppose I am a landlord who owns several houses. I am considering selling one of my houses. The owner of the house next door keeps a very beautiful garden. Her work in the garden adds to the market value of my house, but she does not benefit from that. Suppose, on the other hand, that my neighbour's garden is overgrown and resembles a refuse tip. In this case the value of my house is reduced by my neighbour's actions, but she does not reimburse me. In neither case does the market price of my house reflect the true private costs of supply – I shall receive payment for my neighbour's hard work in her garden (or I will suffer financial loss as a result of her laziness).

Information deficiencies can also lead to market failure; suppose the house is haunted by a particularly malevolent spirit and that I am successful in hiding this fact from potential purchasers. I will receive a price for the house which may exceed the amount which the buyers would have paid had they been aware of the presence of the phantom before their first uncomfortable night in their new abode. External effects and market failure occupy a central role in the study of welfare and public economics. They are of less importance in the context of managerial economics, however, and will not be discussed further here. It is as well to be aware, though, that the market system does not always operate smoothly.

An algebraic analysis

In order to fix some of the important ideas of this chapter, a mathematical analysis may be helpful. Consider first a numerical example in which both the market demand and the market supply functions are straight line functions of price alone. That is, income, tastes and the prices of all other goods are supposed constant. Let demand be given by the equation

$$q_D = 20 - 2p \qquad (2.1)$$

and let supply be given by

$$q_S = 4p - 20 \qquad (2.2)$$

where p is price. Hence if price were £7, demand would be 6 units and 8 units would be supplied. In other words there would be an excess supply of 2 units. Equilibrium is achieved in the model when the amount demanded equals the amount supplied, that is, when

$$20 - 2p = 4p - 20$$
$$p = 20/3 \qquad (2.3)$$
and $q = 20/3$

This is shown diagrammatically in Figure 2.7.

A more general solution to the problem of finding the equilibrium

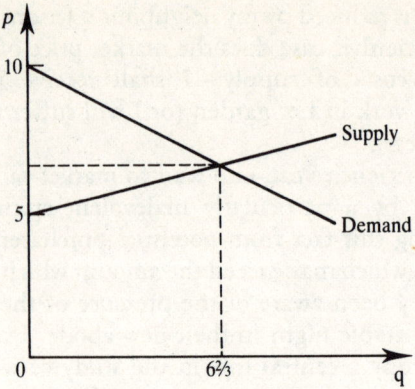

Figure 2.7 The market price

price can be derived if the following general linear demand and supply curves are used.

Demand $\quad q_D = a_0 - a_1 p$ (2.4)

Supply $\quad q_S = b_1 p - b_0$ (2.5)

Then, using the equilibrium condition that $q_D = q_S$,

$$a_0 - a_1 p = b_1 p - b_0$$
$$a_1 p + b_1 p = a_0 + b_0 \quad (2.6)$$

So (where an asterisk denotes the equilibrium value of a variable),

$$p^* = \frac{a_0 + b_0}{a_1 + b_1} \quad (2.7)$$

$$q^* = a_0 - \frac{a_1(a_0 + b_0)}{a_1 + b_1} \quad (2.8)$$

Equations (2.7) and (2.8) give, respectively, the equilibrium price and output for a market characterized by demand and supply curves given by Equations (2.4) and (2.5). The market price depends on the parameters of the demand curve as well as supply side considerations, since a_0 and a_1 appear on the right hand side of Equation (2.7). At the level of the individual firm demand again plays as crucial a role as supply in the determination of prices and quantities; this will be investigated in more detail in later chapters.

DEMAND AND SUPPLY · 23

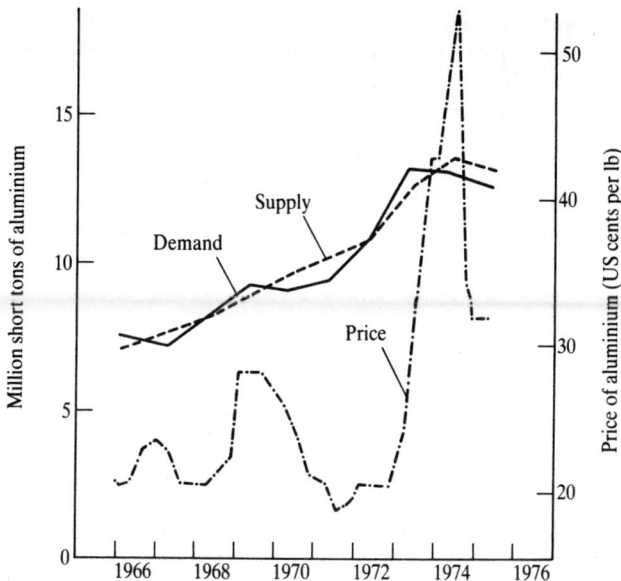

Figure 2.8 The market for aluminium (——— demand; ––––– supply; —·—·— price)

Source: *The Economist*, 1 March 1975, p. 4

Exercise: The price of aluminium

Figure 2.8 charts the Western world's demand for and supply of aluminium over the period 1966–75. The price of the metal (in US cents per lb) is also given. Over half of the world's output of aluminium in 1973 was produced by just five firms (Alcoa, Alcan, Reynolds, Kaiser and Pechiney–Ugine–Kuhlmann). The transport and construction industries are the major users of the metal, but it is also used as a substitute for copper in electrical work.

(a) What factors influence the demand for aluminium?
(b) What factors influence its supply?
(c) In which years did the demand for aluminium exceed its supply?
(d) How did price respond to this excess demand?
(e) In which years did the supply of aluminium exceed the demand for it?
(f) How did price respond to this excess supply?
(g) In some years demand equalled supply. This suggests that the price was at equilibrium at these times. Why might the equilibrium price have risen between 1968 and 1975?

(h) The demand for aluminium is very responsive to the health of the economy as a whole. This is why demand peaked in 1973 — a 'boom' year. If supply continues to be cut beyond 1975 what prediction can be made about the price of the metal during the next upturn in the economy?

(i) What was the likely effect of the price rise of 1973 on the demand for copper?

(j) Why does supply vary less dramatically over time than does demand?

Chapter 3
Elasticity of demand

It is often useful to have a summary statistic which measures the responsiveness of demand or supply to changes in price (or another of their determinants). A firm might not need to know the precise shape of the demand curve it faces if it has sufficient information to answer the question: If we raise our price, what happens to revenue? A particularly useful measure in this context is that of elasticity.

Elasticity is the ratio of the proportional change in some variable, x, to the proportional change in another variable, y, where the change in x is induced by that in y. The elasticity of x with respect to y, say η, is therefore given by

$$\eta = \frac{y}{x} \frac{dx}{dy} \qquad (3.1)$$

Here, dx/dy represents the rate of change of x with respect to y, that is, the slope of the function $x = x(y)$. (Here, the notation $x(y)$ means 'x depends on y'.) To maintain simplicity, most of the functions we shall deal with will be straight line functions of the form

$$y = mx + c \qquad (3.2)$$

where m and c are constants. The slope of such a function is m, and therefore dx/dy is $1/m$; that is, for every extra unit added to x, another m units are added to y.

The full power of the concept of elasticity will become apparent in later chapters, but something of the flavour of the idea and of its applicability should be appreciated at an early stage. Elasticities appear in many different branches of economics – demand analysis, monetary theory, finance, the theory of production functions and exchange rate theory, to name but a few. Indeed, they appear also in many disciplines other than economics: for instance, they are common in engineering, where they are often called 'exponents'. Elasticity is therefore a quite general concept, and its common use in economics in particular makes the investment of acquiring a sound familiarity with it well worthwhile.

Own price elasticity of demand

Probably the most commonly used type of elasticity is known as the own price elasticity of demand. The own price elasticity of demand of good A is the ratio of the proportional change in the quantity of A demanded to the proportional change in the price of A. If the own price elasticity of demand is denoted by η, then

$$\eta = \frac{p}{q} \frac{dq}{dp} \tag{3.3}$$

where p and q represent, respectively, the price and the quantity demanded of good A.

Since demand curves slope downwards from left to right the slope term in Equation (3.3) is invariably negative (this assumes away the possibility of an upward sloping demand curve such as that observed for Giffen goods – such cases are discussed in Chapter 5); so, therefore, is the own price elasticity of demand.

The higher the own price elasticity of demand (in absolute terms), the more sensitive is the quantity demanded to given changes in price, other things remaining equal. Conversely, the lower is the absolute value of η, the less will be the change in the quantity demanded induced by a given change in price. If $\eta = 0$, then no matter how great the change in price, the quantity demanded will remain unchanged; this extreme case is known as perfectly inelastic demand, and is illustrated in Figure 3.1a. The opposite extreme is shown in Figure 3.1b; this is the instance in which $\eta = -\infty$, that is, demand is perfectly elastic, the distinguishing feature of

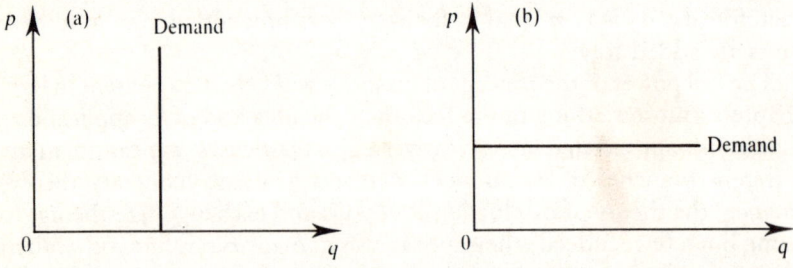

Figure 3.1 (a) Perfectly inelastic demand, (b) Perfectly elastic demand

this case being that a minute increase in the price of the good will reduce demand to zero while a minute price fall will generate insatiable demand.

Few real life demand curves would be so extreme, however. More precisely, few would be so extreme along anything more than short stretches of the curve. Consider the straight line demand curve

$$q = 100 - 2p \tag{3.4}$$

The slope of this function, dq/dp, is -2. If various levels of price are selected the own price elasticity of demand can be estimated over a range of the demand curve. For instance,

when $p = 10$, q must be 80, so at this point $\eta = -2 \times 10/80 = -0.25$

when $p = 25$, q must be 50, so at this point $\eta = -2 \times 25/50 = -1.0$

when $p = 40$, q must be 20, so at this point $\eta = -2 \times 40/20 = -4.0$

Thus, where the demand curve is linear, the absolute value of the own price elasticity of demand rises as price rises, other things remaining equal.

Consider the general linear demand curve

$$q = a - bp \tag{3.5}$$

At the mid-point of such a demand curve, $q = a/2$, $p = a/2b$ and $dq/dp = -b$. The own price elasticity of demand at this point is therefore

$$\eta = -b\left(\frac{a}{2b}\right)\left(\frac{2}{a}\right) = -1 \tag{3.6}$$

In other words, for any downward sloping straight line demand curve, the own price elasticity of demand will equal minus one at a point exactly half-way down the demand curve. Such a point is often said to have unitary elasticity.

Anywhere above the mid-point of the demand curve, $q < a/2$, $p > a/2b$ and $dq/dp = -b$. The own price elasticity of demand is therefore

$$\eta = -b\left(\frac{a+\delta_1}{2b}\right)\left(\frac{2}{a-\delta_2}\right) = -\frac{a+\delta_1}{a-\delta_2} < -1 \tag{3.7}$$

where δ_1 and δ_2 are arbitrary positive constants. Conversely, for points below the mid-point of the general linear demand curve it can easily be shown that $\eta > -1$. At the end points of the demand curve (where either p or q is zero) the own price elasticity of demand will be infinitely negative (where $q = 0$) or zero (where $p = 0$).

Figure 3.2 illustrates what we have established so far about the

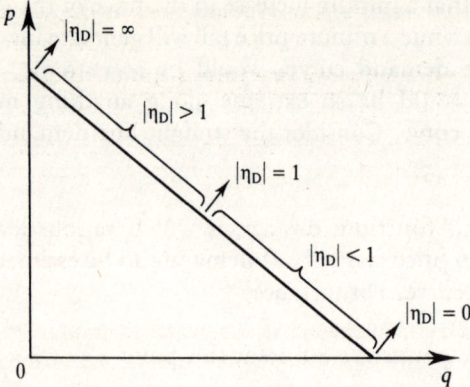

Figure 3.2 Elasticity of demand – the linear demand function

elasticity of the general linear demand curve. The absolute value of the own price elasticity falls smoothly from infinity to zero as we move from left to right along the curve, and is equal to one at the mid-point. Above the mid-point the demand curve is elastic; below the mid-point it is inelastic.

Figure 3.2 begs two questions: first, why use such an apparently complicated measure of the responsiveness of demand to changes in price when simple measures such as the slope of the demand curve are available? Secondly, what, if any, intuitive appeal does the concept of elasticity possess? These questions will be answered in turn.

The slope of the demand curve could certainly be interpreted as a measure of the responsiveness of demand to price changes. But this measure would suffer from a major defect, in that the units of measurement are critical. For example, consider the cattle hide example of Chapter 2. The slope of the demand curve is given by the change in the quantity demanded divided by the change in price, that is, $-0.3/10 = -0.03$. But if the quantities were measured in numbers of hides rather than millions of hides, the slope would be $-30,000$ – a substantial difference! Slope therefore has no meaning unless the units of measurement of price and quantity are also cited; this would clearly be inconvenient. Moreover this disadvantage is not one which applies to elasticity, since elasticity implicitly corrects the slope for scaling factors at each point along the curve.

The second question – that of finding an intuitive meaning for elasticity – is best answered in two stages. First, the importance to the individual firm of an understanding of elasticity will be clarified. Secondly, the identity of the concept of elasticity as a very simple, familiar and intuitively appealing mathematical concept will be established.

The relevance of own price elasticities of demand to a firm

Consider a firm which knows the characteristics of the demand curve it faces, at least in the region near the present price. So long as it is aware of the own price elasticity of its demand curve over the relevant range of prices it is able to tell immediately what effect a change in price will have on its revenue.

Suppose the absolute own price elasticity of demand is less than one. In this instance it is easily shown that $p/q < \mathrm{d}p/\mathrm{d}q$, and so $p\,\mathrm{d}q < q\,\mathrm{d}p$. Consequently an increase in price from p to $p + \mathrm{d}p$ will change total revenue from pq to $(p + \mathrm{d}p)(q - \mathrm{d}q)$. If the price change under consideration is very small (so that $\mathrm{d}p\,\mathrm{d}q$ may be considered negligible) this last expression may be written out in full as

$$\text{Total revenue} = pq + q\,\mathrm{d}p - p\,\mathrm{d}q \tag{3.8}$$

Now since $p\,\mathrm{d}q < q\,\mathrm{d}p$, the price increase of $\mathrm{d}p$ results in an increase of total revenue from pq to $(pq + q\,\mathrm{d}p - p\,\mathrm{d}q)$. In other words, if the absolute own price elasticity of demand is less than one, raising the price of the product serves to raise total revenue (revenue being the product of price and quantity). Conversely, lowering the price of the product would lower total revenue. Similar simple algebraic arguments can be employed to derive the full set of results below; the proofs of these results are left as an exercise for the reader.

If $\eta > -1$, a price rise raises total revenue, a price fall reduces total revenue

If $\eta < -1$, a price rise reduces total revenue, a price fall raises total revenue

If $\eta = -1$, any change in prices leaves total revenue unchanged

These results can be demonstrated in a manner which gives them more impact if a diagrammatic analysis is used. Figure 3.3 shows a price fall from P_1 to P_2 where demand is inelastic. Total revenue rises from the area of the rectangle $0P_1E_1Q_1$ to the area of the rectangle $0P_2E_2Q_2$. Figure 3.4 shows a price fall from P_1 to P_2 where the demand curve is inelastic. In this case total revenue falls, from the area $0P_1E_1Q_1$ to $0P_2E_2Q_2$.

It is therefore sufficient for a firm to know whether or not the own price elasticity of the demand curve it faces exceeds unity for it to be able to ascertain the direction of change of total revenue in response to a price change. A firm whose objective is to maximize its sales revenue will always want to produce at some level, q^*, of output where the own price elasticity of demand is unity, provided it makes sufficient profits to

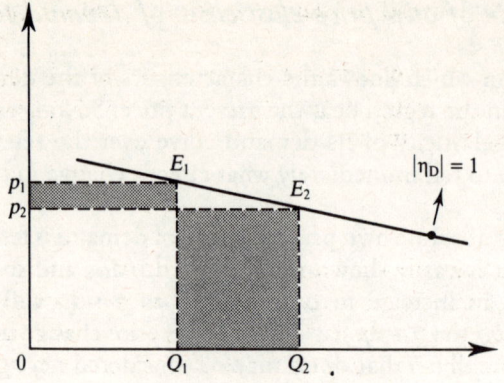

Figure 3.3 Elastic demand

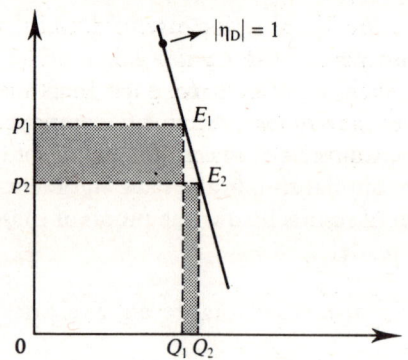

Figure 3.4 Inelastic demand

survive at this output level; at any other value of the own price elasticity, revenue could be raised by either raising or lowering price (and thereby changing output). The desired output of a firm wishing to maximize profit will be discussed in Chapter 8 and 9.

Other important elasticities

As was shown in Chapter 2, demand depends not only on the price of a product, but also on income and on the prices of all other goods. Just as there is an own price elasticity of demand, there also exist income elasticities and cross price elasticities of demand which measure the responsiveness of demand to changes in income and the prices of other goods, respectively.

The income elasticity of demand of good X, denoted by η_Y, is the ratio of the proportional change in the quantity of good X demanded to the proportional change in income, Y.

$$\eta_Y = \frac{y}{q}\frac{dq}{dy} \tag{3.9}$$

Usually demand for a good increases as income increases, so that $\eta_Y > 0$. For some goods, however (for example, coffee with chicory), $\eta_Y < 0$. Such goods are called inferior goods because as incomes rise consumption of such goods is reduced owing to a switch of demand in favour of a more expensive (but preferred) substitute. As well as helping the firms predict future demand (see Chapter 15), a knowledge of income elasticities might be useful for firms in deciding how to advertise a product. An inferior good should be advertised by drawing attention to its price, rather than by building up, say, an aura of sophistication.

The cross price elasticity of demand for good X with respect to good Y, denoted by η_{XY}, is the ratio of the proportional change in the quantity of X demanded to the proportional change in the price of Y.

$$\eta_{XY} = \frac{p_Y}{q_X}\frac{dq_X}{dp_Y} \tag{3.10}$$

If $\eta_{XY} < 0$, then X and Y are said to be complements. If $\eta_{XY} > 0$, then X and Y are said to be substitutes. Formal definitions of complements and substitutes and examples of each follow.

Two commodities, X and Y, are complements if the demand for X is positively related to the demand for Y. Examples of pairs of complementary goods include microcomputers and printers, or video cassette recorders and televisions. Two commodities are perfect complements if the consumption of additional units of either commodity yields no additional utility whatsoever unless extra amounts of the other commodity are also consumed. Such pairs of goods are usually sold together, like left shoes and right shoes. A rare exception to this rule is the case of left and right lenses in a pair of spectacles.

Two commodities, X and Y, are substitutes if the demand for X is negatively related to the demand for Y. Examples of pairs of substitute goods are bitter and mild beers, or Manchester United games and Blackburn Rovers matches. An example of perfect substitutes is a 1985 edition of the Ordnance Survey map of Kent marked 'scale = 1 inch to the mile' and a 1985 edition of the Ordnance Survey map of Kent marked 'scale = 1:63360'.

A firm must be aware of the prices set by firms producing close substitutes and close complements of its own product, and should also be aware of the relevant cross price elasticities if it is to set the price of its own product optimally. In this way the effect on the firm of the behaviour of other firms in the same industry can be incorporated in the price setting mechanism.

Engel curves and cross price demand curves

Just as the demand curve plots demand against the price of a produce (all else assumed constant), the relationship between demand and income, or demand and the prices of other goods can similarly also be plotted graphically.

An *Engel curve* relates the demand for good X to the income of the consumer, assuming tastes, the price of X and the prices of all other goods to be constant. For a normal good (that is, one for which $\eta_Y > 0$) the Engel curve slopes upwards. For an inferior good (where $\eta_Y < 0$) the Engel curve slopes down from left to right. A typical Engel curve is illustrated in Figure 3.5.

A cross price demand curve relates the demand for good X to the price of good Y, assuming constancy of tastes, incomes and all prices except the price of Y. If X and Y are complements the cross price demand curve is downward sloping; if they are substitutes the curve is upward sloping. These two cases are shown in Figures 3.6a and b, respectively.

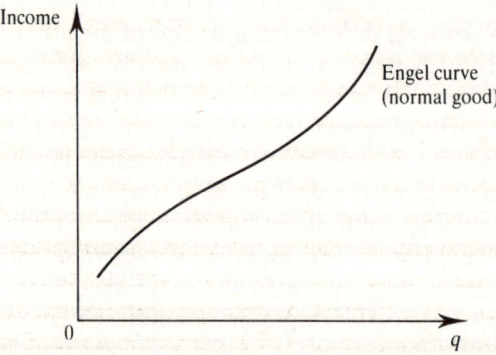

Figure 3.5 Engel curve of a normal good

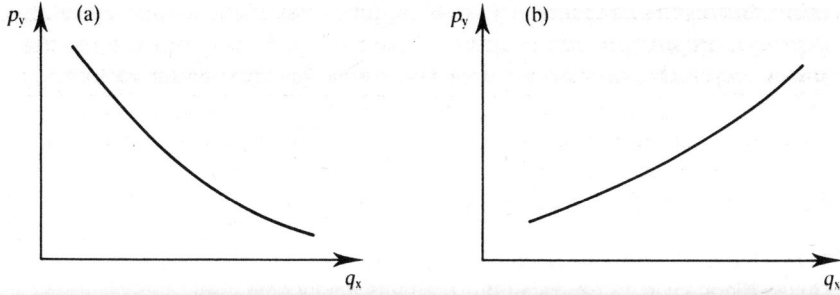

Figure 3.6 Cross price demand curves (a) complements and (b) substitutes

The demand function

The demand, Engel and cross price demand curves may all be viewed as two-dimensional cross sections of the multi-dimensional demand function

$$q_D = q_D(p, Y, p_1, p_2, \ldots, p_n) \quad (3.11)$$

Equation (3.11) means that demand depends on price, p, income, Y, and the prices of all other goods, $p_1, p_2, \ldots, p_n$. For practical purposes of empirical estimation the non-linear form

$$q_D = \alpha p^\beta y^\gamma p_r^\delta \quad (3.12)$$

is often used, where α, β, γ, δ are constants, and p_r is the general price level. The values of the constants can be estimated using statistical techniques like regression analysis. (Regression analysis is discussed in Chapter 4 and Appendix 3.) It can be shown that β, γ and δ are, in fact, elasticities.

■ **PROOF:** Consider the demand function $q = p^a$. Differentiating,

$$\frac{dq}{dp} = ap^{a-1}$$

Multiplying through by p/q,

$$\text{elasticity} = \frac{p}{q}\frac{dq}{dp} = ap^{a-1}p/q = a$$

□ *End of proof*

Thus elasticities are capable of a quite simple mathematical interpretation: an elasticity of variable x with respect to variable y is nothing more sinister than a power of y. In Chapter 15 we shall use the elasticities discussed in the present chapter to calculate a firm's optimal pricing policy, given the forecasted values of various macroeconomic variables.

Exercise: Demand elasticities for food

Table 3.1 shows the own price elasticity of demand for food groups in the United Kingdom in 1972. Table 3.2 presents the income elasticities of demand for food in the United Kingdom in 1972. Table 3.3 gives own and cross price elasticities of the demand for various food groups in the United States in 1957.

(a) What does the sign on the own price elasticities in Table 3.1 indicate about the slope of the demand curve for these goods?

(b) Why is the own price elasticity of demand for meat lower (in absolute terms) than the corresponding elasticities for beef, mutton and pork?

Table 3.1 Own price elasticities
Source: Report of the National Food Survey Committee, MAFF (1974).
© Crown Copyright 1989

Sugar	0.00
Eggs	0.00
Beef and veal	– 1.06
Mutton and lamb	– 0.91
Pork	– 1.19
Meat	– 0.70
Potatoes	– 0.08
Oranges	– 1.01
Pears	– 1.61
Bananas	– 1.22
Bread	– 0.76

Table 3.2 Income elasticities
Source: Report of the National Food Survey Committee, MAFF (1974).
© Crown Copyright 1989

Milk	0.12
Cream	0.90
Cheese	0.34
Beef and veal	0.28
Mutton and lamb	0.39
Pork	0.44
Eggs	0.13
Butter	0.32
Margarine	– 0.28
Fresh fruit	0.59

Table 3.3 Own and cross price elasticities of demand
Source: Wetmore (1959).

	Effect of 1 per cent change in the price of				
Demand for	Meat	Dairy products	Eggs	Fruit	Vegetables
Meat	– 0.60	0.10	0.04	0.08	0.06
Dairy products	0.21	– 0.50	0.02	0.00	0.06
Eggs	0.29	0.08	– 0.58	0.00	0.00
Fruit	0.33	0.00	0.00	– 1.00	0.20
Vegetables	0.22	0.10	0.00	0.18	– 0.70

(c) Why are the own price elasticities of demand for sugar, eggs and potatoes lower than those for meat, pears and bananas?

(d) The own price elasticity of demand for eggs in the United States is estimated to be −0.58. The corresponding figure for the United Kingdom is zero. What might explain this?

(e) The demand for all foods appears to be sensitive to the price of meat — the demand for all types of food (other than meat) rises significantly as the price of meat increases. Why might this be?

(f) The demand for meat seems to vary relatively little in response to changes in the prices of other foods. For what reason?

(g) The own price elasticity of demand for fruit (in both the United Kingdom and the United States) appears to be greater than for other foods. Why?

(h) Explain the sign and magnitude of the income elasticity of demand for margarine.

(i) Why is the income elasticity of demand for cream so high?

(j) Why are the income elasticities of demand for milk and eggs so low?

Chapter 4
Empirical demand functions

To arrive at optimal decisions – whatever the objective function – a firm must have at its disposal information about costs and revenues. So far our attention has been focused on demand and supply in the abstract, but the introduction of empiricism into our analysis of prices and quantities clearly introduces a new set of problems.

Demand conditions, in particular, are notoriously difficult to quantify. While the firm may know how many units of output it can sell at the current price (given the level of personal incomes and the prices of other goods), the firm's perception of the demand for its product at various other prices is often conjectural. Several methods are available, however, which can help a business estimate, with as much accuracy as possible, the demand curve it faces. It is to an overview of these methods that this chapter is devoted.

Four types of demand analysis will be covered. First, statistical analyses which employ regression techniques are examined. The analysis of demand confronts such techniques with a number of difficult problems. Secondly, the use of test markets – experimentation in the field – is discussed. Thirdly, a more limited form of experimentation, namely Gabor–Granger testing, in which a panel of consumers answer a set of carefully constructed questions, is described and evaluated. Finally, we shall consider a method familiar to both theoretical economists and applied market research workers: the consumption technology approach, also referred to as the 'trade-off' model, enables some information to be gathered about the likely demand for certain newly developed products even before such goods are seen by consumers.

Statistical analysis of demand

The methods which underlie statistical analysis essentially derive from the techniques of linear regression. Regression analysis is a tool which is very widely used in applied economics, and indeed forms the basis of a whole sub-discipline, namely econometrics. A brief technical introduction to simple regression is provided in Appendix 3, but a comprehensive treatment lies outside the scope of the present book. Indeed a number of excellent textbooks have been devoted entirely to econometrics (see, for example, Johnston, 1972; Theil, 1971; Judge *et al.*, 1985).

Despite the technical nature of regression methods, the basic principles are quite easily understood. Suppose that the magnitude of one variable, y say, is believed to depend on the value of another variable, x. Suppose further that the relationship between the two variables is believed to be linear; that is, a graph which depicts their relationship would be a straight line. In this case, y is said to be expressed as a linear function of x. An example of such a function is the relationship between the surface area of a wall (x) and the volume of paint needed to cover it (y). If a wall measuring 10 square metres can be covered using 10,000 cubic centimetres of paint, then a wall measuring 20 square metres could be covered by 20,000 cubic centimetres of paint. This relationship can be summarized in the algebraic function

$$y = 1000\,x \qquad (4.1)$$

Now in economics – as in most applications also in the physical sciences – there are few relationships which can be so precisely quantified. Where large numbers of autonomous human beings make independent decisions it is inevitable that any aggregate relationship will be, to some degree, imprecisely measured. For example, consider a good the demand for which is perfectly inelastic with respect to income and the prices of all other goods. A demand curve could be drawn in price–quantity space using data acquired by observation over various time periods ('time series') or across various stores which sell the good at different prices ('cross section'). It is unlikely, however, that such a demand curve would be either a straight line or a smooth curve, because random disturbances to the underlying pattern will be common. It would be more appropriate, therefore, to draw all observations in the form of a 'scatter diagram' (see Figure 4.1). A 'line of best fit' can then be drawn through these observations. This is the straight line which most nearly fits the scatter of observations. (This is in the sense that it minimizes the (sum of the vertical absolute) deviations of the actual observations away from the line.)

The line of best fit can be estimated by eye; simply by looking at a scatter diagram the line around which all the observations are scattered can often be drawn with a reasonable degree of accuracy. In its simplest

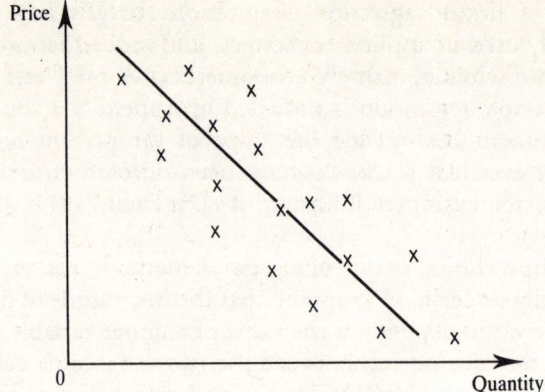

Figure 4.1 A scatter diagram

form, regression analysis is nothing more than a mathematical technique designed to do this with precision.

The ability to estimate a line of best fit by eye vanishes, however, as soon as more complicated functions are to be estimated. Consider, for instance, the introduction of income as a further determinant of demand. The scatter diagram would then have to be drawn in three dimensions (one for price, one for quantity and one for income). The 'line' of best fit would now need to become a two-dimensional plane, and this would certainly not be easy to draw (or even sculpt). In such circumstances, where two or more variables influence the 'dependent' variable, multiple regression analysis really comes into its own. Even so, the principle remains the same, and it is an essentially simple principle: the 'line' of best fit, whose equation is found by regression analysis, is the line which most likely describes the relationship being examined once random distortions have been removed.

At this stage it is appropriate to give a simple overview of the mechanics of regression analysis. In order to estimate the 'line' of best fit, the straight line is chosen which minimizes the absolute value of the (sum of the) discrepancies between the observed value of y and the value of y predicted by the 'line' itself. This then gives us the 'line' which most closely matches the observations plotted on the scatter diagram. Now mathematical convenience dictates that the most convenient way of reducing the sum of absolute discrepancies (or 'regression residuals') to a minimum is to minimize the squared value of the discrepancies. For this reason the technique is often referred to as ordinary least squares (OLS).

In the case of more realistic demand functions regression analysis can be used to estimate an algebraic equation which describes the 'line' of best fit in several dimensions. (Mathematical analysis is especially convenient to the economist because any number of dimensions are available – we are not constrained to refer only to the three dimensions that we can see.) The dependent variable is quantity sold and the set of explanatory variables typically includes the price of the products and general income and price levels. This is not to say that other factors do not influence quantity demanded, nor even that some such factors should not enter the regression equation as explanatory variables. Many variables influence demand, but the most useful approach in a statistical analysis is to identify only the most important determinants of the dependent variable. The dependent variable can then be 'regressed' against these key explanatory variables; enough right hand variables must be included in the equation to guarantee that the regression residuals are random, or else some important systematic variation would remain to be explained. Although a perfect fit is unlikely ever to be achieved, the statistical analysis succeeds in identifying the most important relationships.

Given the tools of regression analysis the basic problem seems simple: using computer software packages and data collected over a number of time periods the firm regresses quantity demanded against price, incomes, prices of complements, prices of substitutes and any other variables deemed important in the context of the particular product in question. Unfortunately, real world applied economics problems are almost never this easy. It is precisely such problems which make an active involvement in applied economics interesting however, and when a solution is the prey the thrill of the chase is highly addictive. Some of the commonest problems encountered in the statistical analysis of demand are discussed below.

1. Misspecification

Consider the hypothetical data shown in Table 4.1. Suppose the demand for buttons is a function of a constant and the price of zips, so that

$$q^d = 5000 + 200p^z \qquad (4.2)$$

Table 4.1 The demand for buttons compared with the price of studs and zips

Year	1985	1986	1987	1988	1989	1990	1991	1992	1993
Boxes of buttons demanded	5100	5100	5130	5120	5130	5142	5144	5140	5148
Price of studs	0.50	0.50	0.65	0.60	0.65	0.68	0.67	0.68	0.69
Price of zips	0.50	0.50	0.65	0.60	0.65	0.71	0.72	0.70	0.74

Suppose further that a button manufacturing firm mistakenly believes the demand for its output to be dependent on the price of studs, and using data from 1985 to 1989 estimates the regression

$$q^d = 5000 + 200p^s \qquad (4.3)$$

By using Equation (4.2) to estimate demand for 1990 and subsequent years the firm would be underestimating the quantity of output which consumers are willing and able to buy; in particular, in 1990 the firm believes it can sell only 5,136 boxes of buttons, whereas in fact it could sell half a dozen more.

The error in the above case is an example of misspecification. While the regression itself has been correctly executed, the firm has incorrectly postulated the form of the demand function by including an irrelevant explanatory variable and excluding a relevant one. Any time a relevant variable is missing from the set of explanatory variables (or any time an irrelevant one is included) the regression estimates are likely to mislead.

Misspecification can also occur if the form of the hypothesized function does not agree with that of the actual function. This can be the case even where the relevant variables have all been correctly identified. For instance, a linear equation might be hypothesized when the true function is non-linear. This would be an example of misspecification.

2. *Multicollinearity*

If two or more explanatory variables (say the prices of substitutes and the prices of complements) move closely together (or, in technical language, are very highly correlated with one another), then it becomes difficult to identify how much each variable is influencing the dependent variable. This is known as the problem of multicollinearity. An intuitive grasp of this problem can be acquired by likening the job of a regression to an identity parade of criminals: the more alike are the men on an identity parade the harder it is to pick the right one out; the more similar the behaviour of the explanatory variables in a regression, the less confidence can one attach to one's estimate of the impact of any one explanatory variable on the dependent variable.

In the context of business, multicollinearity might occur if a firm wishes to examine the impact of a promotional campaign for its product. Suppose that, during the campaign, advertising intensity has increased and the price of the product has temporarily been cut. Suppose also that the campaign is successful in that sales of the good increase. Because advertising and price both changed together, it may be difficult for the firm to determine how much of the increased demand for the good is due to greater advertising and how much is due to lower prices.

There is no cure for multicollinearity, but if the explanatory variables are less than perfectly correlated one with another a variety of techniques is available partially to alleviate the problem. (These include the use of principal components analysis and ridge estimators; see Theil, 1971.)

3. Simultaneity

One possible determinant of the demand for fish is the price of chips. Fish and chips are complements so that as the price of chips falls the demand for fish should rise. That is not the end of the story, however. As the demand for fish rises *upward* pressure is put on the price of chips, again because of the complementarity of the two products. The two variables concerned are simultaneously related to one another – each influences the other so that the single direction of causality implied by the estimation of a single regression equation leaves open the door to misleading results. An analogy which suits the case of a single regression applied to simultaneously related variables would be that of water finding its own level in two vessels connected by a tube and tap: a naive analysis (which does not account for simultaneity) would suggest that if all the water is initially in one vessel it will *all* flow to the other once the tap is opened. Of course, this ignores the fact that water flowing out of one vessel means that water must be flowing *into* the other; but this is precisely the kind of simultaneous relationship which is all too easily overlooked when handling economic data. Taking the simultaneity into full account, the familiar result that water finds its own level, at the same height in both vessels, is reached.

In order to account for the problem of simultaneous equation bias referred to above special least squares regression procedures such as two-stage least squares (2SLS) and three-stage least squares (3SLS) have been developed. Also the statistical technique of full information maximum likelihood (FIML) allows for simultaneity in systems of equations. The interested reader is referred to Johnston (1972).

4. Identification

Consider the scatter diagram shown in Figure 4.2a. The observations all lie around a downward sloping line which may be the demand curve of interest (Figure 4.2b). However, it is quite possible that far from being

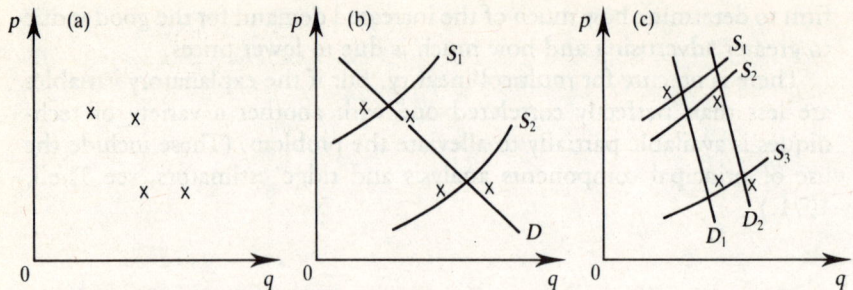

Figure 4.2 The identification problem (a) Scatter diagram (b) Supply shifts (c) Supply and demand shifts

points along a single demand curve, these observations describe points on many different demand curves (Figure 4.2c). Given the information of Figure 4.2 alone, we simply cannot tell what pattern of demand exists because the information does not enable us to identify whether a movement from one position to another is due to shifts of the demand curve or of the supply curve. This, in a nutshell, is the identification problem. Data on quantities purchased and on prices can only be used to estimate the demand curve in a cleared market when it is known that the demand curve has not shifted but the supply curve *has* shifted over the period of study. Otherwise further variables which influence demand but not supply must be included in the regression.

None of the above problems is likely ever to deal a fatal blow to a statistical analysis of demand, provided that the analysis is carefully executed. In practice, close examination of the data betrays problems. For instance, it is instructive to test for the presence of regression residuals which are unusual in some way; they might not be normally distributed, or there may exist some prominent outliers amongst the residuals. Such residuals may be the result of a misspecified equation or of simultaneous equation bias. Statistical tests (which are not discussed here) can reveal the existence of multicollinearity. The identification problem can be tested for by ensuring that not all explanatory variables influence both demand and supply. Once a statistical difficulty has been spotted steps can be taken to correct for it.

It should be emphasized that statistical and econometric analyses are tools most safely used in the hands of specialists. The above discussion of problems encountered in demand analysis is by no means exhaustive, but it is intended to serve two purposes: first, the student and practitioner of management techniques should be aware of the dangers of applying simple least squares or line-fitting techniques in the minefield of real world economic analysis. This is not to suggest that empirical analyses are *necessarily* subject to fatal flaws – quite the contrary – but in order to avoid such flaws statistical studies must be very carefully carried out. Ordinary least squares is simply not appropriate in situations in which one or more of its underlying assumptions is violated, and to try and apply OLS in such circumstances would be somewhat akin to using a compass to guide one to the true north pole. Secondly, a number of technical terms have been introduced and explained. This should provide the reader with at least an intuitive grasp of some of the most important concepts handled by those working in the field of applied economics.

Having solved the problems inherent in the curve-fitting process the demand function can be estimated. An early – and very general – example of a demand function fitted in this way is Tobin's (1950) estimate of the demand for food in the United States between 1913 and 1941. In this study Tobin fitted the log–log function

$$\ln q_t^D = a_0 + a_1 \ln Y_t + a_2 \ln Y_{t-1} + a_3 \ln P_t \tag{4.4}$$

where q^D is the quantity of food demanded; Y is mean income; P is the value of the food price index; the subscript t represents the tth time period; and a_0, a_1, a_2 and a_3 are the coefficients to be estimated. Taking antilogs Equation (4.4) becomes

$$q_t^D = A_0 Y_t^{a_1} Y_{t-1}^{a_2} P_t^{a_3} \tag{4.5}$$

where A_0 is a constant. Using US data for the years 1913 to 1941, Tobin is then able to perform the regression of Equation (4.4) – which is linear in natural logarithms – and arrives at the following estimated demand function:

$$q_t^{D*} = Y_t^{0.45} Y_{t-1}^{0.11} P_t^{-0.53} \tag{4.6}$$

where $q_t^{D*} \equiv q_t^D / A_0$. Thus the demand for food is inversely related to price and positively related to income and lagged income. This is illustrated in Table 4.2 which shows estimated values of q_t^{D*} for a range of possible values of the explanatory variables. Given that the value of income is known (or can be reasonably estimated), the firm can determine how many units of output it can sell at any price it chooses (subject to purely random error). Using this method, Tobin was able to explain 93 per cent of the variation in the demand for food.

While statistical analysis is a very useful and widely used technique for estimating demand functions for products already being sold on the market, a more difficult problem facing many firms is how best to estimate the demand for new products. It is to a discussion of three methods aimed at solving this problem that we now turn.

Table 4.2 The variation in demand with income and price over a period t

q_t^{D*}	Y_t	Y_{t-1}	P_t
4.27	100	80	8
3.80	100	80	10
3.44	100	80	12
4.37	100	100	8
3.89	100	100	10
3.53	100	100	12
4.75	120	100	8
4.22	120	100	10
3.83	120	100	12

Test markets

The most thorough method used to estimate the demand for a new product is that of the test market. The product is sold in a number of geographically distinct but otherwise similar areas at different prices in each area. Local radio, newspapers and – where available – cable TV can be used to advertise the product cheaply. The sales performance of the product in each area can then be evaluated and the demand for the good at different price levels can be compared.

The main advantage of the test market approach is realism. The new product itself is actually sold in competition with others at stores at which the consumer is accustomed to shopping. It is advertised alongside established brands through familiar media. To all intents and purposes, in the areas selected for the test, the good being tested is a genuine new product.

Since the product must be sold at suboptimal prices in some of the test markets, this is a very expensive form of market research test. Furthermore the test must be carried out at a late stage in the development of the product. Here lies an important conflict of interests between the marketing and market research departments of the firm: the former wants to know the likely price of the product as early as possible in the development of the good so that it can gear its advertising to the price and quality of the product; the market research department, on the other hand, prefers to set the price as late as possible in the development process, so that the most information can be used in making the price decision. It follows that a market test designed to provide information about demand for the new product – and hence about the optimal price – cannot on its own be helpful to both departments.

A further disadvantage of market tests lies in the possibility that two areas identified by the firm as similar may in fact have some important distinguishing characteristics overlooked by the firm. For instance, a firm might be able to define 'similar' areas by reference to *per capita* income alone: this might be justifiable in the case of many products, but suppose that the firm in question is a laver bread producer. Market tests might well show that in Area 1 more laver bread is sold than in Area 2, even though in Area 1 a higher price is charged. Does this mean that the demand curve is upward sloping? No. Suppose that Area 1 is in South Wales and Area 2 is in West Scotland. The reason for the seemingly strange result is simple: the firm had overlooked the fact that laver bread is a local delicacy in South Wales. The utmost care has therefore to be taken in selecting test areas which are truly homogeneous.

In an effort to reduce the high cost associated with test markets, many firms employ a small scale version of the test market approach. A mock 'shop' is set up by the company. This shop sells the new product plus a full range of substitutes manufactured by various other companies and sold at their current market price. Consumers are then selected at random to take part in the test, and are given money with which to buy whatever they want from the mock-up store. Over a period of time a range of different prices can be charged for the product (as well as different non-price characteristics such as packaging). In advanced experiments the consumers can even be shown videos of advertisements for the test product and for other brands.

This method has the considerable advantage of relative cheapness; further, it can be used relatively early in the development of the product without running the risk of damaging the reputation of the good over a whole area. However, it has two major disadvantages when compared with the full test market method. First, other firms may not hold the price of their products constant in response to the entry of the new brand. Similarly they might change their marketing strategy once the new brand comes on to the market. It is therefore likely to be very difficult to model the behaviour of rival firms. Secondly, the small scale test is a mock-up; the consumers involved know it is a mock-up and are likely to behave as if it is a mock-up. They would not approach the test as seriously as they would a real life shopping situation.

Even though they are usually much cheaper than full scale market tests, the mock shop tests are still an expensive tool of market research. We next discuss a test which – owing to its cheapness – is particularly popular in the field of market research.

Gabor–Granger tests

The Gabor–Granger test is essentially a survey procedure. Half of the respondents are shown a sample of the new product and are asked whether they would buy the new product at each price on a random list. This procedure is repeated for a similar product already being produced by another firm. The other respondents are shown the established brand first, so that no bias results from showing one brand before the other; otherwise the maximum price a consumer says she is willing to pay for the first brand shown may be higher than the second, simply because no alternative products have been considered.

Although Gabor–Granger tests have been very popular with market researchers, they have come under much criticism elsewhere. In particular, Baumol (1977) has described them as 'blatant and naive'. A number of problems throw doubt on the validity of the results of any Gabor–Granger analysis. First of all, do respondents mean what they say? Do they look closely enough at the product in such a test? Since they are not required to buy the product many consumers may give a quick, glib answer when interviewed, without considering the good at all carefully as they might when buying it.

Secondly, a respondent who is first shown a high random price will respond more favourably to other prices; on the other hand, someone who is first shown a low random price will be less inclined to accept other prices. Averaging over all respondents, there is likely, therefore, to be a bias towards the middle of the range of prices being offered.

Thirdly, different people will base their response on different assumptions. For instance, Ms Adams may answer the questions assuming that there are no brands available besides the two she is being shown. Mr Burkinshaw might assume that more brands are available, all at the same price. Dr Collins might suppose other brands are available, but she does not know the prices of these other brands. When Mr Daniels says he will buy the good, he means he will buy the good sometimes and another brand at other times. When Mrs Evans says she will buy the good, she means always.

Fourthly, different respondents will not buy the type of good concerned as often as each other: I buy three shirts a year, but my brother buys twelve. This is an important factor which many Gabor–Granger tests omit, and stands in marked contrast to the mock shop test where I can spend my money on string vests rather than shirts if my tastes so dictate.

Fifthly, it is likely that the knowledge of real world prices colours the respondents' replies. To illustrate the importance of this consider two soap powders, Cleenee and Razzam, the latter of which is a new product.

A respondent may accept Razzam at £1.00 per packet and reject Cleenee at the same price, simply because he saw packets of Cleenee selling for 95 p in his local supermarket last week. While he is comparing the fictional and random prices of Razzam to those of Cleenee, he also compares random Cleenee prices to real world Cleenee prices. Thus another bias is introduced.

A further problem with both Gabor–Granger tests and market tests is that they are static, snapshot analyses which depict the situation when the new product is still a novelty. They capture the impact effect of advertising and new product promotion, rather than the long run equilibrium effect – which after the market has settled down once more will likely differ quite substantially from the impact effects.

In certain circumstances it is possible to use a particularly inexpensive method of estimating the demand for new products; this method can be used very early on in the development of the product and is not subject to many of the criticisms that apply to the test market and Gabor–Granger approaches. The 'trade off' approach, as it is known, will be the subject of the next section.

The trade-off model

The trade-off method, as applied in present day market research exercises, closely follows the theoretical developments of Kelvin Lancaster (1966) in the area of 'consumption technology'. Rather than concentrating on the goods being produced, Lancaster's approach is to stress the *characteristics* of those goods. That is, instead of viewing the good itself as a provider of utility, the properties possessed by the good which yield utility should each be identified and given separate consideration. The best way to illustrate how this approach can help in estimating the demand for a new product is by way of an example.

Consider shepherd's pie. Suppose two brands of frozen shepherd's pie already exist on the market and are sold by Firms A and B. Firm A's product consists of 2 kg of meat for every 1 kg of potato, and costs £1.50 per kg. Firm B's product, on the other hand, consists of 2 kg of potato for every 1 kg of meat, and costs £1.00 per kg. Assuming that the characteristics of shepherd's pie are determined simply by its ingredients, we already have enough information to draw some conclusions about the demand for a new brand of this product. For instance, we could answer the following question: suppose Firm C wishes to produce its own brand of shepherd's pie, using equal quantities of meat and potatoes. At what price would the demand for C's product fall to zero?

Using the above information, Figure 4.3 can be drawn. The axes on the diagram represent the two characteristics of shepherd's pie, namely meat and potatoes, and the scales are measured in kilograms. The ray labelled 'Firm A' joins all points in characteristics space which can be attained simply by purchasing various amounts of Brand A alone. Thus when 1 kg of meat is purchased exactly 500 g of potato must also be bought if Brand A is the only brand enjoyed. In a similar fashion, the ray labelled 'Firm B' joins all points which can be attained by purchasing various amounts of Brand B alone.

If a consumer has £3 to spend on shepherd's pie, they could, if they wished, buy 2 kg of A and none of B. In this case 1.67 kg of meat and 0.33 kg of potato would be consumed. Alternatively, the same money could buy 3 kg of B and none of A. That would mean buying 2 kg of potato and 1 kg of meat. A final possibility is to buy some combination of the two brands – say 1 kg of Brand A and 1.5 kg of brand B; in this instance 1.17 kg of meat and 1.33 kg of potato would be consumed. The locus of possibilities facing the consumer is given by the line AB on Figure 4.3. This line is called the budget line (or budget constraint) of a consumer who has £3 to spend on shepherd's pie: if they decide to consume 1.17 kg of meat, the most potato that can *possibly* be bought is 1.33 kg, given the £3 limit. The budget line for a consumer willing to spend £6 on shepherd's pie would lie parallel to AB, and would be twice as far from the origin.

As Firm C enters the market it must consider its pricing policy carefully. If its price is so high that point C lies below and to the left of the line AB in Figure 4.3, consumers would be better off buying some mixture of Brands A and B than they would be buying C. For £3 a consumer could

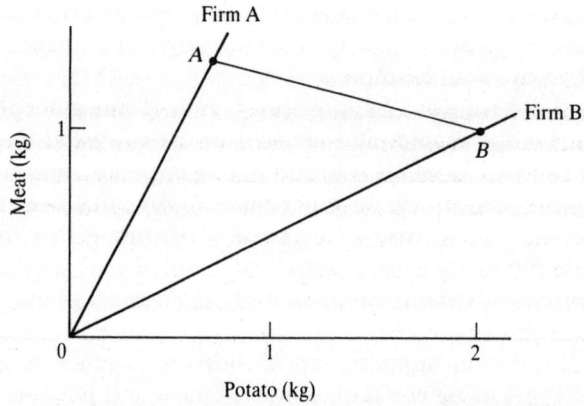

Figure 4.3 The consumption technology approach

EMPIRICAL DEMAND FUNCTIONS · 49

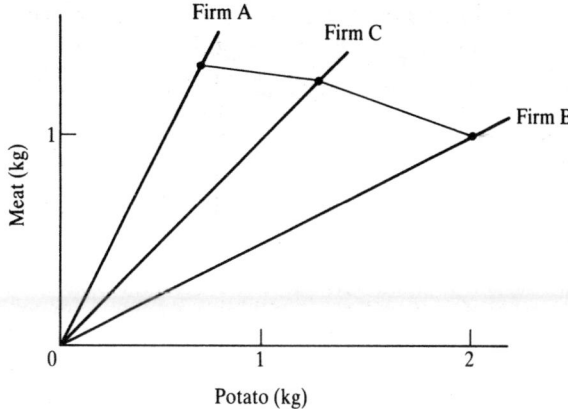

Figure 4.4 Introducing a new product

buy equal quantities of meat and potatoes by purchasing £1.80 of Brand A and £1.20 of Brand B. This would give 1200 g each of meat and potato. Now if Firm C were to charge £1.25 per kg of shepherd's pie, it would cost just £3 to buy 1200 g each of meat and potato by buying Brand C alone. If Firm C charged even a penny more than £1.25, demand for its output would fall to zero, since it would be more economical for consumers to buy a combination of Brands A and B. Suppose, then, that Firm C charges £1.20 per kg, so that £3 would buy 1.25 kg each of meat and potato. The new budget line appears as in Figure 4.4, and Brand C vies with Brands A and B for the consumer's expenditure on shepherd's pie. Note that it would never be optimal for a consumer to consume all three brands of shepherd's pie, since, given only two characteristics, some mix of just two brands can provide any feasible combination of characteristics (ingredients).

Further information regarding consumer tastes and their preferences between Brands A and B can be used by Firm C to construct a fuller demand curve. If the revelation of preferences in a two-firm industry can provide the entrant with information about the utility function generating market demand, then C can use information about price changes and demand in the market before its own entry to estimate a full demand curve for the new product, *even though* the new product is differentiated from those manufactured by its competitors. An example follows.

Suppose the representative consumer allocates £3 per week for expenditure on the output of the shepherd's pie industry considered earlier. Over a period before Firm C's entry A has kept its price constant at 50 p per kg, while B has varied its price from 30 p to 40 p and then to 50 p per kg. Demand for output from A and B and the implied underlying demand for characteristics at various prices of B brand shepherd's pie is

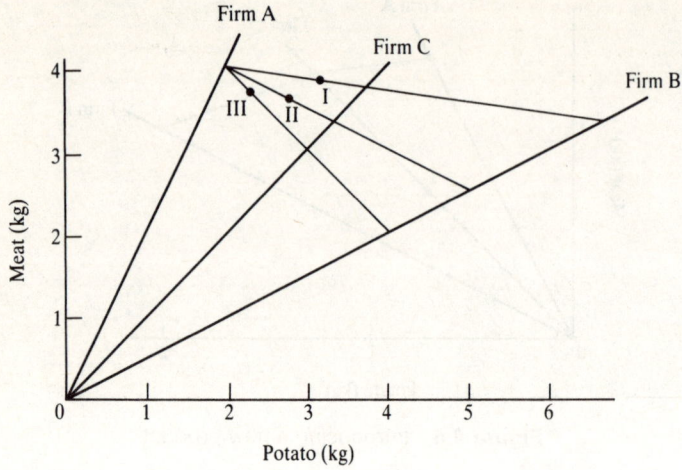

Figure 4.5 The effect of varying the price on demand

given in Table 4.3. The salient features of this table are illustrated in Figure 4.5. Since the preferred characteristic pairings all lie between the rays representing Firms A and C, if Firm C is allowed to enter, then Firm B's demand must fall to zero during the next time period. The demand for characteristics along a given budget constraint will be the same regardless of whether those characteristics are supplied by Firms A and B or Firms A and C. Hence (assuming A's price is still 50 p per kg) the demands for meat and potato when Firm C enters at prices 40 p, 45 p and 50 p are the same as when B prices at 30 p, 40 p and 50 p, respectively.

Converting the characteristics demand back into the demand for the output of Firms A and C enables Table 4.4 to be drawn up. Columns 1 and 3 of this table are a demand schedule for the new good.

Elegant though it is, and useful in many applications, the trade-off model cannot be employed in all environments. Its main drawback is its implicit assumption of divisibility. One vanilla ice cream and one strawberry ice cream might be able to make two strawberry ripples, but one Rolls-Royce and one Mini do not make two Granadas. In an important

Table 4.3 The demand for shepherd's pie from Firms A and B

Point	Price of Brand B (p)	Demand for Brand A	Demand for Brand B	Demand for meat	Demand for potatoes
I	30	4.2	3	3.8	3.4
II	40	4.4	2	3.6	2.8
III	50	5.0	1	3.7	2.3

Table 4.4 The demand for shepherd's pie from Firms A and C

Price of Brand C (p)	Demand for Brand A	Demand for Brand C	Demand for meat	Demand for potatoes
40	1.2	6	3.8	3.4
45	2.4	4	3.6	2.8
50	4.0	2	3.7	2.3

sense, the theory of consumption technology leaves the final stage of production — that of determining the characteristics mix — to the consumer. If the goods concerned are divisible then the characteristics are easily disassembled and put back together again in a preferred combination — like ice cream. It would be either more costly or impossible for the consumer to dismantle and reassemble cars. In general, the less easily divisible are goods in the market concerned, the more costly becomes the final stage of production undertaken by the consumer, and the more scope there is for a new entrant into the industry to produce a viable competitor (like the Granada). In sum then, the characteristics approach can be used to considerable benefit in certain contexts, but its usefulness declines as the products concerned become less divisible.

In the preceding pages four methods commonly used by firms to estimate the demand for their products have been described. None is perfect, and some uncertainty will always characterize the evaluation made by the firm of the demand conditions it faces. Nevertheless, market research techniques have developed rapidly in recent decades and, as a result, the modern day firm is in a much better position to exploit its knowledge of demand than was its counterpart twenty years ago.

Exercise: Demand for Beer in the United Kingdom

Table 4.5 provides data relevant to the analysis of the demand for beer in the United Kingdom from 1978 to 1987. The demand for beer can be estimated using the following logarithmic specification:

$$\ln Q = a_0 + a_1 \ln(p_b/p) + a_2 \ln(p_a/p) + a_3 \ln(Y/p) \tag{4.7}$$

where Q denotes sales of beer; p_b is the price of beer; p_a is the price of wines, cider and perry; Y is the level of personal disposable income; and p is the general price level as measured by the retail price index. The parameters a_0, a_1, a_2 and a_3 represent, respectively, the constant term, the own price elasticity, the cross price elasticity, and the income elasticity of demand for beer.

52 · ECONOMICS FOR MANAGERS

Table 4.5 Demand for beer and its determinants
Source: Annual Abstract of Statistics, HMSO.

Year	Sales of beer (thousand hectolitres)	Price of beer (index)	Price of wines, etc. (index)	General price level (index)	Personal disposable income (£ billion)
1978	67 802	79.0	81.9	197.1	114
1979	68 248	84.6	86.9	227.5	137
1980	65 490	100.0	100.0	263.7	162
1981	62 317	123.2	115.6	295.0	176
1982	60 290	138.7	132.1	320.4	192
1983	62 232	148.6	144.0	335.1	207
1984	62 082	160.9	154.2	351.8	222
1985	61 507	174.4	164.8	373.2	240
1986	61 213	180.9	174.0	385.9	255
1987	61 973	196.5	181.3	402.0	273

(a) If access to a computer supporting an econometrics software package is possible, perform a regression analysis designed to explain the demand for beer. Use the specification suggested above. Refer to the results of this analysis when answering questions (b) to (g) below.

(b) Is the demand for beer elastic, inelastic or of unit elasticity?

(c) To what extent would a brewer's revenue change if the price of beer were to rise by 10 per cent, all else remaining constant? (It may be assumed that *all* breweries raise their prices by the same amount.)

(d) Is the demand for beer responsive to income? If so is it a normal good or an inferior good?

(e) If real incomes are forecast to fall by 5 per cent over the next year, by what proportion should a brewery plan to change its output (assuming all else constant)?

(f) How does the price of other alcoholic beverages influence the demand for beer?

(g) What effect would a tax-induced rise of 10 per cent in the prices of alcoholic drinks other than beer have on the demand for beer (all else constant)?

(h) When a demand curve is drawn on a graph, the axes refer only to the price of the good itself and the quantity demanded. This being so, why is it important to include real income and the price of other alcoholic beverages in the demand function for beer?

Chapter 5
Optimization in economics

The optimum value of a variable, x, is the best value x can take with reference to some particular stated objective, and subject to some given constraints. Economists make very considerable use of the concept of an optimum; if any meaningful economic analysis is possible it must be assumed that economic agents are rational (or at least consistently irrational) in the pursuit of some objective. They will thus seek to maximize some objective function, like utility, profits or sales. Now the scarcity or finiteness of resources available in the known and explorable universe imposes upper limits on the utility, profits or sales which any economic agent can achieve. Optimization problems in economics are therefore almost always constrained problems. For example, a firm tries to maximize its profits subject to the constraint that the demand for its product is limited.

This chapter begins with a simple example of an optimization problem which many of us consciously solve in everyday life. As well as serving as a good example of the general class of problem being discussed, this particular example may serve to convince the sceptical reader that a large number of economic decisions are indeed made rationally (or are arrived at *as if* they were made rationally). Consider a driver on a 120-mile journey whose time is valued at £1 per hour and that petrol costs £2 per gallon. Fuel consumption is positively related to speed so that:

at 25 m.p.h. the car does 50 m.p.g.
at 50 m.p.h. the car does 40 m.p.g.
at 70 m.p.h. the car does 30 m.p.g.

The driver's objective is to minimize cost, that is:

min {1 × time of journey in hours + 2 × number of gallons of petrol consumed}

The driver can exercise some control over the costs by varying the speed of

Speed (m.p.h.)	Total cost (£)
25	9.60
50	8.40
70	9.79

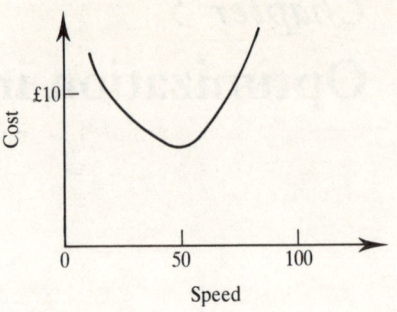

Figure 5.1 Speed and total cost

travel, and can therefore be said to be minimizing cost with respect to the speed of travel. From the above data the table and graph shown in Figure 5.1 are constructed. Cost is seen to be minimized when the speed is 50 m.p.h. Therefore, 50 m.p.h. is said to be the optimal speed. In this example the objective function is the cost function, and the constraints are the technological factors which prevent the car from performing more efficiently.

Returning to the central problem faced by the firm, it will be assumed throughout this chapter that the firm knows the level of output it wishes to produce. The problem tackled in the present chapter is: given the level of output, how cheaply can the firm produce it? Of course, this question can be asked (and answered) for any number of different output levels, and it is by doing precisely this that we shall derive the cost curves which will, in later chapters, form a basis for the analysis of the behaviour of firms. In turn these cost curves play a part in determining the optimal level of output. There is, then, a simultaneous relationship between costs and output. Before examining this further, though, the way in which the firm decides on the best combination of resources for the production of any given output level should be analysed.

The production function

A production function is a mathematical relationship between the quantity of a good produced and the quantities of inputs required to produce it. For simplicity it is often supposed that there are just two inputs into the productive process, namely capital, K, and labour, L. In this instance the production function is simply a mathematical relationship which enables the estimation of output given information about the levels of the inputs, capital and labour.

The simplest type of production function in the economics literature is the Cobb–Douglas production function:

$$Q = AK^a L^b \qquad 0 < a < 1 \qquad 0 < b < 1 \tag{5.1}$$

where Q is output and A, a and b are all constants. At first sight this may look a little daunting, but on closer inspection the nature of the function is seen to be quite simple. Consider the case in which one unit of capital is employed; supposing $A = 1$, $b = 0.5$, the relationship between Q and L takes the form shown in Figure 5.2a. In general, as labour input rises so does output, but the effect of changes in the labour input on output gets smaller as the amount of labour employed increases. A similar argument shows that when labour is fixed (at one unit) and capital is allowed to vary, the production function appears as in Figure 5.2b. The complete production function is illustrated in Figure 5.3.

Many alternatives to the Cobb–Douglas production function have been proposed; these trade off simplicity for generality, and the more advanced functions are very complicated expressions. These will not be

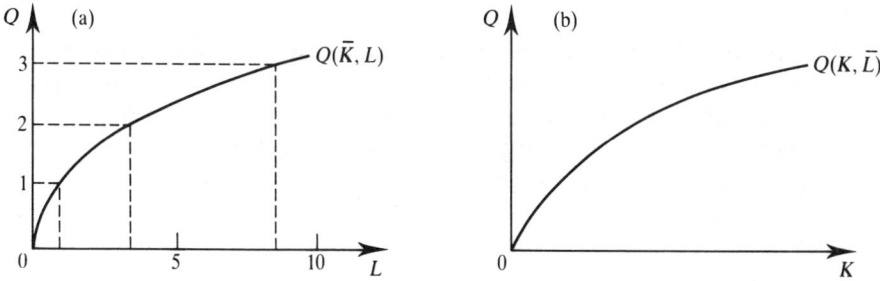

Figure 5.2 The production function: cross sections

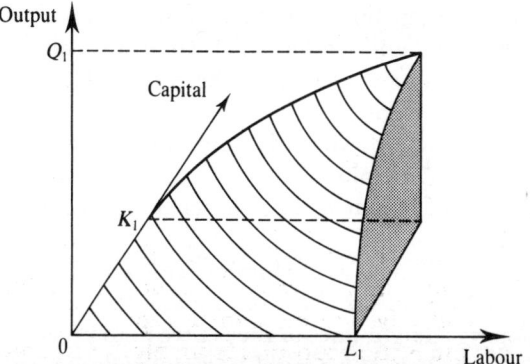

Figure 5.3 The production function

studied here, but the interested reader is referred to Heathfield and Wibe (1987). While advanced production functions improve the theoretical rigour of empirical analyses, the simple Cobb–Douglas production function often works well in practice. For instance, for the United Kingdom engineering industry, 1958–71, the equation

$$Q = 0.5060\, K^{0.4488} L^{0.5988} \tag{5.2}$$

explains over 99 per cent of the variation in value added. (The adjusted coefficient of determination is 0.995.) With a simple function providing results with such 'goodness of fit' it is unlikely that many businessmen will be interested in using more complicated production functions (see Kossentos, 1973; Fuss and McFadden, 1978). Thus the Cobb–Douglas production function (or the 'power function' as it is sometimes called) will suffice in our discussion of the optimization problem faced by the firm.

Isoquants

If there are n inputs into the productive process, an *isoquant* may be defined as a curve which shows, for each possible combination of the first $(n-1)$ inputs, the minimum amount of the nth input which is required to produce a given level of output. In particular, if there are two inputs, labour, L, and capital, K, the definition of an isoquant runs as follows: an isoquant is a curve drawn in (K, L) space which shows, for each possible value of K, the minimum labour input which is required to produce a given level of output.

An intuitive feel for the meaning of an isoquant can be gained if we picture the production function of Figure 5.3 as a mountain; then an isoquant is like a contour line on a map of the mountain – it shows all combinations of capital and labour which are just capable of producing a given level of output, say 10 tonne. Examples of 10- and 20-tonne isoquants are given in Figure 5.4.

Isoquants always slope downwards from left to right: if they did not it would imply that Q^* units of output could be produced either by employing L^* units of labour and K^* units of capital, or by employing $L^* + \delta$ units of labour and $K^* + \epsilon$ units of capital ($\delta, \epsilon > 0$) and that the latter technique is as efficient as the former. This would clearly be absurd.

Isoquants are always convex to the origin; that is, they are always either a downward sloping straight line, or they curve in towards the origin as in Figure 5.4. The curvature of a typical isoquant indicates that inputs are complements of each other, but not perfect complements. If the inputs

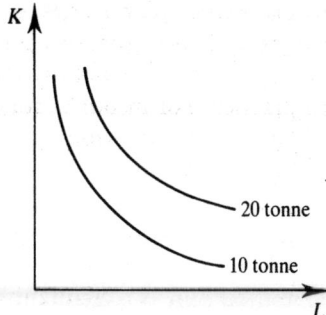

Figure 5.4 Isoquants

were perfect substitutes for one another the isoquants would be linear and downward sloping. If there is any degree of complementarity between the inputs, however, combinations of inputs which use relatively large amounts of one input and relatively small amounts of the other will be less efficient than combinations which mix the two inputs more evenly: this is the consequence of the 'law of diminishing productivity', a supply side variant of the 'law of diminishing marginal utility' discussed in Chapter 2. Put simply, averages are preferred to extremes, and are more efficient.

Isoquants can never intersect one another: if they did it would imply that two different levels of output can simultaneously and efficiently be produced, given the levels of the inputs. This would be nonsensical.

Any set of isoquants which possess the above properties of convexity and negative slope are said to be well behaved. The Cobb–Douglas production function implies the existence of well behaved isoquants. To demonstrate this, consider the function

$$Q = AK^a L^b \tag{5.3}$$

Holding output constant at Q implies

$$L = \frac{\bar{Q}^{1/b}}{AK^a} = RK^{-a/b} \tag{5.4}$$

where $R \equiv (\bar{Q}/A)^{1/b}$ is a positive constant since $\bar{Q} > 0, A > 0$.

$$\frac{dL}{dK} = -\frac{Ra}{b} K^{[-1-(a/b)]} < 0 \tag{5.5}$$

In other words, the rate of change of labour with respect to capital is negative; that is, the isoquants are downward sloping.

$$\frac{d^2 L}{dK^2} = \frac{Ra}{b}(1 + a/b) K^{[-2-(a/b)]} > 0 \tag{5.6}$$

In other words, as K increases the slope of the isoquant becomes more positive (flatter); that is, the isoquants are convex.

The well-behaved nature of isoquants implied by the Cobb–Douglas production function can also be demonstrated by inspection of Figure 5.3. At a given level of output, $\bar{Q}$, the relevant isoquant can be found by looking at the production function mountain from above and painting a line through all points on the mountain which are $\bar{Q}$ metres high. The view of this line from above is the isoquant in (K, L) space. Since the Cobb–Douglas function always gives a smooth mountain and is twice differentiable in capital and labour, the resultant isoquant is said to be well behaved.

So far we have said what an isoquant is and what it looks like, but nothing has been said of what we do with one once we've got one. Isoquants represent one side of the optimization problem. Restating the problem: given the level of output, how cheaply can the firm produce it? If the given level of output is 10 tonne, say, the firm is constrained to lie somewhere on the 10-tonne isoquant. How can the firm select its levels of capital and labour input in such a way as to minimize the costs it must incur to remain on this isoquant? The answer to this question requires the introduction of a new tool of analysis – isocost lines.

Isocost lines and the optimum

An isocost line, as its name implies, joins together all pairs of inputs of K and L which can just be afforded by a firm making a given outlay. Suppose, for instance, that the £600 isocost line is being constructed, and that labour costs £20 per unit and capital costs £30 per unit. Then the firm could employ any of the combinations of capital and labour shown in Figure 5.5. The isocost line is thus a straight, downward sloping line. If

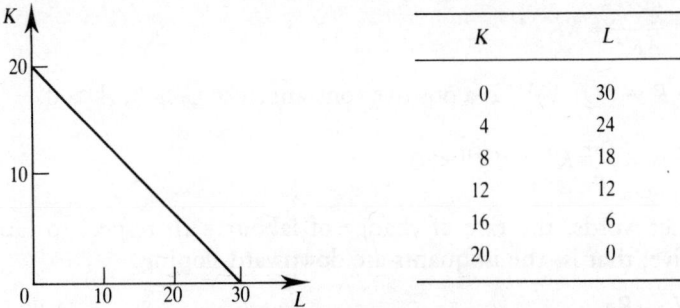

Figure 5.5 An isocost line

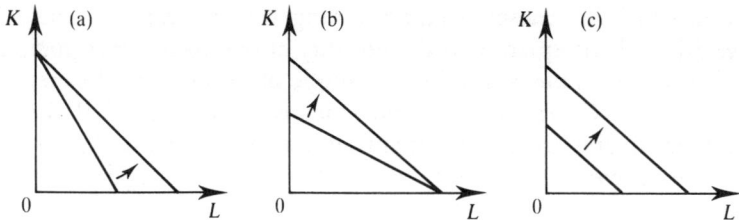

Figure 5.6 Shifts of the isocost line

labour becomes relatively cheaper, the isocost line would rotate counter-clockwise (Figure 5.6a). If capital became relatively cheaper, it would rotate clockwise (Figure 5.6b). If both labour and capital became cheaper, then the whole line would shift away from the origin.

At a given point in time the firm faces constant input prices, but is none the less concerned with a number of different isocost lines: as well as a £600 isocost line, it could construct the £500, £700 or £599.43 isocost lines (or any of an infinite number of others). If it produces on a given isoquant, having already decided on its preferred level of output, the firm will want to produce that quantity as cheaply as possible. In other words it will want to be on the lowest possible isocost line given that it must also be on the specified isoquant.

Suppose that the firm wishes to produce on the 10-tonne isoquant given in Figure 5.7. The £600 isocost line from the previous example is also drawn on this diagram, together with the £700 and £500 isocost lines. Ten tonnes of output could be produced at a cost of £700, either at A or B or any point in between. It would be impossible to produce 10 tonne at a cost of £500. The cheapest way possible of producing 10 tonne is by producing at point C, which would cost the firm £600. This is the only

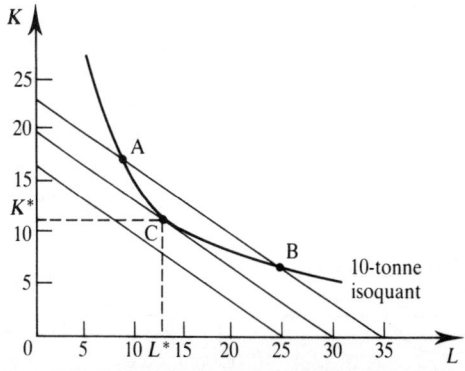

Figure 5.7 The constrained optimum of the firm

point at which the chosen isoquant is tangential to an isocost line. The convexity of the isoquant and the linearity of the isocost lines guarantee that it is not possible to produce 10 tonne of output any cheaper than £600, at point C. The point of tangency is the optimum. If the firm behaves optimally, therefore – that is, if it wishes to produce its 10 tonne at minimum cost – it will employ K^* units of capital and L^* units of labour.

In general, the point of tangency between a constraint and an iso-utility curve (where utility is the objective) represents the solution to the constrained optimization problem. This is an extremely important result which will be used often in the remainder of this book.

Applications of optimization theory

Suppose the government introduced a labour subsidy. The isocost line would pivot counter-clockwise as shown in Figure 5.8. More labour could be hired at a given cost to the firm and given capital input than was the case before the introduction of the subsidy. The case in which the subsidy results in an increase in employment and no change in capital stock is illustrated in Figure 5.8a. However, it is not always the case that the entire amount saved by the firm by the introduction of the labour subsidy will be spent on increasing the size of the firm's workforce. An extreme case is shown in Figure 5.8b, where the nature of the technology faced by the firm is such that the introduction of a labour subsidy actually *reduces* the optimal amount of labour employed as output rises. This would happen if labour is an extremely inferior ('Giffen') good. (A Giffen good is one for which demand falls as the price falls, other things being equal; this can happen because as the price of a good falls, the resources available for

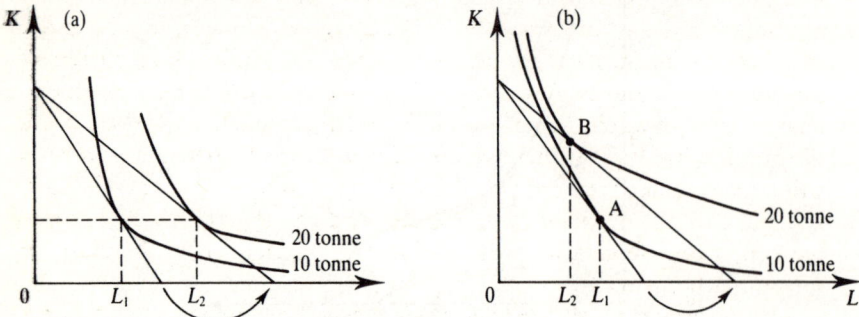

Figure 5.8 Factor price changes

expenditure on that good *or on other goods* increases, all else constant. If the tendency for more of an inferior good to be demanded as price falls is more than offset by the tendency for less of the good to be demanded when purchasing power rises, then that good is a Giffen good.)

An example might help clarify matters. Suppose that capital is 'lumpy' in the sense that the firm's capital consists only of a few large, expensive machines. Hence it may not be able to afford a new machine at pre-subsidy prices. After the introduction of the labour subsidy, however, it may be worth employing one more machine although this means that less labour is hired. This is because the subsidy increases the firm's real income and this change in real income can be used by the firm for whatever purpose it chooses; the firm is not constrained to use the subsidy to hire more labour.

A knowledge of optimization theory is therefore highly valuable to the decision-maker in a modern firm. If the decision-maker were to leave choices about the desired levels of capital and labour employment to intuition the decisions could be the best decisions only by sheer chance, and sometimes may even make changes in completely the wrong direction. Armed with the tools of optimization theory, however, rational decisions can be made based on the declared objectives of the firm and on all available information.

This is not to suggest, however, that managers sit in their offices plotting isoquants and isocost lines on graph paper – real life optimization problems are not as simple as those discussed in this chapter. To begin with, the capital stock takes time to adjust to new levels as new machinery must often be ordered months or even years in advance. So it would not be possible to move directly from point A to B in Figure 5.8b, for example. Secondly, decisions made in one period affect output potential and costs in all succeeding periods; the static, one-period framework adopted in this chapter does not account for this. Instead a dynamic, multi-period approach needs to be taken, and this will involve mathematical techniques of considerably greater complexity than have been developed so far in this book. Thirdly, a typical firm employs far more than two distinct types of input; for instance, the inputs into a university include books, buildings, administrative staff of all grades, computers, laboratory equipment of various kinds and academic staff. If there are n distinguishable inputs into the production process, then the isoquants will be n-dimensional, not two-dimensional as discussed in this chapter. If $n > 3$ then the isoquant cannot be drawn diagrammatically, since space has only three observable dimensions. The problem must therefore be solved mathematically.

The solutions to all these problems will be discussed in the next chapter. They involve certain powerful mathematical techniques which need not concern us at this stage. For the firm, powerful computer software packages are available which enable complicated mathematical optimization procedures to be carried out easily by the manager. Managers do not draw isoquants: they get their computers to do their optimization problem-solving for them. However, a thorough understanding of the diagrammatic presentation of optimization theory in this chapter is necessary if the principles underlying the more general techniques are to be understood.

Application of optimization theory to demand

Just as a firm has a production function, so an individual has a utility function. Just as a firm has isoquants, so an individual has iso-utility or *indifference curves*. Indifference curves will be convex and downward sloping like isoquants, because it is assumed that consumers will in general rather have a broad based mixture of commodities in their possession than a large amount of just one good. (Note that this assumption is closely related to the law of diminishing marginal utility.) A formal definition of an indifferences curve is as follows: an indifference curve is a locus of points in commodity space at which the utility yielded to an individual is constant. That is, the individual is indifferent (or has no preference) between any pair of points on the same indifference curve.

Consumers wish to maximize their utility subject to the constraint imposed by the finite nature of their resources. The so-called budget constraint of the consumer is analogous to the isocost line of the firm. It shows the quantities of goods which the consumer is able to buy given the amount of money available for the consumption of these goods. Just like the isocost line, and for the same reasons, the budget constraint is downward sloping.

In the case of the firm, the objective was to minimize costs at a given level of output; that is, to get onto the lowest possible isocost line given the isoquant. Consumers, on the other hand, want to maximize their utility given their resources – in other words they want to get onto the highest possible indifference curve given the budget constraint. Utility rises as the consumer moves onto indifference curves further from the origin, so optimal consumption is obtained at the point of tangency of the budget constraint and the best attainable indifference curve. In Figure 5.9 a set of indifference curves between eggs and all other goods is illustrated, together with a budget constraint. Curve I_3 is unattainable given the consumer's budget. I_1 is attainable, but the consumer would be

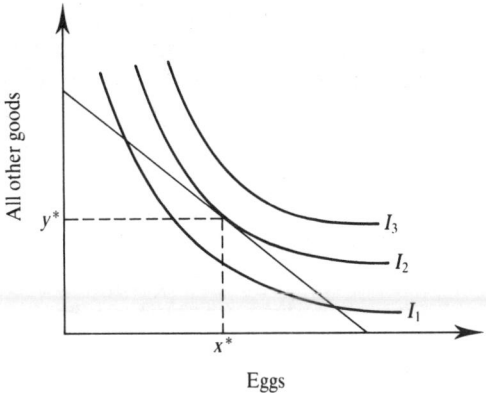

Figure 5.9 The constrained optimum of the consumer

happier on I_2, which is also just attainable, consuming x^* eggs and y^* units of other commodities.

If the price of eggs falls, all other prices remaining unchanged, the budget constraint would pivot counter-clockwise as shown in Figure 5.10a. The consumer will therefore move onto a higher indifference curve since he/she can now afford to buy more eggs, more of other goods (or more of both). If eggs are a normal (that is, not inferior) good, then the consumer will always buy more eggs as the price of eggs falls, other things being equal. Thus consumption of eggs rises from x_1 to x_2, while consumption of all other goods rises (assuming all other goods are also normal) from y_1 to y_2.

If Q eggs can be bought when the price is p_1 and when no other goods are bought, then $2Q$ eggs can be bought when the price is halved from p_1 to p_2. Thus the budget line rotates from P–Q to P–$2Q$. Assuming optimal behaviour on the part of the consumer, x_1 eggs are demanded at price p_1 and x_2 are demanded at price p_2. Using this information points along the demand curve can be defined, as shown in Figure 5.10b. As can be seen, this demand curve is downward sloping, exactly as one would expect of a demand curve for a normal good.

Thus optimization theory can be applied on the demand side of the microeconomy to demonstrate how optimal consumer behaviour leads to the downward sloping type of demand curve faced by the typical firm. Our main concern with optimization is in the context of the behaviour of the firm itself though, and it is on that we shall continue to concentrate as more advanced optimization theory is introduced in Chapter 6.

64 · ECONOMICS FOR MANAGERS

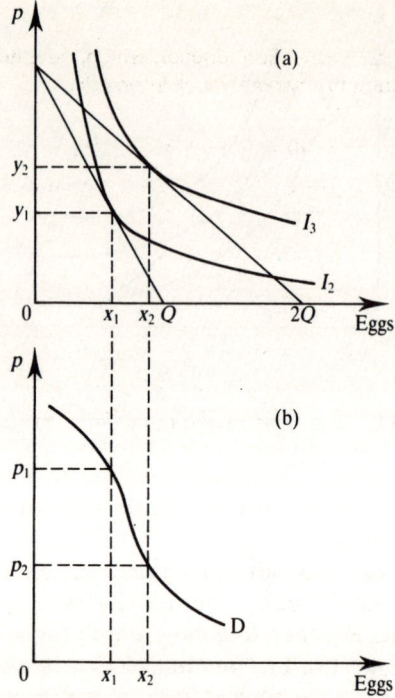

Figure 5.10 Indifference analysis and the demand curve

Exercise: Production functions in UK manufacturing

Table 5.1 shows the output of manufacturing industry in the United Kingdom in 1960 (measured by £million gross value added) which would have been achieved given the levels of input of labour and capital indicated. Labour input is measured in thousands of workers, and capital input is measured by the net value of the capital stock (in £million). The table has been constructed using the production function estimated by Mizon (1977), where

Table 5.1 Production function for UK manufacturing

Capital	Labour (in '000s)				
	10	15	20	25	30
100	18	24	30	36	41
80	17	23	29	34	39
60	16	22	27	32	37
40	14	20	24	29	33
20	12	17	21	24	28

$$Q = K^{0.24} L^{0.77} \tag{5.7}$$

This is a Cobb–Douglas production function which, despite its relative simplicity, explains output remarkably well in practice.

(a) Use the above information to draw the 24-unit isoquant.

(b) Suppose that labour costs £6 million per 1,000 men to employ. (Capital costs £1 million per unit.) How cheaply can 24 units of output be produced?

(c) How much labour would be employed at this point?

(d) How much capital?

(e) Suppose labour becomes more expensive to hire than was assumed in question (b) above. In particular, suppose labour now costs £21,000 per worker. How cheaply can 24 units of output now be produced?

(f) How much labour is now employed?

(g) How much capital?

(h) Suppose that, in the short run, firms cannot alter the amount of capital which they are using. So firms are constrained, in the short run, to use the amount of capital calculated as the answer to (d) above, even when labour costs rise. How cheaply can 24 units of output be produced (in the short run) immediately after the increase in labour costs?

(i) Why does the answer to (h) differ to that of (e)? What does this example teach us about the costs of production in the short run and in the long run?

Chapter 6
Mathematical programming in economics

The idea of optimization, and in particular optimization subject to a constraint, was introduced in Chapter 5. For a given level of output it was seen how firms wishing to minimize their costs do so by using the input levels indicated by the point of tangency of the relevant isoquant and the lowest attainable isocost line. The task to be tackled in the present chapter is that of constructing a mathematical version of the isoquant–isocost diagram. There are several reasons for doing this.

First, an algebraic analysis affords greater precision than does a graphical analysis. Together with this comes a more rigorous understanding of the concepts involved. Secondly, as computers have become cheaper and more accessible to even small businesses, and as business software has become increasingly available, the means of conducting a rigorous mathematical analysis has become easier to acquire. Consequently such exercises are now much more widely used in practice than ever before. Thirdly, graphical analysis is possible only for the simple case of Chapter 5 in which only two factors of production (such as labour and capital) exist. Use of the techniques described in this chapter, on the other hand, enables any number of factors of production to be incorporated into the analysis. Finally, as students familiar with operational research techniques will be aware, linear and non-linear programming methods can be used in solving a wide variety of problems for the firm, not all of which can be depicted graphically.

The sequence of topics covered in this chapter is as follows: the method of Lagrange multipliers is introduced in the context of a simple programming problem. The complexity and generality of the problem is then increased by relaxing, in turn, the assumptions that there are only two dimensions and one constraint, that some of all inputs must be used, and that the entire budget must be spent. Finally, a special case – that of

Reading of this chapter may, without loss of continuity, be deferred until after Chapter 14 if the student so wishes.

linear programming – is introduced, this being a method very frequently used by businessmen in arriving at day-to-day decisions.

The method of Lagrange multipliers

Following the analysis of Chapter 5 a production or utility function is defined. This might be represented in very general terms as

$$u = u(x_1, x_2) \qquad (6.1)$$

where u represents production or utility, and x_1 and x_2 are the variables which determine u. To be specific, if u is the number of postbags produced by a postbag manufacturer, then x_1 might be the square yards of sackcloth and x_2 might be the number of workers employed by the firm. Output can be increased by increasing the input of either x_1 or x_2. Alternatively, u could be a measure of my degree of satisfaction (or utility). In this latter case x_1 and x_2 might represent the amount of food I eat and the amount of beer I drink, respectively. The production (or utility) function might be Cobb–Douglas, that is

$$u = x_1^\alpha x_2^\beta \qquad (6.2)$$

where α and β are constant, or it could have any of a number of other possible forms. It is not necessary to specify the precise nature of the function at this stage, however, so for the time being we shall work with the general utility function of Equation (6.1).

Finding the maximum of a utility function is much like finding the summit of a mountain – when you can no longer go up no matter which way you turn, you know you're there. If adding a tiny amount more of x_1 neither increases nor decreases utility, and if adding a tiny amount more of x_2 neither increases nor decreases utility, then we must be at either a maximum, a minimum or a ridge – either the peak of a mountain or the trough of a valley. In mathematical terms such a point is represented by the first order conditions for an unconstrained maximum of Equation (6.1).

$$\frac{\partial u}{\partial x_1} = \frac{\partial u}{\partial x_2} = 0 \qquad (6.3)$$

That is, the partial first derivative of utility with respect to each of the arguments in the utility function must equal zero. To determine whether a point satisfying Equation (6.3) is a maximum or not the following technique is used. If, as inputs of both x_1 and x_2 increase from levels below the optimum to levels above the optimum, the gradient changes from being uphill to being downhill, then the point is indeed a maximum. In mathematical terms, the second order conditions for a maximum are given by

$$\frac{\partial^2 u}{\partial x_1^2} < 0 \quad \text{and} \quad \frac{\partial^2 u}{\partial x_2^2} < 0 \qquad (6.4)$$

The type of maximization problem solved by Equations (6.3) and (6.4) is illustrated in Figures 6.1 and 6.2 by the point X. Figure 6.2 is an aerial view of the 'mountain' in Figure 6.1 and the contour lines are iso-utility curves (indifference curves or isoquants). Figure 6.2 bears exactly the same relationship to Figure 6.1 as does Figure 5.4 to Figure 5.3. As one moves from one iso-utility curve to a second, one's utility increases if the following condition is satisfied, and decreases otherwise: the nearest point on the second curve to point X must be closer to point X itself than is the nearest point on the first curve to point X. Hence utility increases as one moves from A to B in Figure 6.2, but decreases as one moves from A to C.

Point X represents the best of all worlds, and for this reason is often referred to in the literature as a bliss point. Bliss points are of interest when studying the consumption of certain pairs of products – for instance, small amounts of water and manure both increase a gardener's utility, but too much of either is damaging. In most cases, though, it is the consumer's limited ability to pay for more of a good which limits consumption of the product. For this reason the simple optimization rule given in Equations (6.3) and (6.4) is not sufficiently powerful to be adopted as a solution to the *general* optimization problem. We need to incorporate into the analysis a mathematical version of the isocost or budget line.

The budget constraint can be represented algebraically as

$$p_1 x_1 + p_2 x_2 = w \qquad (6.5)$$

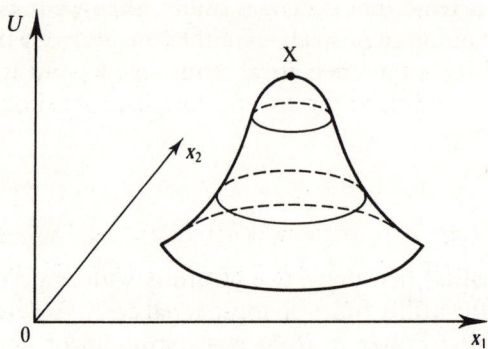

Figure 6.1 The utility function

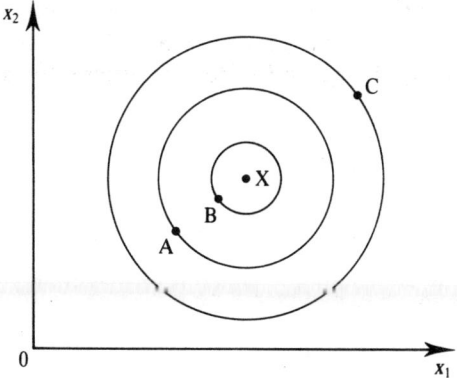

Figure 6.2 The bliss point

where p_1 and p_2 denote the prices of inputs x_1 and x_2, respectively, and w denotes the upper limit of expenditure on these two inputs. To begin with the case in which the entire budget is spent will be discussed. That is, it is assumed that no bliss points lie to the left of and below the budget line.

In solving the constrained optimization problem the method of Lagrangian multipliers is used. To restate the problem formally, we wish to maximize

$$u = u(x_1, x_2) \tag{6.1}$$

subject to the budget constraint

$$p_1 x_1 + p_2 x_2 = w \tag{6.5}$$

The solution proceeds in three stages. First, the Lagrangian function, $\mathscr{L}$, is set up. The Lagrangian function is equal to the unconstrained utility function, $u(x_1, x_2)$, *minus* the product of a Lagrangian multiplier, π, and an expression which is zero if the budget constraint is satisfied. (The meaning of the Lagrangian multiplier, π, will become clear. It is a constant which may be interpreted as the marginal utility, or 'shadow price', of the constrained resource – in this case it is the marginal utility of money.) Hence,

$$\mathscr{L} = u(x_1, x_2) - \pi(p_1 x_1 + p_2 x_2 - w) \tag{6.6}$$

The second step is to partially differentiate the Lagrangian function, $\mathscr{L}$, with respect to the inputs of the utility function, x_1 and x_2, and to set the results to zero. This gives

$$\frac{\partial \mathscr{L}}{\partial x_1} = \frac{\partial u}{\partial x_1} - \pi p_1 = 0 \tag{6.7}$$

$$\frac{\partial \mathcal{L}}{\partial x_2} = \frac{\partial u}{\partial x_2} - \pi p_2 = 0 \qquad (6.8)$$

If a bliss point exists to the left of and below the budget line, then $\pi = 0$. Equations (6.7) and (6.8) then reduce to the more familiar Equation (6.3) since the budget constraint is no longer effective. If no bliss point is attainable, given the budget constraint, then $\pi > 0$ and it will not now be the case that the marginal utility of each input equals zero; since, in the absence of the constraint, total utility would be greater, the marginal utility of the ith input is now πp_i which is greater than zero.

Thirdly, partially differentiate the Lagrangian function, $\mathcal{L}$, with respect to the Lagrangian multiplier, π, and set the result equal to zero. This guarantees that the constraint of Equation (6.5) is satisfied.

$$\frac{\partial \mathcal{L}}{\partial \pi} = w - p_1 x_1 - p_2 x_2 = 0 \qquad (6.9)$$

This done, Equations (6.7) and (6.8) can be manipulated to give, respectively,

$$\frac{\partial u}{\partial x_1} = \pi p_1 \qquad (6.10)$$

$$\frac{\partial u}{\partial x_2} = \pi p_2 \qquad (6.11)$$

Dividing Equation (6.10) by Equation (6.11) gives

$$\frac{\partial u}{\partial x_1} \bigg/ \frac{\partial u}{\partial x_2} = \frac{p_1}{p_2} \qquad (6.12)$$

That is, the ratio of the marginal utilities of the inputs equals the ratio of their prices. This makes good sense: at their point of tangency the slopes of the indifference curve and budget line are clearly equal, and these slopes represent, respectively, the ratio of marginal utilities and the ratio of prices. Put another way, Equation (6.12) is simply stating that to maximize utility, the extra utility derived per extra penny spent on each input should be the same for all inputs. In other words there is, at the optimum point, no way to increase total utility simply by transferring some expenditure from the purchase of one input to that of another.

Rearranging Equation (6.9) gives

$$p_1 x_1 + p_2 x_2 = w \qquad (6.5)$$

which is the original budget constraint. Together Equations (6.5) and (6.12) state that at the optimum, the slope of the indifference curve should equal that of the budget constraint and that the solution lies on the budget constraint. The only point which can satisfy both Equations (6.5) and (6.12), then, is the point of tangency of the indifference curve and the budget line (or of the isoquant and isocost line). Equations (6.5) and (6.12) – the outcomes of our three step procedure – therefore represent the solution of the constrained optimization problem set out in Equations (6.1) and (6.5). A diagrammatic interpretation of the solution is given in Figure 6.3.

Hitherto only two inputs and one constraint have been considered. This is a convenient starting point because the solution is capable of diagrammatic representation. One of the most important advantages of mathematical analysis over graphical analysis, however, is its ability to consider any number of inputs and constraints; when working with algebra we are no longer confined by the two-dimensional nature of the paper on which we draw – nor, for that matter, by the three-dimensional nature of the space in which we live! The next step, then, is to consider the constrained optimization problem with n dimensions and m constraints.

Extension to n dimensions and m constraints

Consider a firm using n inputs subject to m constraints. The inputs may be unskilled labour, skilled labour, management, conveyor belts, land, rivets and cloth. The constraints may be a budget constraint, a rationing of inputs (such as an inelastic supply of skilled labour) or a government imposed constraint (as in the case of a limit to investment which, if exceeded, would result in the firm being referred to the Monopolies and Mergers Commission).

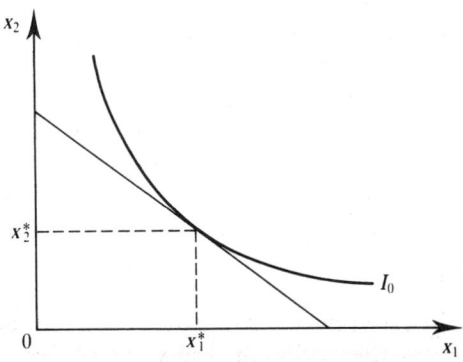

Figure 6.3 The constrained optimum

The problem to be considered is

maximize $\quad u = u(x_1, x_2, x_3, x_4)$ \hfill (6.13)

subject to
$$\sum_{i=1}^{4} p_i x_i = w \tag{6.14}$$

$$\sum_{i=1}^{4} r_i x_i = c \tag{6.15}$$

$$x_i > 0 \quad \forall i \tag{6.16}$$

where the symbol $\forall$ means 'for all'.

The problem used as an example is, therefore, one with four dimensions and two constraints. The solution proceeds exactly as before. First the Lagrangian function is set up. There will now be two Lagrangian multipliers, π_1 and π_2, which refer respectively to the two constraints Equations (6.14) and (6.15). One of these constraints might be regarded as a budget constraint, and will take exactly the same form as the constraint encountered in the last section. The second constraint might be a 'ration coupon' constraint which takes the following form: if only $\bar{x}_2$ units of x_2 exist in the world, then $r_2 = 1$, $r_i = 0$, $\forall i \neq 2$ and $c = \bar{x}_2$. The Lagrangian function is given by

$$\mathscr{L} = u(x_1, x_2, x_3, x_4) - \pi_1 \left(\sum_{i=1}^{4} p_i x_i - w \right) - \pi_2 \left(\sum_{i=1}^{4} r_i x_i - c \right) \tag{6.17}$$

The second step is to differentiate $\mathscr{L}$ with respect to each of the x_i, and set the results to zero:

$$\frac{\partial \mathscr{L}}{\partial x_1} = \frac{\partial u}{\partial x_1} - \pi_1 p_1 - \pi_2 r_1 = 0 \tag{6.18}$$

$$\frac{\partial \mathscr{L}}{\partial x_2} = \frac{\partial u}{\partial x_2} - \pi_1 p_2 - \pi_2 r_2 = 0 \tag{6.19}$$

$$\frac{\partial \mathscr{L}}{\partial x_3} = \frac{\partial u}{\partial x_3} - \pi_1 p_3 - \pi_2 r_3 = 0 \tag{6.20}$$

$$\frac{\partial \mathscr{L}}{\partial x_4} = \frac{\partial u}{\partial x_4} - \pi_1 p_4 - \pi_2 r_4 = 0 \tag{6.21}$$

In the third step, $\mathscr{L}$ is differentiated with respect to each of the Lagrangian multipliers, π_1 and π_2, and the results are again set to zero.

$$\frac{\partial \mathscr{L}}{\partial \pi_1} = \sum_{i=1}^{4} p_i x_i - w = 0 \tag{6.22}$$

$$\frac{\partial \mathscr{L}}{\partial \pi_2} = \sum_{i=1}^{4} r_i x_i - c = 0 \tag{6.23}$$

As in the earlier example, the ratio of the marginal utilities of any two inputs can easily be derived. For instance, the ratio of the marginal utilities of x_1 and x_2 can be found by dividing Equation (6.19) by Equation (6.18)

$$\frac{\partial u}{\partial x_2} \bigg/ \frac{\partial u}{\partial x_1} = \frac{\pi_1 p_2 + \pi_2 r_2}{\pi_1 p_1 + \pi_2 p_1} \tag{6.24}$$

and no further simplification can take place. The rule that the slopes of the indifference curve (isoquant) and the budget line (isocost line) should be equal no longer applies when more than one constraint may operate – unless, that is, there is some *a priori* reason why π_2 should equal zero, in which case the ration constraint does not effectively restrict consumption of any input.

At this point a numerical example might serve to fix ideas.

NUMERICAL EXAMPLE I

Suppose a firm wishes to find out how much output it is possible to produce given a budget of £250,000. Assume that the firm's production function is a constant returns to scale Cobb–Douglas function, and that the shares to labour and capital are equal. The problem can therefore be stated as:

maximize $\quad Q = K^{0.5} L^{0.5}$ \hfill (6.25)

subject to $\quad rK + wL = 250\,000 \qquad K > 0; \quad L > 0$ \hfill (6.26)

where r represents the price of capital, (the 'user cost') and w is the price of labour (the wage rate).

Suppose that in the above example $r = 0.1$ and $w = 2.5$. This implies an annual user cost of capital of 10 per cent and a wage rate of £2.50 per man hour if capital is measured in terms of value of stock and labour is measured in man hours.

The solution proceeds by first setting up the Lagrangian function:

$$\mathscr{L} = K^{0.5} L^{0.5} - \pi(0.1\,K + 2.5\,L - 250\,000) \tag{6.27}$$

Differentiating $\mathscr{L}$ by each of the unknowns and setting the results to zero gives:

$$\frac{\partial \mathscr{L}}{\partial K} = 0.5 L^{0.5} K^{-0.5} - 0.1 \pi = 0 \tag{6.28}$$

$$\frac{\partial \mathscr{L}}{\partial L} = 0.5 K^{0.5} L^{-0.5} - 2.5 \pi = 0 \tag{6.29}$$

$$\frac{\partial \mathcal{L}}{\partial \pi} = 0.1K + 2.5L - 250\,000 = 0 \tag{6.30}$$

Dividing Equation (6.29) by Equation (6.28)

$$\frac{K^{0.5}L^{-0.5}}{L^{0.5}K^{-0.5}} = \frac{2.5\,\pi}{0.1\,\pi} \tag{6.31}$$

Multiplying both sides by L gives

$$K = 25L \tag{6.32}$$

From Equation (6.30) we have

$$0.1K = 250\,000 - 2.5L \tag{6.33}$$

Equations (6.32) and (6.33) present a pair of simultaneous relationships between the two remaining unknowns – capital, K, and labour, L. The only values of K and L which can satisfy both equations at once are the optimal inputs of capital and labour, namely $K^* = 1{,}250{,}000$ and $L^* = 50{,}000$. That is, the firm should use £1.25 million worth of capital and 50,000 man hours of labour (around 27 employees) in order to produce some 1,342 units of output per year. This is the greatest amount of output it is possible to produce given that the total annual cost of production should not exceed £250,000.

Figure 6.4 shows the problem solved above in diagrammatic form. The concave, football-shaped function is the production function, Equation (6.25). The plane ABCD is the isocost constraint, Equation (6.26) in three

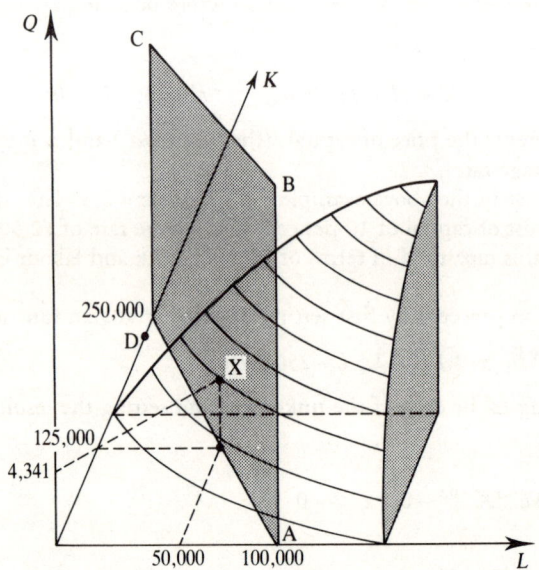

Figure 6.4 Constrained optimization in 3D

dimensions, and cuts through the football like a knife. The object is to find the point, X, where the knife intersects the football at the highest possible altitude. The optimal inputs of capital and labour, and the best possible output can then be read off the axes as the co-ordinates of point X. While conceptually simple enough, the three-dimensional nature of the problem makes diagrammatic analysis very difficult and rather more confusing than its mathematical equivalent.

Two potentially important problems remain with the mathematical programming techniques described so far in this chapter. First of all, an implicit assumption has been made in the earlier discussion, namely that non-zero amounts of all inputs are consumed. Secondly, cases in which a bliss point lies within the area attainable by the producer or consumer have not been considered. It is to a discussion of these problems we now turn.

Non-linear programming in economics

First consider the case in which not all inputs into the production or utility function are consumed. An example of such a situation is illustrated in Figure 6.5. The budget constraint AB represents the total amount to be spent on the two inputs x_1 and x_2. Each indifference curve I_0 and I_1 represents a given amount of utility (or output, etc.). The highest attainable indifference curve is I_1 which touches the budget constraint at A but is not tangential to the budget constraint at this point. Given the shape of the budget line and of the indifference curves, such a point of tangency would have to lie somewhere left of the vertical axis, implying that negative amounts of x_1 are used. Since it is impossible to

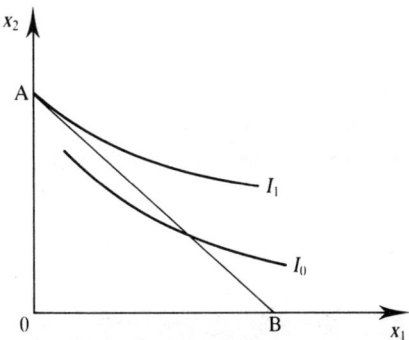

Figure 6.5 A corner solution

'unconsume' something, the best attainable position is at A, a so-called corner solution where none of input x_1 is bought. Although point A does lie on the highest attainable indifference curve, the slope of the indifference curve I_1 at this point does *not* equal that of the budget line. Hence the required solution is not one which satisfies Equation (6.12).

It is not at all difficult to amend the earlier Lagrangian method so that the possibility of encountering such corner solutions is allowed for. Consider the problem

maximize $\quad u(x_1, \ldots, x_n) \quad$ (6.34)

subject to $\quad \sum_{i=1}^{n} p_i x_i = w \quad$ (6.35)

and $\quad x_i \geq 0 \quad \forall i \quad$ (6.36)

Note that Equation (6.36) is now no longer a strict inequality (as was the case in the earlier examples – see, for instance, Equation (6.16)). For each of the inputs, x_i, there are two possibilities; these are dealt with in turn.

(a) Input x_i is not consumed. In this case it is clear that the decision-maker chooses not to buy any of x_i because the marginal utility of purchase is exceeded by the marginal cost. It follows that if $x_i = 0$, then

$$\frac{\partial u}{\partial x_i} < p_i \pi \quad (6.37)$$

(b) Input x_i is consumed. In this instance the problem does not differ from that studied earlier when there were no corner solutions allowed. Once more the rule for deciding how much of x_i to consume is to equate the marginal utility of extra consumption to the marginal cost.

$$\frac{\partial u}{\partial x_i} = p_i \pi \quad (6.38)$$

Combining Equations (6.37) and (6.38) we get the optimal conditions for the revised optimization problem given in Equations (6.34) to (6.36)

$$\frac{\partial u}{\partial x_i} \leq p_i \pi \quad (6.39)$$

$$\sum_{i=1}^{n} p_i x_i = w \quad (6.35)$$

$$x_i \geq 0 \quad (6.40)$$

$$\left(\frac{\partial u}{\partial x_i} - p_i \pi\right) x_i = 0 \tag{6.41}$$

Hence either x_i is consumed – in which case Equation (6.39) is a strict equality and Equation (6.40) a strict inequality – or x_i is not consumed – that is Equation (6.40) is an equality and Equation (6.39) a strict inequality.

The solution is still too rigid to serve as a general optimization rule, however. It still restricts the economic agent to spending all the budget as seen in Equation (6.35). This constraint will now be relaxed. The reason for doing this is that bliss points may exist which mean that it would simply not be optimal for the economic agent to consume up to the limit of the budget. Such an attainable bliss point is illustrated in Figure 6.6. The mathematical analysis developed so far – if applied to the problem shown in the diagram – would suggest point B as an optimum; an 'interior' solution exists, however, and utility is maximized, not at B, but rather at the bliss point A. Note that at A a change in income at the margin would have no effect on the amounts of x_1 and x_2 consumed, since small shifts of the budget constraint neither alter the position of A nor make A unattainable. It follows that the marginal utility of money, π, will be zero if an attainable bliss point exists.

To relax the assumption of a strict equality in the budget constraint, the optimization problem must first be restated as:

maximize $\quad u(x_i, \ldots, x_n) \tag{6.34}$

subject to $\quad \sum_{i=1}^{n} p_i x_i \leq w \tag{6.42}$

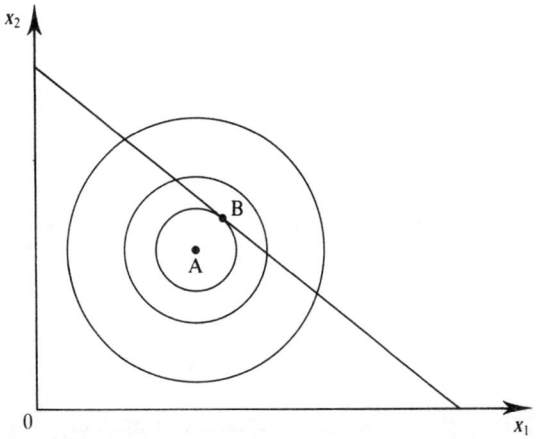

Figure 6.6 Bliss points and the constrained optimization problem

$$x_i \geq 0 \tag{6.40}$$

The Lagrangian function is

$$\mathcal{L} = u(x_1, \ldots, x_n) - \pi \left(\sum_{i=1}^{n} p_i x_i - w \right) \tag{6.43}$$

exactly as in the simpler problems faced hitherto.

By relaxing the budget constraint to Equation (6.42) two possibilities emerge:

(a) The agent spends all the budget, in which case

$$\sum_{i=1}^{n} p_i x_i - w = 0 \quad \text{and } \pi > 0 \tag{6.44}$$

If the agent spends the last unit of income then that last unit of money spent must have given some utility. This rationalizes the positive sign adopted by the marginal utility of money, π, when the entire budget is spent.

(b) The agent does not spend the entire budget. This can only be the case because a bliss point has been reached, that is because the marginal utility of money is zero. Hence

$$\sum_{i=1}^{n} p_i x_i - w < 0 \quad \text{and } \pi = 0 \tag{6.45}$$

Combining conditions given in Equations (6.44) and (6.45), and observing that at least one of these two conditions must hold for behaviour to be optimal, the following conditions are derived:

$$\sum_{i=1}^{n} p_i x_i - w \leq 0 \tag{6.46}$$

$$\pi \geq 0 \tag{6.47}$$

$$\left(\sum_{i=1}^{n} p_i x_i - w \right) \pi = 0 \tag{6.48}$$

The full solution to the problem set out in Equations (6.34), (6.40) and (6.42) is given by the equations and inequalities Expressions (6.39)–(6.41) and (6.46)–(6.48). This system of equations and inequalities enables a single optimal solution to be derived, indicating the best possible levels of input of each x_i. A numerical example of a problem of this type will appear later in this chapter. First, however, the various strands of thought encountered in the foregoing pages will be presented in a formal manner as the general non-linear optimizing problem with n dimensions and m constraints.

The general optimizing problem

In the completely general case, with n dimensions and m constraints, the optimizing problem is given by Equations (6.52) to (6.54).

$$\text{maximize} \quad u(x_i, \ldots, x_n) \tag{6.34}$$

$$\text{subject to} \quad g_j(x_i, \ldots, x_n) \leq 0 \quad \forall j \tag{6.49}$$

$$\text{and} \quad x_i \geq 0 \quad \forall i \tag{6.36}$$

There are n dimensions with $i = 1, \ldots, n$, and m constraints with $j = 1, \ldots, m$.

The Lagrangian function is given by

$$\mathscr{L} = u(x_i, \ldots, x_n) - \sum_{j=1}^{m} \pi_j g_j(x_i, \ldots, x_n) \tag{6.50}$$

Let g_j^i denote the cost to the optimizer of consuming each unit of the good x_i measured in terms of how much closer to the jth constraint the consumption of one extra unit of x_i brings him. In other words g_j^i is the derivative of the g_jth constraint with respect to x_i. For instance, if g_j is a budget constraint then g_j^i is the price of good x_i. If g_j were a ration coupon constraint, on the other hand, g_j^i would equal the number of ration coupons the optimizer must give up in order to acquire one extra unit of x_i.

The set of optimizing conditions for the problem set out in Equations (6.34), (6.36) and (6.49) is:

$$\frac{\partial u}{\partial x_i} - \sum_{j=1}^{m} \pi_j g_j^i \leq 0 \quad \forall i \tag{6.51}$$

$$x_i \geq 0 \quad \forall i \tag{6.36}$$

$$\left(\frac{\partial u}{\partial x_i} - \sum_{j=1}^{m} \pi_j g_j^i \right) x_i = 0 \quad \forall i \tag{6.52}$$

$$g_j(x_1, \ldots, x_n) \leq 0 \quad \forall j \tag{6.49}$$

$$\pi_j \geq 0 \quad \forall j \tag{6.53}$$

80 · ECONOMICS FOR MANAGERS

$$g_j(x_1, \ldots, x_n)\pi_j = 0 \quad \forall j \quad (6.54)$$

The system of equations and inequalities given in Expressions (6.36), (6.49) and (6.51) to (6.54) is known as the set of Kuhn–Tucker conditions for the solution of the general optimization problem. They summarize all the results derived earlier in this chapter.

NUMERICAL EXAMPLE II

Consider a firm whose inputs are capital, K, and labour, L. Given the following information, derive the Kuhn–Tucker conditions and hence the output maximizing levels of the two inputs.

The production function is

$$Q = K^{0.5} L^{0.5} \quad (6.25)$$

There is a budget constraint of £50 and the factor prices of capital and labour are 0.1 and 0.7, respectively. No more than 5 units of labour are available for employment.

The first step in the solution of this problem is to set up the Lagrangian function:

$$\mathscr{L} = K^{0.5} L^{0.5} - \pi_1(0.1 K + 0.7 L - 50) - \pi_2(L - 5) \quad (6.55)$$

The first term on the right hand side of Equation (6.55) is the production function itself. The second term is the budget constraint multiplied by π_1, the first of the Lagrangian multipliers, which represents the marginal utility of money. The third term encapsulates the limit on the availability of labour – either π_2 (the marginal utility of labour) is zero and less than five units of labour are used, or $(L - 5)$ is zero and all the available labour is employed.

From Equations (6.36), (6.49) and (6.51) to (6.54) the Kuhn–Tucker conditions for the problem at hand are easily derived:

$$0.5 K^{-0.5} L^{0.5} - 0.1 \pi_1 \leq 0 \quad (6.56)$$

$$0.5 K^{0.5} L^{-0.5} - 0.7 \pi_1 - \pi_2 \leq 0 \quad (6.57)$$

$$K \geq 0 \quad (6.58)$$

$$L \geq 0 \quad (6.59)$$

$$0.5 K^{0.5} L^{0.5} - 0.1 \pi_1 K = 0 \quad (6.60)$$

$$0.5 K^{0.5} L^{0.5} - 0.7 \pi_1 L - \pi_2 L = 0 \quad (6.61)$$

$$0.1 K + 0.7 L - 50 \leq 0 \quad (6.62)$$

$$L - 5 \leq 0 \quad (6.63)$$

$$\pi_1 \geq 0 \quad (6.64)$$

$$\pi_2 \geq 0 \quad (6.65)$$

$$0.1K\pi_1 + 0.7L\pi_1 - 50\pi_1 = 0 \tag{6.66}$$

$$L\pi_2 - 5\pi_2 = 0 \tag{6.67}$$

These equations and inequalities contain four unknowns. Although there are four equations, these are not sufficient to provide solutions for all the unknowns as the equations are themselves non-linear. The inequality conditions can be used in conjunction with the equalities, however, to derive the unique solution. As is often the case with non-linear problems, numerical procedures must be used to find the solutions for optimal K, L, π_1 and π_2. The solution in this case is $K^* = 465$, $L^* = 5$, $\pi_1 = 0.518$ and $\pi_2 = 4.459$. Both the labour constraint and the budget constraint effectively prevent further increases in output, since the marginal utility of labour at the optimum, π_2, and the marginal utility of money at the optimum, π_1, are both strictly positive. The optimal level of inputs are also both strictly positive; the optimal level of inputs are 465 units of capital and 5 units of labour.

Routine use of the Kuhn–Tucker conditions and simple manipulation of the resulting equalities and inequalities thus make possible the derivation of optimal inputs of labour and capital, subject to the various constraints in existence. Since the technique can be used for any number of dimensions and constraints it is very much more powerful than the diagrammatic analysis introduced in Chapter 5. Moreover, just as is the case for the statistical approaches described in Chapter 4, the ever-increasing availability of 'user friendly' computer software enables businesses to employ techniques of this kind cheaply and quickly.

Linear Programming

An important special case of the non-linear programming models discussed above is that of linear programming (LP). This is especially important because of its particularly widespread use in the business world. Its popularity is no doubt due to its simplicity. This, in turn, follows from the linear nature of both the optimand and the constraints. Equations (6.34), (6.36) and (6.49) can therefore be re-written as:

Maximize $\quad U = a_1x_1 + a_2x_2 + \ldots + a_nx_n \tag{6.68}$

subject to $\quad b_{i1}x_1 + b_{i2}x_2 + \ldots + b_{in}x_n \leq B_i \quad \forall i \tag{6.69}$

and $\quad x_1, x_2, \ldots, x_n \geq 0 \tag{6.70}$

Now Equations (6.68) to (6.70) could, of course, be solved using the Kuhn–Tucker conditions. But the simple set-up of the system enables us to take advantage of a particularly easy method of solution.

Note that the linear nature of the optimand and constraints can limit the number of solutions which may exist. Only in extreme cases where the direction of preference is orthogonal to a constraint (for instance, when the budget line is perfectly parallel to a linear indifference curve) will this not be so. To explain why, consider Figure 6.7. This shows an economic agent's preferences between two goods, x_1 and x_2. The indifference curves (or isoquants, or isoprofit lines) are linear and parallel to one another. Utility (output, profit) rises as the agent moves up along the line indicating direction of preference. The two constraints define the limits of the attainable set of affordable combinations of x_1 and x_2. It is easily seen that there are only three candidates for the optimal solution, namely A, B and C. In this example A is the point at which the solution to the constrained optimization problem lies. Had the contours of the preference function $(I_1, I_2, \ldots)$ been flatter, the solution might have been at B. Had they been steeper, the solution might have been at C. But the solution could not have been anywhere other than at A, B or C, because these three points are the only corners, or 'vertices' of the attainable set. The analyst need not consider any other points in the analysis.

The method most frequently used in the solution of LP problems is known as the simplex algorithm. This is a set of steps (usually performed by computer) developed by Dantzig (1951). The procedure first identifies the location of the vertices of the attainable set, and then selects the one which optimizes the objective function. The method is particularly appealing because it need not always even require the identification of all vertices in order to determine the solution. Figure 6.8 illustrates the way in which the simplex method works. The operation of the method is best explained by reference to a numerical example.

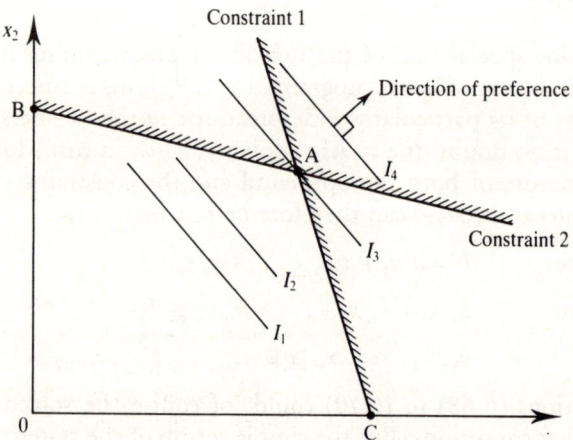

Figure 6.7 Linear programming applied to a choice of two goods, x_1 and x_2

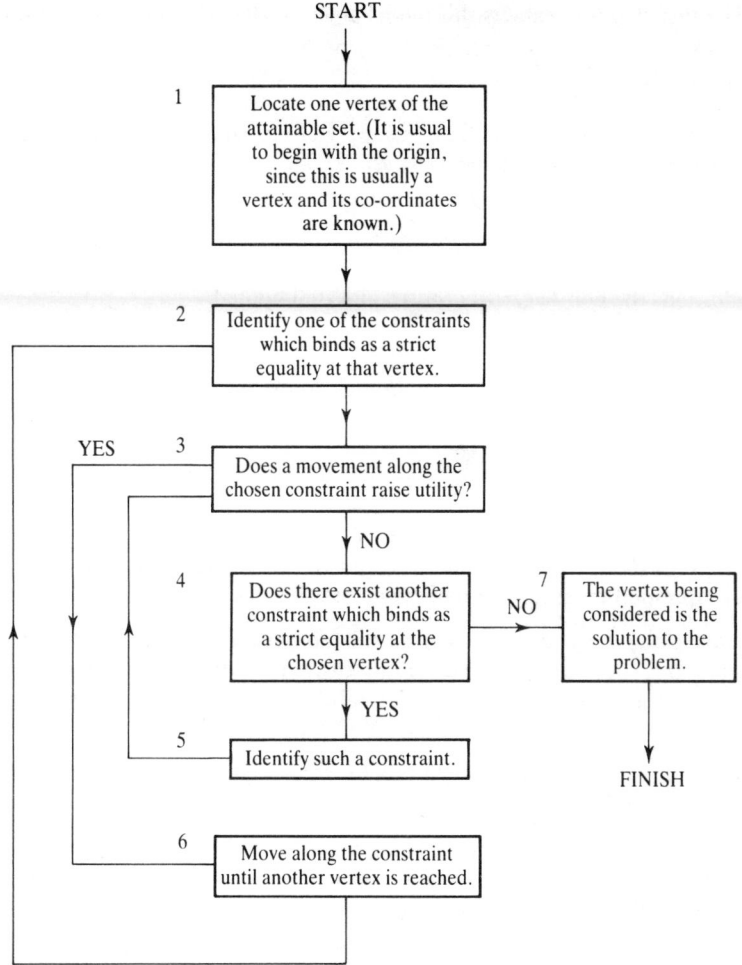

Figure 6.8 The simplex algorithm

NUMERICAL EXAMPLE III

Consider a firm which produces two goods, x_1 and x_2. It employs 50 units of labour, L, and 100 units of capital, K. Both capital and labour are suitable for use in the production of either good, and inputs of both capital and labour are to be regarded as fixed. The profit margins on each unit produced of goods x_1 and x_2 are 50 p and 70 p, respectively. In order to produce one unit of x_1 the firm requires 2 units of capital and 5 units of labour. Production of one unit of x_2 requires 10 units of capital and 2 units of labour. Solve for the profit maximizing output of x_1 and x_2.

The first step is to express this model algebraically. The optimand is profits, given by

$$\text{Max } U = 0.5x_1 + 0.75x_2 \tag{6.71}$$

The constraints represent the limited supply of capital and labour respectively, and may be represented algebraically as:

$$x_1 + 5x_2 \leq 50 \tag{6.72}$$

$$5x_1 + 2x_2 \leq 50 \tag{6.73}$$

In addition, the non-negativity constraints are imposed:

$$x_1, x_2 \geq 0 \tag{6.74}$$

We now use Figure 6.8 to guide us through to the solution:

1 Choose the origin, where $x_1 = x_2 = 0$

2 Identify the constraint $x_1 \geq 0$

3 Does a movement along this constraint raise utility? Moving from $(x_1, x_2) = (0, 0)$ to $(1, 0)$ would raise profits from zero to 0.5. The answer to this question must therefore be 'yes'.

6 Move along the $x_1 \geq 0$ constraint until another vertex is reached. Progress along this constraint can be halted by either Equation (6.72) or Equation (6.74). Assuming $x_2 = 0$ still, Equation (6.72) allows $x_1 \leq 50$ while Equation (6.73) allows $x_1 \leq 10$. A vertex therefore exists at (10, 0).

2 The only constraint operative at (10, 0) which has not yet been explored is Equation (6.73).

3 Does a movement from (10, 0) along Equation (6.73) raise utility? Moving from (10, 0) to (0, 25) would raise profits from 5 to 18.75. The answer to this question must therefore be 'yes'.

6 Move along the $5x_1 + 2x_2 \leq 50$ constraint until another vertex is reached. Progress along this constraint can be halted either by Equation (6.72) or Equation (6.74). Assuming $5x_1 + 2x_2 = 50$ still, Equation (6.72) allows $x_2 \leq 8.7$ while Equation (6.74) allows $x_2 \leq 25$. A vertex therefore exists at (6.5, 8.7).

2 The only constraint operative at (6.5, 8.7) which has not yet been explored is Equation (6.72)

3 Does a movement from (6.5, 8.7) along Equation (6.72) raise utility? Moving from (6.5, 8.7) to (0, 10) would lower profits from 9.775 to 7.5. The answer to the question posed here must therefore be 'no'.

7 The vertex under consideration, where $x_1 = 6.5$ and $x_2 = 8.7$, represents the profit maximizing solution. This completes the simplex algorithm

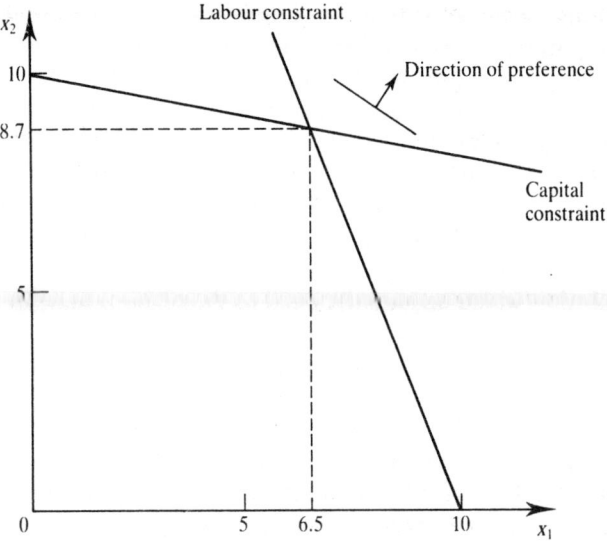

Figure 6.9 Linear programming: the solution

The result obtained by application of the simplex method to the above LP problem can be checked by deriving the Kuhn–Tucker conditions. These are satisfied by the above values of x_1 and x_2, and $\pi_1 = 0.120$ and $\pi_2 = 0.076$ where π_1 and π_2 represent, respectively, the Lagrangian multipliers on the capital and labour constraints. (Evaluation of the Kuhn–Tucker conditions for this example is left to the reader as an exercise.) The example is illustrated diagrammatically in Figure 6.9.

The simplex method is useful because it provides a simple algorithm which may be used in the solution of LP problems, even when the problem concerns many more dimensions (or x variables) than have been considered here. Quite complicated problems concerning the optimal allocation of resources can be solved easily using the LP methods outlined in this section. The appeal of the method is, therefore, quite considerable.

Concluding comments

The methods of mathematical optimization are in widespread use in modern businesses. Particularly popular is the tool of linear programming, whose great appeal lies in its simplicity. Nevertheless, more general programming methods (such as non-linear programming) are gaining in popularity as more powerful computing facilities become more generally available. Like forecasting methods, optimization methods lie in the province of the specialist, but a sound grasp of the basic concepts underlying the methodology helps any manager.

Numbers sometimes imply any unwarranted degree of precision. Programming models which fully take into account problems of industrial relations are as rare as forecasting models which predict wars. These methods are tools, and managers should not use them as strait-jackets. An optimal solution which implies the need to shed labour may, in practice, be difficult to achieve. But the model which led to such a solution is unlikely to have costed out management–union negotiations for the reduction of manpower. The world described by the model is an approximation to the real world, not the real world itself.

Having thus qualified the use of mathematical models in general management, some students might ask: Why bother? The answer to this question – and it is a convincing answer – is that more information is surely to be preferred to less, if that information is available (as it is) at low cost. So long as managers appreciate the limitation of mathematical programming, such techniques can be of great value indeed. The popularity of the methods is testimony of their usefulness.

Exercise: Mathematical optimization in UK manufacturing

Solve the problem posed at the end of Chapter 5 using the Kuhn–Tucker method.

Chapter 7
Costs

In the foregoing chapters optimization methods were used to calculate the optimal employment of factors of production, such as labour and capital, by a firm. An extension of this application, to be described below, involves deriving cost curves for the firm. Cost curves relate the cost of production to the quantity of output produced. They are drawn on the general assumption that the firm wishing to produce a given quantity of output does so as cheaply as possible, given certain constraints on the time required to make adjustments in the mix of inputs employed. In particular, the firm will require more time to make changes in its capital stock (plant and equipment) than in its pool of labour, since labour inputs are more easily variable; at least two sets of cost curves must therefore be defined: one to describe costs before capital can be adjusted (the so-called *short run*) and one to describe costs after capital has fully adjusted to its optimal level (the *long run*). These sets of cost curves which refer, respectively, to the short run and the long run will be described in more detail at a later stage.

The total cost (TC) curve shows the relationship between the output level, q, and the costs of producing that output as efficiently as possible. As output rises one would expect total costs to rise, but it is likely that the rate at which total costs rise varies over the range of output being considered. This will be so in both the short run and the long run, though for different reasons. In the short run costs initially fall as output rises because the firm possesses a fixed stock of machinery and other capital; as labour employment rises, the most efficient mix of inputs is approached. Consequently the cost of producing a typical unit of output (the 'unit cost' or 'average cost') would fall. Inputs of labour should not be allowed to rise indefinitely, though, because a situation might be reached where too many cooks spoil the broth. So the cost of producing each unit of output would start to rise as output increases. Picture one man in a large factory, tending 1,000 machines. He spends so much time running from one machine to another that he fails to service any of them satisfactorily.

On the other hand, if the factory were to enjoy the services of 10 million workers, each worker would be so busy bumping into his colleagues that he would not be able to work effectively.

In a simple model in which capital inputs are fixed and labour is the only variable factor of production, labour productivity is the only source of cost variation. If, in such a model, the unit cost falls as output rises, then each unit of labour employed must be becoming more productive. The firm is said to be experiencing increasing productivity. Otherwise the firm experiences diminishing productivity. In the short run, there must always be a level of output above which diminishing productivity occurs.

So much for the short run; consider now what might happen when *all* inputs are freely variable. Here too, costs are likely to vary with output. There are several reasons for this. Costs will fall as the expansion of the firm enables it to exploit bulk-buy deals; certain costs – such as administration costs – rise only slowly as output rises; large firms can support their own research and development (R and D) staff, and reap the benefits of innovation. All these factors are likely to reduce the cost of producing the representative unit of output as the total production of the firm increases. On the other hand, when organizations become very large, bureaucracy might creep in to impose additional costs on the business.

Where all inputs into the production process are variable and the costs borne by the firm *per unit of output* are falling as total output rises, economies of scale are said to exist. If, on the other hand, unit costs rise with output (when all inputs are variable), then diseconomies of scale exist.

Both long run and short run total cost curves can be derived directly from the isoquant map of a firm. Figure 7.1 shows an isoquant map of an imaginary firm, complete with certain of its isocost lines. Capital stock is fixed at $\bar{K}$ in the short run. In other words the firm currently employs $\bar{K}$ units of capital and it can neither increase nor decrease its capital stock instantaneously. New machines, once ordered, take time to arrive; furthermore, machines already employed by the firm will continue to be operated since, once bought, the machines represent fixed costs – the firm would have to pay for the machines whether they are in use or not.

Figure 7.1 shows the 1-, 2-, 3-, 4- and 5-tonne isoquants, together with a number of isocost lines (where costs are measured in £ thousands). If the firm wishes to produce its output as cheaply as possible it must operate on the lowest attainable isocost line at each level of output. In the long run (where both capital and labour can be varied) these points will be defined by the tangency of isoquants and isocost lines. In the short run, however, although the labour input is fully flexible (that is, overtime, new hiring and short-time are all at the firm's own discretion), capital input is fixed

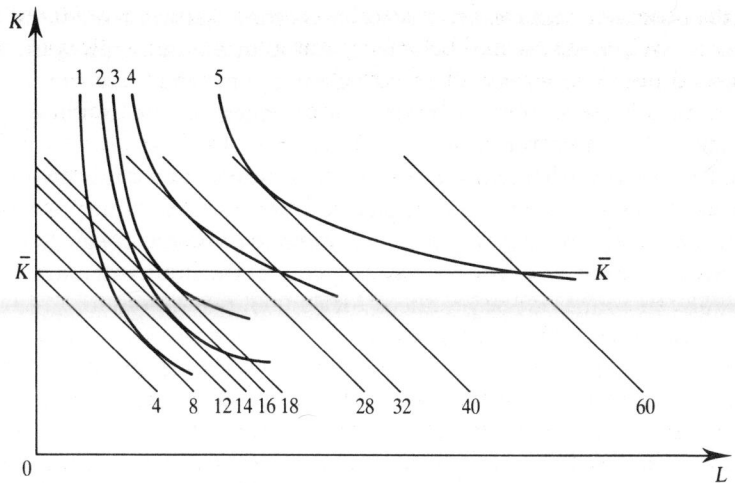

Figure 7.1 An isoquant map

at $\bar{K}$. Short run costs are therefore defined by the intersection of the relevant isoquant and the line $\bar{K}$-$\bar{K}$.

If firms operate efficiently (producing given output at the least possible cost) their short and long run cost schedules will appear as shown in columns 1, 2, 5 and 6 of Table 7.1. These figures are derived directly from the isoquant map shown in Figure 7.1. Consider first the short run total cost curve. The firm is constrained to employ a combination of capital and labour which lies along the $\bar{K}$-$\bar{K}$ line. This means that it must incur a minimum of £4,000 costs per period (since the combination of $\bar{K}$

Table 7.1 Short and long run costs (units of output in £000s)

	Short-run costs			Long-run costs		
Output (q)	Total cost	Average cost	Marginal cost	Output (q)	Total cost	Average cost
0	4	—		0	0	—
			} 8			
1	12	12		1	8	8
			} 4			
2	16	8		2	14	7
			} 6			
3	18	6		3	18	6
			} 8			
4	32	8		4	28	7
			} 12			
5	60	12		5	40	8

units of capital and no units of labour lies on the £4,000 isocost line). One tonne of output can be produced for £12,000 in the short run, since the 1-tonne isoquant intersects the $\bar{K}$-$\bar{K}$ line at a point which coincides with the £12,000 isocost line. Similarly, two tonnes can be produced for £16,000 in the short run, and so on.

In the long run the firm is free to vary its capital input; it is no longer compelled to employ $\bar{K}$ units of capital. Consequently zero output can be produced at zero cost, and the least cost method of producing given levels of output is defined by the points of tangency of the isoquants and isocost lines. So one tonne can be produced for £8,000, two tonnes for £14,000, and so on.

Once the costs have been tabulated in this way the short and long run total cost curves can be drawn (as in Figure 7.2) by plotting costs against output. Note that the short run total cost curve (SRTC) lies everywhere above the long run total cost curve (LRTC) except at the single point where the long run desired capital stock and the actual capital stock are equal ($q = 3$). The inverse S-shape of the functions drawn in Figure 7.2 is typical of total cost functions in general. It should be noted, however, that in practice diseconomies of scale usually occur only at very high levels of output (often above the levels at which a single firm would normally produce).

In addition to total costs in the long run and the short run, the so-called average and marginal cost schedules will be of interest to the firm. The reasons for the firm's interest in average and marginal costs will become clear in the next two chapters, but for the time being let us concentrate on defining the concepts.

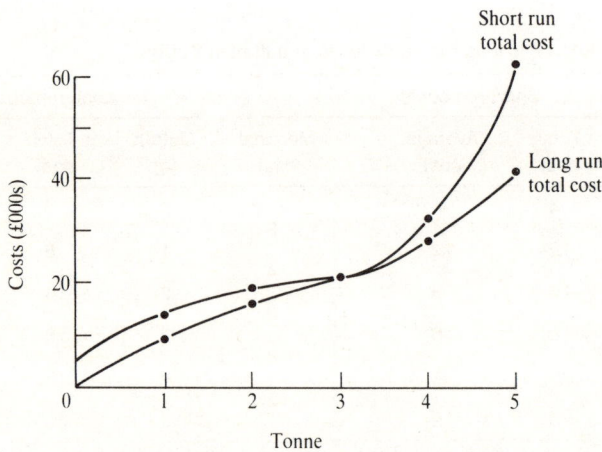

Figure 7.2 Total cost curves

The average cost schedule (AC) relates the cost of producing the average unit of output to the level of output. Hence

$$AC \equiv \frac{TC}{q} \qquad (7.1)$$

The marginal cost schedule (MC) describes the rate at which total cost changes in response to a unit change in the level of output produced. Hence

$$MC \equiv \frac{dTC}{dq} \qquad (7.2)$$

In particular, if output is x units, $MC = TC\{\text{when } q = x + 0.5\} - TC\{\text{when } q = x - 0.5\}$. Marginal and average cost schedules are reported in columns 3, 4 and 7 of Table 7.1. Just as total cost curves could be drawn from the data in that table, so can average and marginal cost curves, and these are illustrated in Figure 7.3. The average cost curves – both short run (SRAC) and long run (LRAC) – resemble horseshoes; the short run marginal cost curve (SRMC), while also U-shaped, initially falls below the SRAC then rises at a faster rate than average costs, passing through the minimum point of the SRAC. Thus the SRMC somewhat resembles a tick. These shapes are typical of empirically established cost schedules, and cost curves which look like this are frequently said to be 'well behaved' (see,

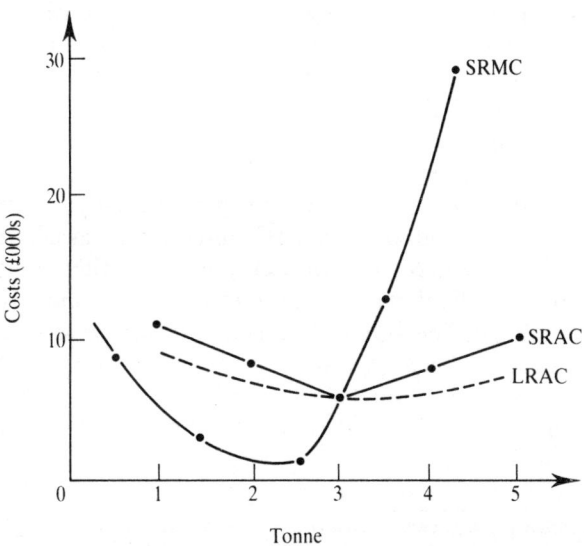

Figure 7.3 Average and marginal cost curves

for instance, Bays, 1986; Hayes, 1987; Johnes and Haycox, 1986; Johnston, 1960).

Note that the marginal cost curve of Figure 7.3 intersects the (short run) average cost curve at the latter's minimum. This must always be the case, since average cost can only be constant if it equals marginal cost. If the cost of producing the marginal unit exceeds average cost, then average cost must be pulled up by the addition of extra output. Conversely, if the cost of producing the marginal unit is less than average cost, then average cost must be falling.

Cost curves play a crucial role in determining how much of a product a firm will be prepared to supply, and they are also often crucial in price-setting. Thus the price of gold-plated Rolls-Royces is high largely because it costs Rolls-Royce a lot to produce such cars. But it should always be remembered that costs are only one part of the price-setting story; flowers are expensive at Valentine's day and Mother's day not because they cost more to produce at these times, but because demand is high.

Fixed and variable costs

An important distinction can be made between costs which are fixed and those which are variable in the short run. Fixed costs are paid on inputs (like capital or land) which are fixed in the short run. Once it has been decided to employ such inputs over, say, the next month, payment for such factors of production must be made independently of whether or not production actually takes place at the anticipated levels. These payments might then be regarded as thrown away for the remainder of the month; they must be paid regardless of whether or not any output is produced at all. Fixed costs are therefore invariate with respect to output. They are also sometimes referred to as overheads and they exist only in the short run. The intercept of the total cost curve, TC, and the vertical axis in Figure 7.2 is the level of total fixed costs. In the example used earlier, total fixed costs (TFC) are £4,000. All other costs are variable (total variable costs, TVC) as shown in Figure 7.4. The TC and TVC curves are always vertically parallel, the vertical distance between these curves representing the £4,000 fixed cost which, as was said earlier, is constant with respect to output.

Average fixed cost (AFC) and average variable cost (AVC) schedules are derived by dividing TFC and TVC, respectively, by output at each level of output. AFC declines as output rises because while the numerator (TFC) remains constant, the denominator of the identity $AFC \equiv TFC/q$ clearly rises with output. Consequently AFC falls at a decreasing rate as output increases. Average variable costs, on the other hand, first fall and then

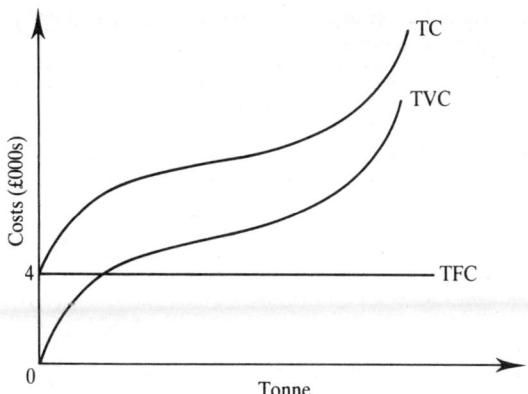

Figure 7.4 Fixed and variable total cost curves

later rise as output increases. Both AFC and AVC curves are illustrated in Figure 7.5.

A rational firm will continue to produce output in the short run so long as its revenue exceeds its total variable cost. In this way, even if it cannot make a short run profit, by producing at the optimal level of output the firm can at least contribute to the reduction of the losses entailed by its fixed costs. If there is no prospect of profits by the time payments for fixed inputs must again be made (the end of the short run), the firm will cease production at that time, *but not before*. If the firm cannot even cover its variable costs it will cease production immediately.

Table 7.2 shows the TFC, AFC, TVC and AVC schedules which are derived from the isoquant map of Figure 7.1. A firm producing 3 tonne of output and which secures a total revenue of £14,500 cannot cover total

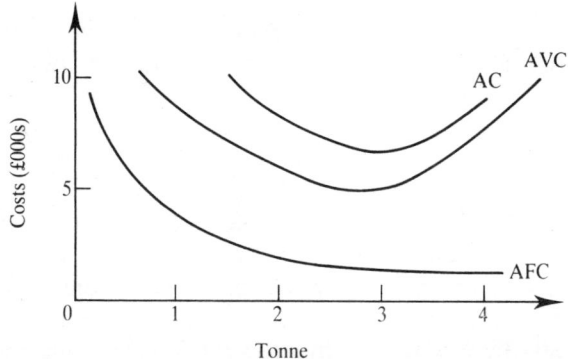

Figure 7.5 Fixed and variable average cost curves

Table 7.2 Fixed and variable costs compared for quantity, q (units of output in £000s)

q	TFC	AFC	TVC	AVC
1	4	4	8	8
2	4	2	12	6
3	4	$1\frac{1}{3}$	14	$4\frac{2}{3}$
4	4	1	28	7
5	4	$\frac{4}{5}$	56	$11\frac{1}{5}$

costs and therefore makes a loss. However, such a firm will stay in business *in the short run* as it can cover *variable* costs and make some contribution to fixed costs. Once fixed costs for the next period become payable the firm quits the industry; only if total revenue falls below total variable cost, and if there is no prospect of future recovery, would the firm choose to go out of business instantaneously.

Cost curves and product curves

We have seen in the last few pages how the production function and the prices of inputs determine the cost structures of a firm. Exactly the same factors determine the productivity of the various inputs. That is, the addition to output resulting from the addition of a small amount of a single input, holding all other inputs constant, is dependent on the shape of the isoquant map near the points of tangency of isoquants and isocost lines. The concept of productivity will be of particular importance in the sequel; this will be introduced here in order to emphasize the special relationship between productivity and costs.

The total productivity of labour (TPL) schedule is derived by plotting output (along the vertical axis) against labour input (where capital is held constant). Recall that in the short run variations in output result from changes in labour employment alone, and that capital costs the firm a fixed £4,000. From Table 7.1 it can be seen that the labour cost incurred in order to produce 0 tonne of output would be £0 (since $4000 - 4000 = 0$). To produce 1 tonne of output, the value of labour input must be £8,000 (since $12\,000 - 4000 = 8000$). Continuing in this vein, the TPL schedule shown in Table 7.3 (columns 1 and 2) can be constructed. It cannot be overemphasized that to construct this table capital input is held constant. Moreover, it is convenient to assume that labour is elastically supplied, so that the employment of labour varies in proportion to its total cost.

Table 7.3 Productivity of labour schedule (units of output based on '000s workers)

Labour input (L)	TPL (q)	APL	MPL
0	0	–	
			0.125
8	1	0.125	
			0.250
12	2	0.167	
			0.250
16	3	0.187	
			0.083
28	4	0.143	
			0.036
56	5	0.089	

The average product of labour (APL) is defined as the ratio of the total product of labour to the amount of labour being employed, that is $APL \equiv TPL/L$. The marginal product of labour (MPL) is defined as the rate of change of the total product of labour with respect to the amount of labour; that is $MPL \equiv dTPL/dL$. Further, the marginal product of labour when $L = x$ may be thought of as approximately equal to the difference in TPL when $L = x + 0.5$ and TPL when $L = x - 0.5$. Both APL and MPL schedules have been calculated for the example under consideration and are reported in the third and fourth columns, respectively, of Table 7.3.

When the APL and MPL schedules are plotted against L on a graph, as in Figure 7.6, an interesting fact emerges. The APL and MPL curves look very much like the short run AC and MC curves upside-down. The reason for this is simple: the increasing returns which make the AC slope

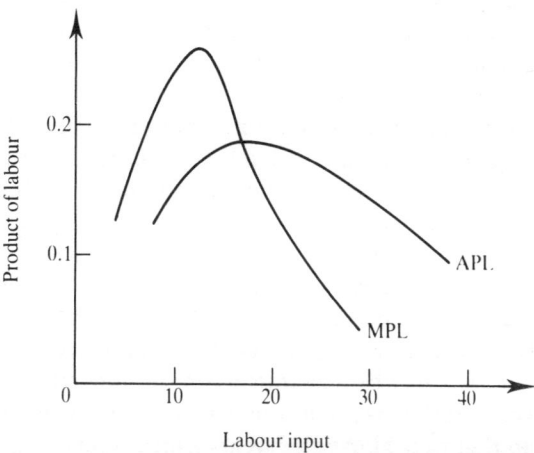

Figure 7.6 Average and marginal product of labour curves

downwards initially are themselves the result of the increasing average product of labour; the decreasing returns which ultimately cause the AC to fall result directly from a decreasing average product of labour. The cost functions and the product functions are inextricably linked to one another; specifically, as one reaches a minimum the other reaches a maximum. For this reason the total product of labour function is said to be the dual of the total cost function.

The marginal product of labour schedule is of particular importance in the labour market, since the demand for labour is governed in large part by worker productivity. (Indeed, if the price at which the firm sold its output in the product market were fixed at 1, the marginal product of labour schedule would correspond exactly to the demand curve for labour.) The demand for labour is a concept which need not detain us further here, however, but is one to which we shall return in Chapter 13.

The cost of capital

One of the major costs faced by a firm is that of capital – the plant and machinery which is used in the production process. In practice, decisions made by the firm concerning investments in capital are complicated by the fact that the life of capital equipment is typically quite long. The firm must therefore be aware, when purchasing new capital, that the decision to do so can affect production for many years into the future. In some sectors (like the chemicals or brewing industries) capital equipment can remain in use for thirty years or more, though in others (such as the computer industry) it can become obsolete within a couple of years. In virtually every sector, capital is fundamentally different from labour in that while labour can, in general, be hired at short notice and for short periods, capital is bought and can neither be acquired nor disposed of quickly. Moreover, labour is hired on terms which (usually) guarantee that *period by period* it produces a value of output which is at least as great as the wage; in other words, the costs of labour are incurred at the same time as the benefits of its production are enjoyed. Capital is different. The costs of acquiring capital are usually incurred before the benefits of the investment are realized.

It follows that static, one-period analyses do not provide a sufficiently powerful technique for assessing the value of capital investment. Instead a technique must be used which enables a comparison to be made between the costs of capital at the time of its purchase and the stream of production attributable to that capital over the years which follow.

A further problem hinders the comparison of costs and returns which are realized in different time periods. A pound spent by a firm now is worth more than a pound earned by the firm at some time in the future. This is so for a number of reasons. First, inflation erodes the value of money as time passes. Secondly, a bird in hand is worth two in the bush; money which is promised for the future is worth less than money which is owned now because a degree of risk inevitably attaches to the promise of future returns, and the firm may be risk averse. Thirdly, a pound owned now could – if the firm so chose – be saved in a bank, and could therefore earn interest. This is clearly not an option if the pound is not already in the possession of the firm but rather is one which will become available only in the future.

To keep matters simple in what follows, it will be assumed that there is zero inflation and that firms are risk neutral. Hence the only disparity between the value of a pound now and that of a pound promised for one year from now is attributable to the rate of interest. If the rate of interest is, say, 10 per cent, then one pound now is worth the same as $1 \times 1.10 = £1.10$ one year hence. Moreover, one pound now is worth the same as $1.10 \times 1.10 = £1.21$ two years hence or $1.21 \times 1.10 = £1.33$ three years hence. This means that a pound promised for three years' time is equivalent to just 1/1.33, or 75 pence paid today. A pound promised for 8 years' time would be worth just under 50 pence today.

If, on the other hand, the interest rate is just 5 per cent, then one pound now is worth the same as £1.05 one year hence, £1.10 two years hence and £1.16 three years hence. So a pound promised for three years' time would be equivalent to just 86 pence today. A pound promised for 15 years' time would be worth just under 50 pence today. Note that this all happens even in a world without inflation.

Now if the interest rate is high (over 10 per cent, say), the returns which a firm can expect to arise in ten years' time from an investment made now will carry relatively little weight in the calculation of whether the investment is worthwhile or not. An example of this is the Channel Tunnel linking Britain and France. Such a large project takes so long to construct that the returns can only be realized in the distant future. Once they have been discounted, therefore, the returns seem small in relation to the costs, since the costs must all be borne before the returns start to come in. It is largely for this reason that the Tunnel remained a 'pipe dream' for a century before its eventual construction; it is for much the same reason that difficulties were experienced in raising the required finance for the project once the decision to go ahead had been taken.

If the interest rate can be assumed constant over the lifetime of an investment, a convenient formula can be used to calculate the worth of a project in present day values. Denoting by r the rate of interest (so that if the interest rate is 5 per cent, $r = 0.05$), it is easily seen that each pound earned in year t is worth $£1/(1+r)^t$ now. This is because a pound saved now will be worth $£(1+r)$ in one years' time, $£(1+r)(1+r)$ in two years' time, and so on; put another way, in order to secure a bank balance of £1 this year, an individual would need to have saved $£1/(1+r)$ one year ago, or $£1/(1+r)^2$ two years ago. The *net present value* of one pound received two years ago is therefore $£(1+r)^2$, and the net present value of one pound received two years hence is just $£1/(1+r)^2$. The net present value of a project can be defined as the difference between the present day values of the returns and the present day values of the costs.

Hence,

$$NPV = \sum_{t=0}^{T} \frac{R_t}{(1+r)^t} - \sum_{t=0}^{T} \frac{C_t}{(1+r)^t} \qquad (7.3)$$

where NPV denotes net present value; R_t is the returns to the investment realized in period t; C_t are the costs of the investment incurred in period t; and $0, \ldots, T$ is the time horizon over which the project takes place.

If $(R_t - C_t)$ does not vary from year to year and the project is of long duration (so that T tends to infinity), Equation (7.3) can be simplified to

$$NPV = (R_t - C_t)(1+r)/r \qquad (7.4)$$

The above analysis suggests the following criterion for determining whether or not an investment should be made by the firm. So long as the NPV associated with a capital investment project is positive, the firm should go ahead with the project.

A related criterion which is sometimes used as an alternative to the NPV rule discussed above is the *internal rate of return* (IRR). The IRR of a project is the discount rate, i, which reduces the NPV to zero. That is, the IRR is the value of i which satisfies the equation

$$NPV = \sum_{t=0}^{T} \frac{R_t}{(1+i)^t} - \sum_{t=0}^{T} \frac{C_t}{(1+i)^t} = 0 \qquad (7.5)$$

The internal rate of return criterion for investment may be stated as follows. So long as the IRR exceeds the market rate of interest, the firm should invest in the project under consideration.

The NPV and IRR criteria commonly yield the same results, and both are in widespread use. The NPV does, however, possess certain advantages over the IRR criterion. In particular, there may, in certain circumstances, exist more than one value of i which satisfies Equation (7.5). In other words, the internal rate of return may not be unique. For example, suppose that a given project is expected to last for four years, and that $(R_t - C_t)$ for the four periods, respectively, is expected to be -20, $+32$,

+ 19 and − 33. With an interest rate of 15 per cent the net present value of the project would be 0.5, and so the recommendation is that the project should go ahead. There are, however, two real positive solutions for i (and one real negative solution). The internal rate of return is either 10 per cent or 50 per cent. The result of applying the IRR criterion is therefore ambiguous. This situation arises when the sign attached to the annual net returns changes more than once over the lifetime of the project. For this reason most practitioners prefer to use the NPV criterion when making decisions about investment projects.

The connection between investment and the interest rate is one which will be explored further in Chapter 11. Meanwhile our attention in the next chapter will be concentrated on the way in which demand and costs influence the pricing behaviour of firms in a variety of different types of market.

Exercise: Costs in a hospital ward

Schedules relating the average cost of health care to the number of mentally handicapped patients resident on a hospital ward have been estimated by Johnes and Haycox (1986). One of these average cost curves can be summarized by the data in Table 7.4. From these data, perform the following tasks:

(a) Calculate the total cost curve.

(b) Find the total fixed cost.

(c) Evaluate the total variable cost.

(d) Construct the marginal cost schedule.

(e) Derive the average fixed cost schedule.

Table 7.4 Average cost of health care by size of ward

Number of patients in ward	Average cost (£)
1	33 763
10	18 078
15	12 700
20	9 706
25	9 095
30	10 866
40	21 558

100 · ECONOMICS FOR MANAGERS

(f) Evaluate the average variable cost.

(g) Draw the average cost, average variable cost and marginal cost curves. Notice that the marginal cost curve intersects both the average cost curve and the average variable cost curve at their lowest points. Why is this?

(h) Assuming that capital costs are fixed and that labour is the only variable input, calculate the average product of labour.

(i) Calculate the marginal product of labour.

(j) Draw the curves you have derived in the answers to (h) and (i) above. Examine these together with the average cost and marginal cost curves which were drawn as the answer to question (g). How do the two sets of curves compare?

(k) What is the optimal (least cost) ward size?

Chapter 8
Optimizing profits

Hitherto we have considered the theory of demand and the structure of the costs of a firm. It was hinted earlier that it is not only the costs of production that determine price, but that demand factors also contribute. Now it is time to combine costs with the demand side to establish a full theory of price-setting behaviour. As will be seen later, an important influence on the manner in which prices are set is the structure of the market for which the good in question is being produced. In this chapter several features of the analysis are developed which lead to rules of thumb which may profitably be employed by firms operating in any type of market. Different types of market structure are then described in greater detail.

First, the way in which the demand side enters the firm's system of pricing must be introduced. Just as there are cost curves for a firm, each firm also faces revenue curves. Consider the revenue for a firm which faces the demand curve shown in Figure 8.1. If price is 60 p no output is demanded, so total revenue will be zero. Reducing the price to 40 p produces a demand for 3,000 units per week and a total weekly revenue of £1,200. By further reducing the price to 30 p, 4,500 units will be demanded and total revenue rises further to £1,350 per week.

Just as in the case of costs, various measures of revenue can be employed. In particular, we can derive total revenue, average revenue and marginal revenue schedules.

Total revenue (TR) is the gross income of the firm. It is equal to the number of units sold multiplied by the price of each unit. It exceeds the surplus profits of the firm by an amount equal to the total cost.

Average revenue (AR) is the revenue the firm earns from the average unit sold; hence $AR \equiv TR/q$.

Marginal revenue, (MR) is the change observed in total revenue as a consequence of a unit change in the level of output sold; hence $MR \equiv dTR/dq$. Further, the marginal revenue when output is x may be thought of as approximately equal to the difference between total

102 · ECONOMICS FOR MANAGERS

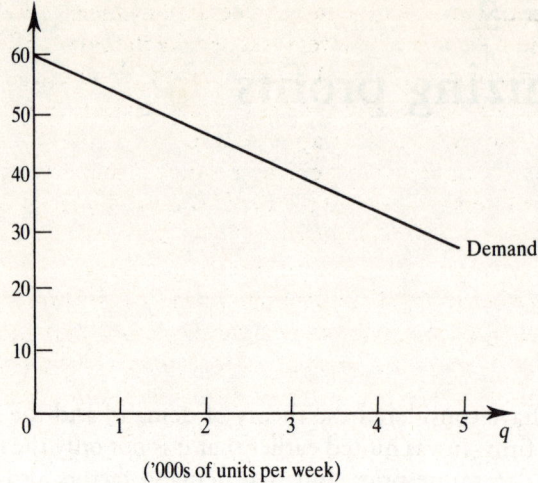

('000s of units per week)

Figure 8.1 A demand curve

revenue when output is $x + 0.5$ and total revenue when output is $x - 0.5$.

Using information from the demand curve of Figure 8.1 and the above definitions, a table of revenues like Table 8.1 can be constructed. This shows total, average and marginal revenues for every level of output. It is analogous to the costs data calculated in Table 7.1.

Marginal revenue is zero at the point at which total revenue peaks, since at this point a very small change in output has zero effect on revenue. Recall that where total revenue is constant, the own price elasticity of demand is 1. Recall also that, for a linear demand curve, unit own price elasticity of demand occurs at the mid-point. It follows that the marginal revenue curve must slope downwards at twice the gradient of the

Table 8.1 Total, average and marginal revenues related to output

$q(\times 10^3$ week)	TR (£)	AR (p)	MR (p)
1	533.33	$53\frac{1}{3}$	
			40
2	933.33	$46\frac{2}{3}$	
			$26\frac{2}{3}$
3	1200	40	
			$13\frac{1}{3}$
4	1333.33	$33\frac{1}{3}$	
			0
5	1333.33	$26\frac{2}{3}$	
			$-13\frac{1}{3}$
6	1200	20	

average revenue curve. In the more general non-linear case, the MR curve lies below the AR curve whenever (as is usually the case for firms which are less than perfectly competitive) the AR curve is downward sloping. Note also that since $TR = pq$ and $AR = TR/q$, the average revenue and demand curves are identical; this is always the case.

Having derived the revenue curves it is now possible to analyse the way in which a firm sets the price of the product it produces. The behaviour of the firm in this respect depends crucially on the objective function or the goal which it sets itself. Its price-setting strategy will be different according to whether the firm wishes to maximize its profits, or maximize its sales revenue, or maximize some other objective, or maximize nothing at all. For convenience just one particular option will be assumed for the remainder of this part of the book – that of profit maximization. In certain circumstances, however, other objectives may be of importance, and these alternative objectives will be given due treatment in Chapter 16. Meanwhile, since profit maximization appears to reflect the behaviour of many real life firms, at least to the extent of being an adequate first approximation, the assumption that profit is the firm's objective function is adopted.

Profit is defined as the payment to those who own the firm made as a return on their financial commitment to the firm. It may conveniently be divided into two components. The first of these is *normal profit*, the minimum level of profit which the owners must make in order for them to maintain their financial commitment to the company. This is properly regarded as part of the costs of production and is included as such in the total cost curve. Any revenue which the firm is able to make in excess of total costs also goes to the owners as a surplus profit; this profit is known as a *supernormal profit* and is defined as the difference between total revenue and total costs. The firm will not produce in the long run if it does not earn normal profits. A profit-maximizing firm will attempt to achieve the largest possible supernormal profits. If the TR and TC curves appear as in Figure 8.2 maximum profits will be secured at q^*, where the vertical distance between the two curves is greatest (in the range where revenues exceed costs).

As output rises from q_1 the slope of TR is initially greater than that of TC, and so revenue is increasing faster than costs and hence profits rise. Between q_1 and q_2 however, the slope of TR is steadily declining and that of TC begins to rise. Thus there must come a point when the relative magnitudes of the slopes of TC and TR are reversed; that is, a point beyond which TC rises more steeply than TR and beyond which profits are therefore declining as output rises. This point is q^*, where the two curves are (vertically) parallel to one another. This occurs where the rate of change of total costs with respect to output equals the rate of change of

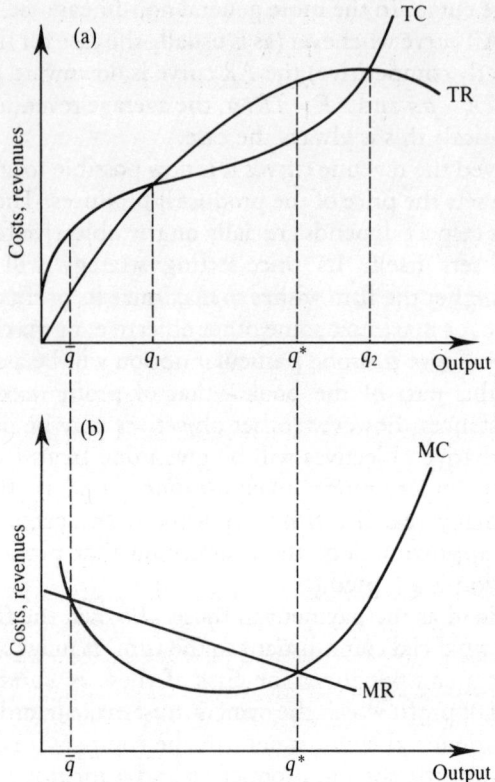

Figure 8.2 Cost and revenue curves: profit maximization. (a) Total costs and revenues, (b) Marginal costs and revenues

total revenue with respect to output. The rate of change of total costs, dTC/dq, has already been defined as marginal cost. Similarly, the rate of change of total revenue, dTR/dq, has been defined as marginal revenue. The condition for profit maximization may therefore be restated as: output should be set at a level at which marginal costs equal marginal revenue. More formally, if total revenue, R, is given by $p(q)q$, and total cost, C, is defined to be a function of output such that $C = C(q)$, then supernormal profits are given by $p(q)q - C(q)$. Differentiating profit with respect to output and setting the result equal to zero implies $dp/dq + p(q) - dC/dq = 0$. Since dC/dq is marginal cost and $dp/dq + p(q)$ is marginal revenue, this implies that the first order condition for profit maximization must be that marginal costs and marginal revenues should equal one another.

Further examination of Figure 8.2 confirms that for profit maximization, MC must cut MR from below, at output q^*. (If MC cuts MR from above *losses* are being locally maximized.)

To restate the rule: profits are maximized at that level of output at which MC intersects MR from below.

Market structure

The above analysis holds good for any type of market. The way in which the rule operates, however, varies somewhat between different kinds of market structure. While $MC = MR$ always guarantees that profit will be maximized in the period under consideration, the profit made will depend not only on costs and on market demand, but also on such factors as the number of firms in the market, the ease of entry into the market of new firms, the contractual obligations of economic agents, the nature of legal constraints, and the efficiency of information flows. These considerations all fall under the umbrella of the term 'market structure'. In the remainder of this chapter two particular types of market structure will be studied: perfect competition and monopoly. These are both extreme cases which exist only rarely in the real world. However, they are extremely valuable as scenarios with which the real world firms can be compared, and they are also especially useful in that the economic analysis is particularly simple in these two polar cases. A third type of market structure, known as oligopoly, will also be defined here, but extensive analysis of decision-making under oligopoly is deferred to Chapter 9.

Perfect competition occurs in an industry characterized by the following properties:

(a) *There is a large number of firms in the industry and a large number of buyers.* The second of these requirements suggests that, other things being equal, firms producing output for final consumption are more likely to be perfectly competitive than firms which produce machines for sale to other firms. The requirement that there should be a large number of firms implies that the firms will each be fairly small.

(b) *Entry into and exit from the industry by any firm is costless and unrestricted.* This rules out any industries in which the smallest profitable scale of operation is high, such as the oil, chemical or heavy metal industries. Firms must be able to enter or leave the industry quickly and cheaply.

(c) *Inputs move freely between firms and industries.* Thus, for example, if a worker finds that a higher wage can be earned by working elsewhere, a transfer will be made to the highest paid job available. Similarly, capital transfers instantaneously to the use where it earns the highest interest for those who own it.

(d) *All firms and consumers have perfect knowledge of market conditions*. Consequently books of stamps sold at a discount at Christmas time will always be bought in preference to sheets of stamps, since everyone is assumed to know about the special offer.

(e) *The output of the various firms in the industry is indistinguishable*. It is therefore easy to define an industry as a group of firms which all produce exactly the same product. Dressmakers' pins, paper clips, pieces of chipboard and cotton wool are examples of goods which rarely differ in their characteristics when produced by different firms. The indistinguishability of the output of different firms is important in that, given perfect information, no consumer will ever buy the output of a certain firm if another firm offers the same product at a cheaper price.

Although in some markets (such as stock-markets, barrow boys, rag and bone men, back street motor repair garages, ticket touts) perfect competition is an adequate approximation to reality, in general it is to be regarded as a benchmark against which real life structures are compared.

Monopoly occurs when a single supplier, known as a monopolist, produces all the output of an industry, and where its product has no close substitute. Barriers to entry into the market exist which prevent other firms wishing to supply the product from doing so. Such barriers include:

(a) ownership of natural resources by the monopolist (such as the barriers to entry to the petrochemical industry imposed by the ownership of oil by a small number of companies).

(b) high cost of entry into the industry (for example the gas industry in Britain is a (virtual) monopoly: to compete successfully with British Gas a new firm would have to provide a second complete pipe network at considerable expense).

(c) patents, copyrights (for instance EMI is the sole supplier of Beatles recordings).

(d) legal barriers. (These, until recently, severely restricted entry into the television industry in an attempt to maintain a high quality of programmes.)

The Monopolies and Mergers Commission can investigate firms or coalitions of firms controlling 25 per cent or more of a market. This does *not* mean that such firms are monopolies in the strict sense of the term used in this book. It does, however, mean that firms controlling a large share of their market may be capable of exploiting the lack of competition for their own benefit and at the expense of the rest of the economy.

Oligopoly occurs when a small number of firms account for a large proportion of the output in an industry. Hence in an oligopoly there exist many buyers and few sellers. Characteristic of this type of industry is the existence of product differentiation. Unlike perfect competition, where the relative smallness of firms gives them a certain anonymity, the small number of firms in an oligopoly enables them to use brand names and to make minor variations in the nature of the product in order to accumulate brand loyalty on the part of their customers. Demand may exist for the output of firms which sell their product at a higher price than their rivals. Thus different firms may price differently and firms may frequently change their prices as they haggle for position and for greater profits. All this makes oligopoly a tremendously exciting and challenging field, both for study and for active involvement. Moreover, since it is now the commonest market structure in all advanced Western economies, a familiarity with oligopoly is of particular importance to the student of management techniques. We shall return to a full discussion of this topic in the next chapter.

Perfect competition

In the study of perfect competition, analysis proceeds at two levels: that of the industry and that of the firm. At the industry level, the industry demand curve is the horizontal summation of the demand schedules of all buyers. The industry supply schedule is the horizontal summation of the supply schedules of all sellers (remembering that some sellers may only be attracted into the industry at higher price levels). Price is determined at industry level by the intersection of the industry demand and supply curves (see Figure 8.3). This is so because if price exceeds p^* a surplus results which would leave some firms unable to sell their output and would eventually result in those firms making a loss and withdrawing from the market; if, on the other hand, price was lower than p^*, new firms would be attracted into the industry since there is an excess demand for the product which is waiting to be satisfied. Only when the price equates market demand and market supply will the number of firms in the industry – and hence the market supply curve itself – be stable.

All firms must price at p^*, where market demand and market supply curves intersect one another. Any firm which charges more than p^* for its output will immediately lose all its customers to other firms, since the customers know they can buy an identical product elsewhere for just p^*. Conversely any firm which charges less than p^* for its output would realize that all other firms would also have to cut their price in order to survive, and that once this is done new firms would enter the industry to compete away any extra profits being made. Consequently all firms accept the market price, p^*. Perfectly competitive firms are thus said to be price-takers. A look at nearly competitive real world industries confirms this and adds flesh to the bones of the theoretical model: barrow boys all charge much the same for their apples, since each knows that if he does not accept the market price the barrow boys around him will react in a manner contrary to his interests. The demand curve faced by any individual firm is therefore horizontal, or perfectly elastic. While it may at first sight appear odd that the market demand curve should have a slope different to the demand curves of individual firms, it should be remembered that the market demand curve is the sum of the demands of individual *consumers*, not firms.

As has already been established, the demand curve and the AR curve are identical and have zero slope in the case of a perfectly competitive firm; it has already been shown that the marginal revenue curve slopes downwards at twice the rate of the average revenue curve. Since 'two times nothing is nothing', it follows that the MR curve is exactly the same as the AR and demand curves. All are horizontal, indicating that the price

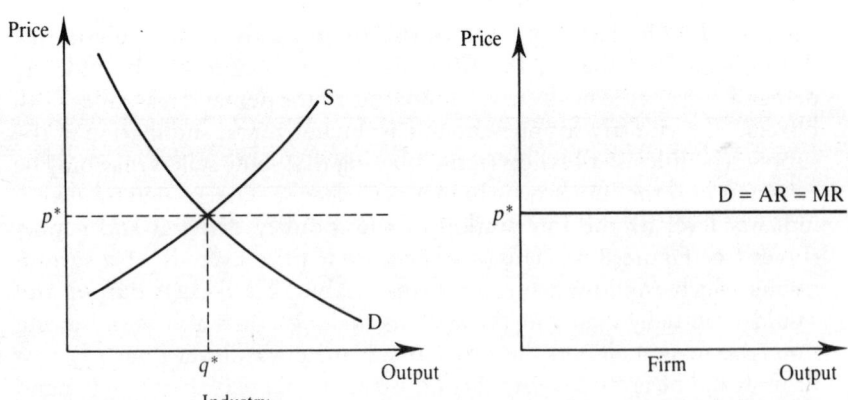

Figure 8.3 The perfectly competitive industry

Figure 8.4 Demand curve faced by a perfectly competitive firm

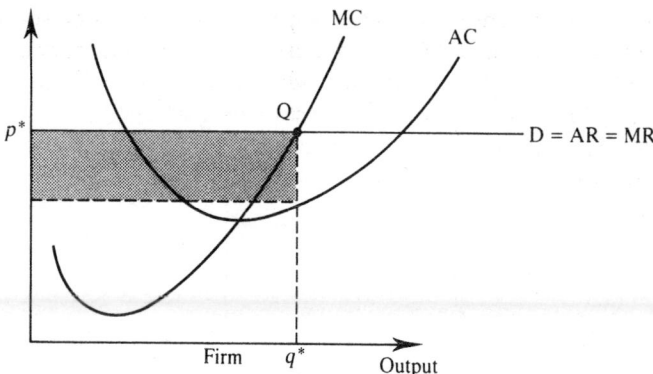

Figure 8.5 Supernormal profits in a perfectly competitive firm

is fixed at industry level and that the firm is powerless to change price via supply side variations. This demand curve is illustrated in Figure 8.4.

The average and marginal cost curves of a perfectly competitive firm have the familiar shape. These are illustrated, together with the revenue curves, in Figure 8.5. In the diagram the firm is shown at a short run equilibrium position: it is producing at q^*, where its marginal cost and marginal revenue are equal. Thus it is maximizing profits. By producing at this level, the firm's total revenue (the product of average revenue and q^*) exceeds its total cost (the product of q^* and average cost). This difference is equal to the shaded area in the diagram, and this area represents the value of supernormal profits being made.

This is not the end of the story, however. The conditions of perfect knowledge, perfect input mobility and freedom of entry and exit which characterize perfect competition serve to ensure that in response to the abnormal profits being made in this industry, new firms are attracted into the market. New firms can be set up only in the long run since they must employ capital (which is fixed in the short run) in order to produce. In the long run, then, with the entry of new firms, the market supply curve shifts down and to the right. This reduces market price and so shifts the demand curve faced by each firm downwards (see Figure 8.6). This process of entry of new firms will continue until all firms in the industry are making just normal profits. This position is reached when the price falls to p^*_2. At this stage all the incumbents are surviving, and there is no incentive for any new firms to enter the industry. Note that the price is thus set at the minimum of the short run average cost curve.

In the long run it is possible not only for new firms to enter the industry but also for established concerns to alter their stocks of capital. Firms which employ the optimal capital and labour mix will be at an advantage

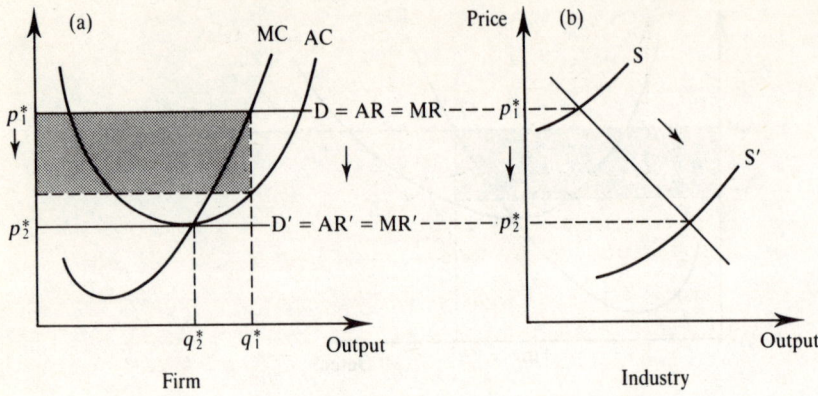

Figure 8.6 Entry of firms into a perfectly competitive industry

vis-à-vis firms which do not; it is essential that firms use the best available mix of inputs at all times, since they will otherwise be competed out of business by more efficient firms which are able to undercut their price. In the long run, then, there is a tendency for perfectly competitive firms to operate at the minimum not only of the short run average cost curve, but also of the long run average cost curve. This means that firms in a competitive industry will tend to produce as efficiently as possible. This is a feature of perfect competition which makes it particularly useful as a benchmark against which the efficiency of alternative market structures can be measured. Once the new equilibrium has been reached, with output and price set at the minimum of the long run average cost curve, the industry is said to be at long run equilibrium, since all firms are maximizing profit (at zero supernormal profit) and there is no incentive for any change in the number of firms active in the industry.

It is also possible that, owing to a shift in tastes away from the output of the industry under consideration, the market price is so low that all firms in the industry make a loss. Such a situation is illustrated in Figure 8.7. Firms which must shortly pay their fixed costs shortly go out of business, thus reducing the total supply of output to the market. The market supply curve then shifts up and to the left, thereby raising price and inducing an upward shift in the demand curve faced by individual firms. (Note that there is no shift in the market demand curve – the 'stayer' firms simply benefit from the demand which was previously satisfied by the 'quitter' firms.) This reduces the loss which was made by those firms which remain in the industry. After more firms exit (when their fixed costs become payable) the remaining firms are left making normal profits once more. Thus the exit, as well as the entry, of firms produces a tendency to move towards long run equilibrium in perfect competition.

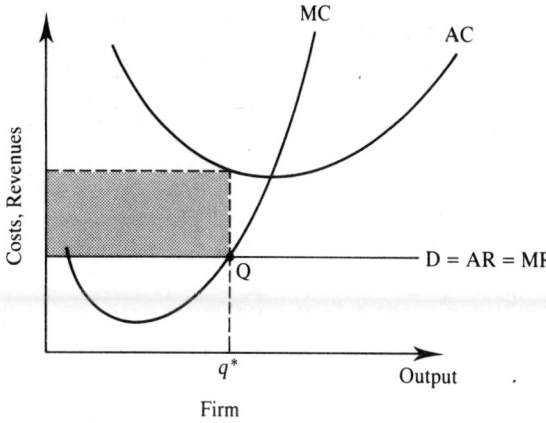

Figure 8.7 Losses in a perfectly competitive firm

The position of the perfectly competitive firm in long run equilibrium is illustrated in Figure 8.8. The long run equilibrium position of a firm in perfect competition is therefore characterized by

$$MC = MR = AC = AR \qquad (8.1)$$

and is located at the minimum of the long run average cost curve. Marginal cost equals marginal revenue so that the firm maximizes profit; marginal revenue equals average revenue at all levels of output; and average cost equals average revenue so that no supernormal profits are made which would attract entry into the market by new firms.

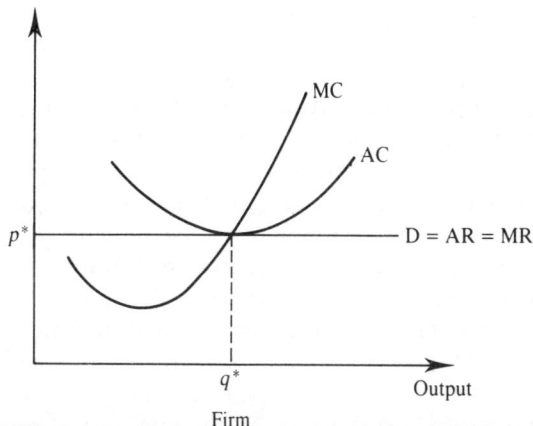

Figure 8.8 Equilibrium of a perfectly competitive firm

112 · ECONOMICS FOR MANAGERS

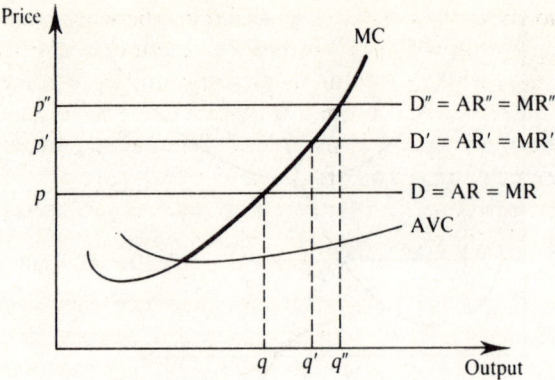

Figure 8.9 The supply curve under perfect competition

Comparison of the points labelled Q in Figures 8.5 and 8.7 indicates that if, as it does, the perfectly competitive firm produces output at the point where demand equals supply, the supply curve of such a firm is its marginal cost curve. Strictly speaking, the supply curve is that portion of the marginal cost curve which lies above average variable costs, since the firm will not supply any output if it cannot cover its variable costs. The supply curve of the firm is illustrated again in Figure 8.9.

Perfect competition and welfare economics

Given the extreme nature of many of the assumptions underlying perfect competition, it may appear surprising that this type of market structure enjoys considerable prominence in the economic literature. While it is true that markets have been getting less competitive over the last hundred years, the reason for the popularity of the perfectly competitive system in the literature is not purely historical – how often do we read of *the* village blacksmith, surely an instance of local monopoly? The appeal of perfect competition is not simply one of an approximation to many real world industries. The fact that the marginal cost curve of perfectly competitive firms is their supply curve, and that therefore such firms always set price equal to marginal cost, is of great importance. Marginal cost pricing, in the absence of market failure, maximizes economic welfare.

To prove this assertion, first note that since the marginal utility curve is identical to the demand curve, total consumer utility is represented by the area under the demand curve. Secondly, the total cost of production to the firm is given by the area under the marginal cost curve (in the long run, since no fixed costs exist). The difference between total utility and total cost represents economic welfare (or economic surplus). It is the amount of utility which economic agents enjoy over and above the opportunity cost of their activity. Economic welfare is maximized at the point at which the marginal utility (demand) equals marginal cost. In the case of perfect competition this is where demand equals supply.

Perfect competition has, therefore, the following extremely appealing property: by selfishly trying to maximize their own individual utility and profits, a large number of consumers and firms are *unwittingly and unintentionally* serving to maximize the welfare of society as a whole. As a result, perfect competition occupies a central role in welfare economics, not as a description of reality, but as a model of a world in which the economic system works as efficiently as possible, and to the greatest possible benefit of the economic actors within the economy.

While it is a highly idealized model, the system of perfect competition provides an extremely useful point of reference. Moreover, firms in many industries may approximate perfect competition closely enough for the model to be of at least some practical use. Where the scope for product differentiation and brand loyalty is limited this is often the case. For instance, farmers, estate agents, firms in the fishing, brewing, baking and stationery industries are close to being price-takers. While supernormal profits can certainly be made in these industries such profits are typically low. Many firms may therefore find it worthwhile to behave *as if* they were perfectly competitive since the greater complexity of pricing rules under, say, oligopoly may mean that such rules cost more to implement than they save.

Monopoly

In the case of monopoly the firm is the sole supplier to the market, and so the demand curve faced by the firm is identical to the market demand curve. Since the market demand curve is downward sloping, so also are the firm's average revenue and marginal revenue curves, the latter being twice as steep as the former.

The equilibrium position of the monopolist is illustrated in Figure 8.10. Its profits are maximized where MC = MR, and so it will produce at the level of output, q^*, which satisfies this equality. At this level of output, the market clearing price, which ensures no shortages or gluts and which maximizes the firm's profits, is p^*. This is the highest price at which the firm can sell all it produces, since it is the price at which demand is just q^*. For the given cost of producing q^* units,

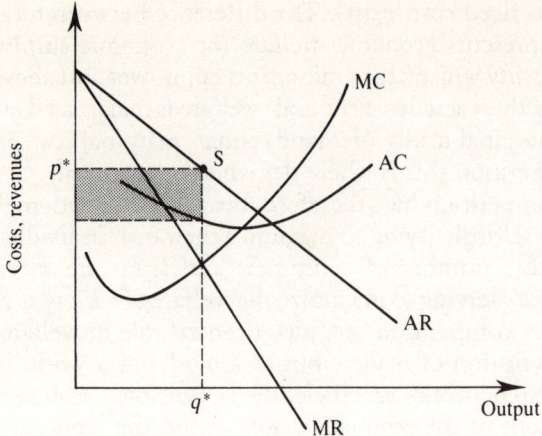

Figure 8.10 Equilibrium of a monopoly

$TC = q^* \cdot AC(q^*)$, therefore, revenue is maximized by setting price to p^*, so that $TR = p^* \cdot AR(q^*)$. The shaded rectangle of Figure 8.10 represents supernormal profits.

Barriers to entry prevent these supernormal profits from being competed away, and so, in contrast to the perfect competition model, the short run and long run equilibria of a (profitable) monopolist are identical to one another so long as the monopolist is employing the optimal stock of capital. Several points are worthy of particular note in the monopoly model. First, a monopolist does not have a supply curve. Point S in Figure 8.10 is where demand equals supply, but no locus of price-quantity pairs exists which can be called a supply curve. This is so because – unlike the case of perfect competition – the intersection of MC and MR does not occur on the demand curve. The extent to which an outward shift in demand raises price is thus a function not only of the shape of the marginal cost curve, but also of the elasticity of demand.

Secondly, a monopolist does not price at marginal cost. Monopoly does not therefore confer as much welfare on society as does perfect competition. For this reason, monopolies are regarded as potentially damaging to the public interest, and may be made subject to the scrutiny of the Monopolies and Mergers Commission. If the Commission finds the monopoly guilty of action contrary to the public interest it may recommend to the Secretary of State for Trade and Industry that such action should be terminated. In the case of a merger between two or more companies which would give those companies a substantial degree of monopoly power in a market, the Commission can recommend that the merger should not go ahead if it is deemed a 'bad thing'.

Thirdly, in general, monopolies produce less output and charge a higher price than would the same industry placed in the invisible hands of perfect competitors. This is because in perfect competition the price–output pairing is given by the minimum point of the long run average cost curve, while – as can be seen in Figure 8.10 – the monopolist produces at a point away from the minimum of its average cost schedule. For this reason monopolies are said to be inefficient since they do not minimize their costs per unit of output. However, an exception to this general rule may apply in certain cases. If the monopoly is able to exploit its position as a single seller to reduce its costs (perhaps by employing monopsony – or single buyer – power in the input markets, or by developing new products or methods of production) then its cost curves will be lower than the corresponding schedules of a competitive firm. This situation is illustrated in Figure 8.11. In this diagram the monopolist's cost curves are the same as those of Figure 8.10. The AC curve under perfect competition reaches a minimum at the same price level as does the AC of each perfect competitor, and the corresponding quantity level equals the product of the output of the representative firm and the number of firms in the industry. (Points of the perfectly competitive AC away from the minimum are shown in the diagram, although the precise shape of the curve cannot be determined simply by aggregating individual firms' cost curves.) Note that the monopolists' MC lies below and to the right of the perfect competitor's MC. Consequently the monopolist produces *more* and sells at a *lower* price than would the competitive firm. It should be emphasized, however, that this instance of a beneficial monopoly is very much the exception rather than the rule in modern economies.

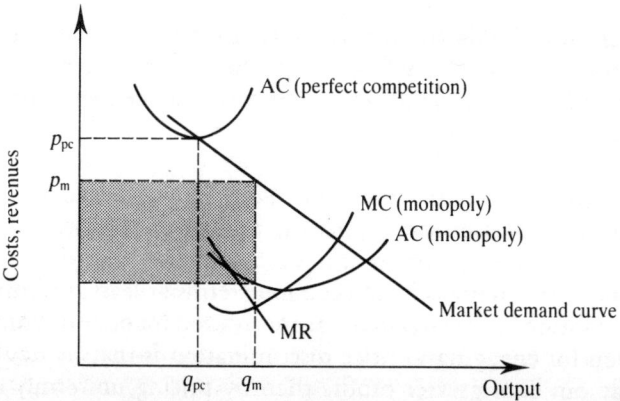

Figure 8.11 Perfect competition versus monopoly

Monopoly and price discrimination

Price discrimination exists when different buyers or groups of buyers are charged different prices for the same good on grounds other than cost. It cannot take place under competitive conditions since any firm discriminating against a particular group of buyers (by charging them a price higher than cost) would soon find its price undercut by a rival firm. Discrimination is, therefore, a phenomenon of particular interest when monopolies are being considered.

For price discrimination to take place it must be possible for the monopolist to separate the various markets in which it sells its output. If a good is sold at a higher price to Ms Adams than to Ms Brown it must be impossible for Ms Brown to buy an extra unit of the good and resell the good to Ms Adams. Markets may be separated in a number of ways:

(a) Geographically (beer is more expensive in London than in Manchester, but it would not be worthwhile for Londoners to travel to Manchester just to buy their beer).

(b) Temporally (off-peak train tickets are much cheaper than peak fares, though the costs of operating trains are unlikely to vary through the day. Peak time travellers must travel at a given time of day in order to get to work).

(c) By type of consumer (electricity is more expensive for firms than for households).

(d) By the nature of the product (the same firm can sell the same good or service to different consumers at different prices if the product is personal in nature. Examples include health care, haircuts and spectacles).

(e) By the use of bulk-buy discounts. (Firms may charge different prices to customers who may be distinguished by the size of their orders. Examples include long term contractual agreements for servicing industrial equipment).

Even if the industry is a monopoly and the markets are separable, a third condition must be met if price discrimination is to occur: the elasticity of demand must be different in each market. Otherwise the distinction between the markets is, in economic terms at least, meaningless.

So far nothing has been said of the motivation for price discrimination. The reason for engaging in price discrimination is that by doing so the monopoly can earn greater profits than by pricing uniformly across all

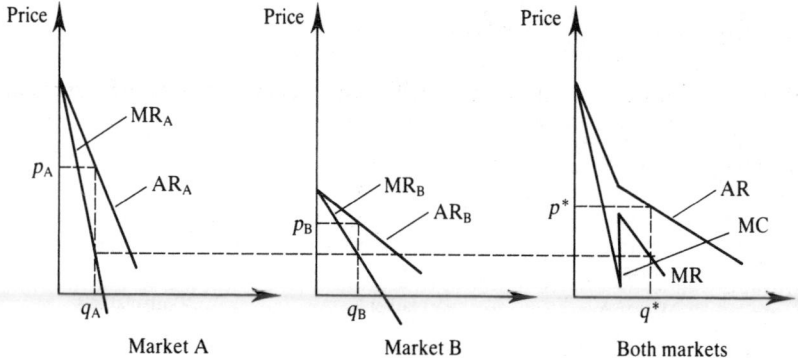

Figure 8.12 Price discrimination under monopoly

markets. The validity of this assertion is demonstrated by reference to Figure 8.12.

■ **PROOF:** Total cost is the same regardless of whether or not discrimination takes place. If the price charged in both markets were p^*, marginal revenue in Market B (where demand is relatively elastic) would exceed that in Market A (where demand is relatively inelastic). By selling more units in Market B and fewer in Market A, the firm could therefore raise its total revenue until it is maximized where the marginal revenue is the same across all markets. In order to do this the price charged in Market A must rise and that in Market B must fall, to p_A and p_B, respectively.
□ *End of proof*

Examples of price discrimination are many and varied. Peak and off-peak rail fares, student railcards, matinees at the theatre or cinema are all examples. A particularly interesting instance is the system of bargaining for goods used in many countries, where sellers haggle for price with buyers on an individual basis; the more elastic the buyers demand curve, the greater the resistance to pay higher prices for the good. It is thus a rare example of perfect price discrimination, where all buyers pay for the good an amount equal to the utility they derive from it.

Just as market power attaches to sellers in a market which does not provide competition, so can sole buyers assume power of a similar kind. A sole buyer in a market is called a monopsonist. Price discrimination occurs also in the labour market. A monopsonistic firm can discriminate between separately identifiable groups of workers. Here the demand for labour is determined by the intersection of the marginal cost of labour

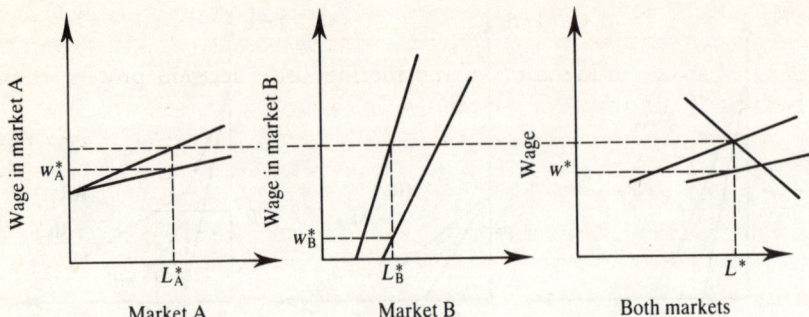

Figure 8.13 Wage discrimination under monopsony

and the value of the marginal product of labour. As can be seen from Figure 8.13, those groups of workers which supply their labour inelastically will be discriminated against, in that they receive a lower wage. Thus unionized labour, which supplies labour elastically at high wages only is rewarded with a higher wage than non-unionized labour, the supply of which is less elastic. If w^* were paid across all markets, the marginal cost of employing non-unionized labour would be higher than that of employing unionized labour, and so it would reduce costs to transfer employment opportunities in the direction of unionized labour. In doing so the wage offered to unionized labour rises above w^* while that offered to non-unionized labour falls.

Advertising and monopoly

In addition to price, some firms are able to compete for a larger share of the consumer's budget by engaging in other forms of competition. One of the most important forms of non-price competition is advertising. Perfectly competitive firms do not advertise, because their products are indistinguishable from those of other firms in the same industry. Firms operating in industries which are nearly perfectly competitive may advertise a little in an attempt to differentiate their product from that produced by other companies; the closeness of available substitutes will nevertheless constrain such firms to set their price at a level very similar to that of competing products. Firms operating in oligopolistic industries tend to advertise more than their counterparts in other types of market, since each company must keep up with (and try to outstrip) the advertising efforts of its rivals in order to retain its share of the market. Monopolies enjoy a position where close substitutes do not exist, and they can therefore use advertising to boost demand for their output without fear of enhancing the sales of rival suppliers. The remainder of this chapter is devoted to a consideration of the monopolist's decision process when both price and advertising intensity are controlled by the firm.

Advertising raises both demand and costs. That it raises demand is obvious by its mere existence – if it did not, firms would not bother with it. The impact of advertising on costs depends on the media used and on the intensity of advertising effort, but it is rare indeed for advertising to be available free of charge to the firm. It costs *something* even to paint the name of the firm on the side of a van. The argument now proceeds by way of an example.

Suppose, then, that the demand and total cost functions faced by the firm are given by Equations (8.2) and (8.3), respectively.

$$p = 30 - q_D + 10A - A^2 \tag{8.2}$$

$$TC = q_S + A \tag{8.3}$$

where p denotes the price of the firm's output; A is advertising intensity; TC is total cost; and q_D and q_S denote, respectively, the quantities demanded and supplied. In addition to these two equations, an equilibrium condition, Equation (8.4), is needed to close the model;

$$q_D = q_S = q \tag{8.4}$$

where q is the equilibrium output level. The firm is assumed to seek to maximize its profit. To solve the model the demand function is first multiplied through by q to give the total revenue function:

$$TR = 30q - q^2 + 10qA - qA^2 \tag{8.5}$$

Profits can now be represented as the difference between total revenue and total cost:

$$\pi = 30q - q^2 + 10qA - qA^2 - q - A \tag{8.6}$$

Substituting from Equation (8.2) for q yields

$$\pi = 31p - p^2 + 10Ap - A^2p - 11A + A^2 - 30 \tag{8.7}$$

The first order conditions for maximizing profit are:

$$\frac{\partial \pi}{\partial p} = 31 - 2p + 10A - A^2 = 0 \quad \text{and}$$

$$\frac{\partial \pi}{\partial A} = 10p - 2Ap + 2A - 11 = 0 \tag{8.8}$$

These imply, respectively, that

$$p = 15.5 + 5A - A^2/2 \tag{8.9}$$

and

$$A = (11 - 10p)/2(1-p) \tag{8.10}$$

Equations (8.9) and (8.10) are two equations in two unknowns. Solving simultaneously for p gives

$$p = 15.5 + 5(11 - 10p)/2(1-p) - [(11 - 10p)/(1-p)]^2/8 \tag{8.11}$$

This can be solved (by numerical methods) to give $p = 28$. Substitution of this value into Equation (8.12) gives the solution for A. Hence $A = 5$. Since $\delta^2\pi/\delta p^2 < 0$ and $\delta^2\pi/\delta A^2 < 0$, the second order conditions for profit maximization are met.

The firm should therefore set price to 28 and advertising intensity to 5 in order to maximize profits in this example. If it does so, then it will be able to sell 27 units of output, and will make a profit of 724. To demonstrate that this is indeed a profit-maximizing position, the profit which the firm would make under a variety of price and advertising conditions are shown in Table 8.2.

Table 8.2 Profits under various price and advertising intensity assumptions

Advertising intensity	Price		
	25	28	30
4	692	698	692
5	715	724	720
6	690	696	690

The method described above can be used also to determine the profit-maximizing combination of price and advertising intensity under conditions of oligopoly. In the latter instance, however, the situation is complicated somewhat by the fact that the firm does not know the combinations of advertising and price that its rivals will select. This is important because under oligopoly the actions of one firm will affect all other firms in the market. This means that the optimal combination of price and advertising intensity is subject to uncertainty, as indeed is the amount of profit obtainable by any one firm. The presence of uncertainty in an oligopolistic setting requires the introduction of new techniques of analysis. This will be the subject of the next chapter.

Exercise: Pricing in the electricity industry

The electricity industry in the United Kingdom may be characterized as a monopoly. Deaton (1975) has estimated the own price elasticity of demand for

Table 8.3 The demand for electricity
Sources: Estimated from data in Deaton (1975), the *Annual Abstracts of Statistics* (HMSO) and the Annual Report of the Electricity Council.

Price (£ per GWh)	Quantity demanded (GWh)
5 000	260 574
6 000	227 240
7 000	193 907
8 000	160 574
9 000	127 240
10 000	93 907

electricity in 1970 to be -1.203. This (together with information about 1970 sales and revenue) enables the demand schedule shown in Table 8.3 to be constructed. Costs in the industry can (without much loss of realism) be assumed to be a constant £5,000 per GWh, regardless of the level of output.

(a) What was the profit-maximizing level of output?

(b) What price would guarantee profit maximization?

(c) What profit would be made if the price were set at this level?

(d) What would the answers to questions (a), (b) and (c) have been had the market structure been assumed perfectly competitive instead of monopolistic?

(e) In fact, price was set at around £7,000 per GWh. That is, between the monopoly (profit-maximizing) price and the perfectly competitive price. How many GWh of electricity were sold at this price?

(f) How much profit was made?

(g) What factors might explain the decision to set the price below the profit-maximizing level?

Chapter 9
Coping with uncertainty

An oligopoly is an industry in which a small number of firms accounts for a large proportion of output. Hence there are many buyers and few sellers. The output of one firm in an oligopolistic industry is a close substitute for the output of other firms in the same industry. Output is not homogeneous across firms, as in perfect competition, however. Oligopoly is the commonest market structure in existence in modern Western economies. Unfortunately it is also the most difficult to analyse, since a number of special techniques are required to deal with the element of uncertainty which arises in oligopolistic markets.

The approach of this chapter will be to review a number of approaches to the oligopoly problem. First, a model very reminiscent of the optimization models of Chapter 5 will be described. Later the more powerful mathematical tools of game theory and statistical decision theory will be introduced; these enable the firm methodically to cope with the problems of risk and uncertainty, respectively. Before proceeding further, however, the reasons why oligopoly begets risk and uncertainty must be expounded.

The discussion about the theory of the firm in the last chapter concentrated on a market structure which is either monopolistic or perfectly competitive. Supposing the market demand curve is known with certainty, both the monopolist and the perfect competitor must know with certainty the demand curves their firms face; this is because in the one case the firm and the industry are synonymous, while in the other case the firm is a price-taker. An oligopolistic firm, on the other hand, faces a somewhat different situation. Even if total industry demand is known, the demand for the output of one firm will depend not only on the price set by that firm, but also on prices set by all other firms in the industry. Since different firms produce (slightly) different goods, the demand for the output of a different firm will remain positive even if a similar good is available elsewhere at a lower price; however, demand for the firm's output will vary positively with the prices set by rival firms, other things being equal.

Hence, no firm can predict with certainty what the demand for its output will be in the next period simply because no firm can tell what prices its rivals in the industry will be charging. This is the root cause of uncertainty in oligopolies.

Frankel's model of pricing under uncertainty

The first model to be considered in the present chapter is that devised by Frankel (1973) which explains a firm's price and output decisions when demand conditions are characterized by risk. Risk exists where a single decision results in one of a number of outcomes, and the particular outcome which results does so with a known probability.

Define a family of isoprofit rate curves in price–output space. Each isoprofit rate curve (PRC) joins together all price–output pairs which would yield a given profit per pound of investment. The PRCs are convex to the origin.

■ **PROOF:** This assertion follows by observing that

$$\pi = PQ - bQ \tag{9.1}$$

where π represents profits, P is price, Q is output and b is a constant. PQ thus represents total revenue and bQ is total cost (which is assumed linear in output). Dividing both sides by investment, I, gives the profit rate,

$$\pi/I = Q(P-b)/I \tag{9.2}$$

Along any single PRC the profit rate is constant and so

$$P = \frac{\pi}{I}\frac{I}{Q} + b = \frac{kI}{Q} + b, \text{ say.} \tag{9.3}$$

Thus Q is inversely related to P so that as Q rises P falls, but falls at a decreasing rate, since

$$\frac{\partial P}{\partial Q} = \frac{-kI}{Q^2} < 0 \qquad \frac{\partial^2 P}{\partial Q^2} = \frac{2kI}{Q^3} > 0 \tag{9.4}$$

☐ *End of proof*

A family of PRCs can be drawn onto a graph in (P, Q) space; a sample of such curves appears in Figure 9.1. The 0 per cent profit rate curve represents points at which only normal profit is being earned; the 15 per cent PRC, on the other hand, joins all combinations of prices and

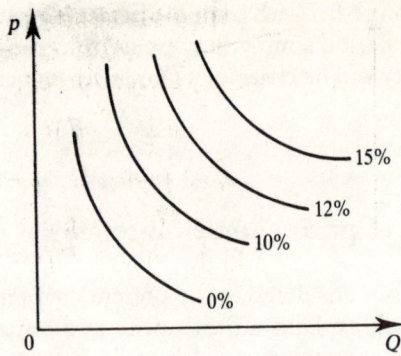

Figure 9.1 Isoprofit-rate curves

quantities which would, if realized, yield a profit which is 15 per cent greater than investment. Since a higher profit rate implies a higher value of k, it follows that of two PRCs, the one representing the higher rate of profit must lie nearer the north-east than the other. Just as no two isoquants, indifference curves or (in meteorology) isobars can intersect one another, neither can two PRCs intersect one another; if they did, it would imply that two profit rates simultaneously exist at one (P, Q) pairing, which is clearly absurd.

A second family of curves needs also to be defined. These are 'isoprobability subjective sales' curves, or PSS. These are found by asking the management of the firm, at each of a number of different prices, P, and for each of a number of different levels of output, Q: What, in your opinion, is the probability that you will sell at least Q units per period, if the price is set at P?' If the answer is 'I think there's a fifty–fifty chance', then the (P, Q) pairing must be on the 0.50 PSS. If the answer is 'Oh, we'll *definitely* sell that many', the (P, Q) pairing is on the 1.00 PSS. If the answer is 'I'd say the odds are about nine-to-one against' then the pairing is on the 0.10 PSS. There must be some price level, P_0, at which the executive is not 100 per cent confident of making any sales whatsoever; there must also be some level of sales, q_0, which the executive cannot be certain of achieving however low the price. Similarly, there are price and sales levels, p_1 and q_1, where $p_1 > p_0$ and $q_1 > q_0$, which cannot be more than 75 per cent sure of being achieved. Since the PRCs cannot intersect either of the axes and since the PSS must intersect both axes, there must be some areas along each PSS where the second derivative of price with respect to output is lower than is the case along the nearby PRCs. Since these are the areas of interest, it will henceforth be assumed, with no essential loss of generality, that the PSS curves are concave to the origin. Such curves are illustrated in Figure 9.2.

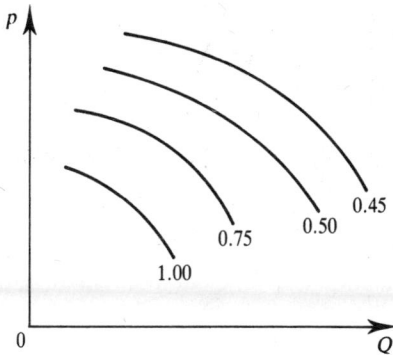

Figure 9.2 Isoprofitability subjective sales curves

Combining the PRCs of Figure 9.1 with the PSS curves of Figure 9.2 produces a diagram like the one shown in Figure 9.3. This diagram enables us to say something about the pricing decision of a firm facing a risky demand. If the firm wishes to aim at a profit rate of 10 per cent, the diagram shows that its best chance of achieving this goal is a 75 per cent chance, which is achieved by producing at X, the point of tangency of the 10 per cent PRC and the best attainable PSS curve. Thus the firm would set price equal to p^*. How, though, does the firm decide on its target profit rate? This depends on its attitude to risk.

Suppose the firm is risk-neutral. That is, it expresses no preference between being given £x with probability y and being given £nx with probability y/n. The optimal price–quantity pairing must lie somewhere on the locus CC of points of tangency which maximizes the product of the profit rate and the probability of selling all output. This is at point X on Figure 9.3, since $0.75 \times 10 > 0.45 \times 15 > 0.50 \times 12 > 1.00 \times 0$.

A risk-loving firm is indifferent between being given £x with probability y and being given £nx with probability y/m where $m > n$. Such a firm would tend to opt for higher profit rates and set higher prices than a risk-neutral firm. Conversely, a risk-averse firm will tend to aim for lower profit rates and set lower prices.

Given the attitude of the firm to risk, there may be a number of 'expected profit' maximizing points such as X. For instance, if the firm is risk-neutral and the 0.3 PSS curve lies tangent to the 25 per cent PRC, the expected profit at this latter point is the same as at X. The firm must then choose between these two points, but the theory can tell us nothing about which of the points the firm will select. Note further that expected profit need not change smoothly as one moves up along CC; for instance, at point Y expected profit is lower than at either X or Z. The model is not, therefore, capable of defining a unique optimum.

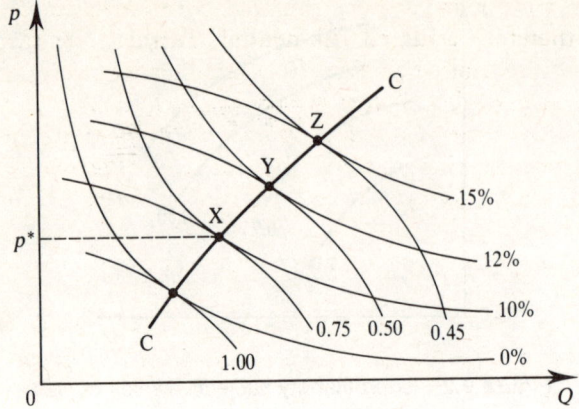

Figure 9.3 Frankel's model

Even if the optimum is unique, the optimal choice of price-output pairing may vary from firm to firm for one or both of two reasons:

(a) The isoprobability sales curves are subjective. They are based on the intuition of individual managers rather than on objective criteria, and will therefore vary from firm to firm according to the perception of the managers.

(b) The degree of risk aversion varies from firm to firm. This again depends on subjective considerations.

While Frankel's model provides a very plausible formalization of the way in which decisions are made in the face of risk, its value is as a descriptive tool only. No prescriptive statements can be made by an economist studying the model simply because nothing is known about the *actual* isoprobability sales curves. By assuming risk-neutrality and a knowledge of the firm's profit function under each of a finite number of states of nature, however, more can be said. It is to this we now turn.

The theory of games

In the present section we consider the theory of games. This theory facilitates further our understanding of the way in which decisions can rationally be taken under conditions of risk. An economist who can only explain the past is of much less value to the firm than one who can go further and say: 'and this is what we should do next'. In order to do this, however, an

COPING WITH UNCERTAINTY · 127

assumption must be made about the firm's attitude to risk. In the sequel firms are therefore assumed risk-neutral. Further, the firm must be assumed to face a choice between a finite number of options; that is, there is a limit to the number of different prices which the firm could possibly select. Finally, assume that there is only a finite number of states of nature which may occur. For instance, in an industry consisting of only two firms, A and B, Firm A faces a finite number of states of nature because Firm B is choosing between only a finite number of price options; B's price is A's state of nature and *vice versa*. In other words, the environment in which A makes the pricing decision, and which will influence A's profit, is determined by the price which B sets. By constraining both the set of available choices and the set of possible states of nature to lie between predetermined bounds it becomes possible to compare the profits made by Firm A at various price levels in each state of nature.

Game theory is a set of mathematical techniques which can be applied to a situation where two or more 'players' (in this case firms) are in conflict with each other. To illustrate the way in which game theory works, consider a two firm industry (or a 'duopoly'). Both firms are considering their pricing strategy for the next period. Either firm may lower price, raise price or maintain the current price. Thus there are nine possibilities, represented by the nine boxes of the matrix in Table 9.1. The figure in the top right hand corner of each box represents Firm A's profit when the pricing strategies of A and B are those which are represented by that box. The figures in the bottom left hand corners represent Firm B's profit.

Suppose A and B both know each other's profit matrices. Whatever A decides to do, Firm B will not raise its price, because regardless of A's price B can always make more profit by keeping its price unchanged (45 > 44, 50 > 48 and 55 > 54). Firm A realizes that B will not raise its price, and observes also that, regardless of whether B lowers price or keeps its price

Table 9.1 The payoff matrix — example 1

Firm B \ Firm A	lower price	no change	raise price
lower price	46 / 46	45 / 51	48 / 53
no change	48 / 45	50 / 50	52 / 55
raise price	55 / 44	54 / 48	54 / 54

unchanged, A's profits are greatest when A raises its price (48 > 46 > 45 and 52 > 50 > 48). Firm A therefore plans to raise its price. Knowing this to be the case, Firm B compares its alternatives: if it lowers its price its profits will be £53, whereas if it keeps its price constant it will make £55 as profit. Firm B therefore plans to keep its price constant.

The above is an example of a strictly determined game. Given the profit matrices of Firms A and B, the outcome of the 'game' (the strategic choice made by each firm) will be the same each time the 'game' is played. Whenever the profit matrices of the firms are those shown above the result will be the same: Firm A will raise its price, Firm B will maintain the price it charged in the previous period. In the period following the price change A will make a profit of £52 and B will make a profit of £55.

When the firms are competing with one another, therefore, a total of £107 will be earned by the industry as profit. If the firms were to co-operate with one another, on the other hand, an agreement could be reached whereby both firms raise price. In this instance total industry profit would be £108 (54 + 54), and the firms could share this profit between them however they see fit. *Collusion, or co-operation, between oligopolistic firms can always yield at least as great a profit to the oligopolists themselves as can non-co-operation, or competition.* This is an important observation, and collusion (of various kinds) represents an important aspect of oligopoly. When all firms in an oligopoly collude they can, in effect, act as a monopolist and can fully exploit the potential of the industry for making supernormal profits; when this happens uncertainty disappears – at least for the duration of the agreement.

The example of game theory given above was one of a strictly determined game. Such examples are likely to be rare in practice, particularly when there may be more than two firms in the oligopoly and when each firm faces a broader menu of price changes. Nevertheless the possible existence of strictly determined games demonstrates that even in non-co-operative oligopolies it is conceivable that firms will in every period act in a manner consistent with optimization of profit subject to the limited information available. The risk and uncertainty of oligopoly need not always turn pricing strategy into a guessing game. However the problem of 'games' which do not produce an unambiguous solution remains.

The example discussed above is somewhat unusual in the sense that each firm is assumed to have full knowledge of both its own profit matrix and that of its rival. Suppose, now, more realistically, that each firm knows its own profit matrix, but not that of its rival. The solution arrived at earlier – which was contingent on Firm A realizing that Firm B would never raise its price – can no longer be reached. In order to solve the game in this more realistic scenario, a further assumption must be made concerning what constitutes 'reasonable' behaviour on the part of firms.

One assumption which is often made in this situation is known as the *maximin* assumption. Each firm starts by assuming that the strategy chosen by its rival will produce the least favourable state of nature possible. In the earlier example, the worst possible state of nature for Firm A occurs if B lowers its price, so A assumes that B will indeed do this. Similarly, the worst possible state of nature for Firm B occurs when A lowers its price, and so B assumes that A will do this. The next step for each firm is to maximize its expected profit, given the assumed state of nature. Thus A raises its price (since 48 > 46 > 45) and B lowers its price (since 46 > 45 > 44). The maximin rule, therefore, suggests that A's price will rise and B's will fall in the next period.

The maximin rule in this instance gives a different solution to the full information rule discussed earlier. In fact, neither need be optimal. In the particular example discussed above, the full information rule provides an optimal solution, in the sense that no string of events can lead to A receiving a greater profit than £52 *and* B receiving more than £55. The maximin rule, in this example, does not give an optimal solution since both firms can earn greater profits by not following the maximin rule than by following it.

Two further examples follow. In Table 9.2, neither the full information rule nor the maximin rule provides an optimal solution. In Table 9.3 both do. Closer examination of these two matrices reveals that in Table 9.2 the full information rule proposes that A should keep its price constant while B lowers price; the maximin rule suggests that neither firm should change its price; the optimum solution, meanwhile, would be for A to raise its price while B keeps its price constant. In Table 9.3, on the other hand, if A raises its price and B keeps its price constant the full information and maximin rules are both satisfied and, furthermore, the profits of each firm are optimized.

Table 9.2 The payoff matrix – example 2

Firm B \ Firm A	lower price	no change	raise price
lower price	51 / 45	54 / 51	53 / 55
no change	52 / 46	53 / 50	54 / 55
raise price	48 / 44	50 / 48	44 / 54

Table 9.3 The payoff matrix – example 3

Firm B \ Firm A	lower price	no change	raise price
lower price	51 / 44	54 / 49	53 / 55
no change	52 / 45	53 / 50	54 / 55
raise price	48 / 44	44 / 48	50 / 54

The point of the foregoing discussion is simply this: both the full information rule and the maximin rule are 'reasonable' rules which may be used to govern price setting under risk. Neither rule, however, can guarantee that profits will be maximized. Risk simply does not permit such a guarantee to be made. In many industries firms can feel sufficiently confident in each other's actions to approach an optimum only when they co-operate with one another. While non-co-operation and risk may not, therefore, allow an optimum to be reached, the adoption of either the full information or maximin rule often constitutes the best a firm can do. The reasons why maximin and full information rules do not always guarantee optimum profits can easily be explained: maximin fails to take account of all the information in the matrix, looking, as it does, at only one column and one row in the final decision. Full information can fail when one firm has no preference between alternative prices given its most favourable state of nature.

One problem remains with the game theoretic approach to risk: certain situations can occur in which neither the maximin nor the full information rule can produce a pricing strategy prescription. In other words, games may be intractable. Such a case is illustrated in Table 9.4. Neither rule is capable of telling either firm what price is the 'best' to charge, because no state of nature can unambiguously be labelled the best or the worst. Moreover, Table 9.4 is interesting in that no clear optimum exists. The profits of Firms A and B cannot simultaneously be maximized. A game of this kind, in which the standard rules of behaviour cannot produce a solution, is said to be non-strictly-determined. The usual price strategy prescription to emerge from a non-strictly-determined game is as follows: if you think that strategy x is your best strategy y per cent of the time, then play strategy x for y per cent of the time. Hence in a typical spell of 100 price-setting periods you should choose to set your price at x in y of these periods. So that your rival remains uncertain about your strategy

Table 9.4 The payoff matrix – example 4

	Firm A lower price	no change	raise price
Firm B			
lower price	51 / 45	54 / 55	53 / 50
no change	54 / 46	53 / 50	54 / 55
raise price	48 / 49	55 / 48	44 / 54

in the coming period (and so that it cannot therefore enjoy the luxury of pricing under certain knowledge of its state of nature) choose *at random* the particular periods in which x is played.

While non-strictly-determined games are likely to be of considerable importance to the firm, further discussion of them lies beyond the scope of this text. Readers interested in learning more about this subject are referred to Luce and Raiffa (1957) and Peston and Coddington (1967). Game theory is extensively used in several areas of economics in addition to oligopoly theory; see Laver (1980) for a particularly interesting and strikingly simple example. The theory of games is also widely used in the social sciences and in the analysis of military strategy. Advanced game theoretic techniques are used in the solution of a variety of engineering problems; missiles pursuing a moving target are programmed to use such methods to optimize their pursuit paths. While its applicability is quite widespread though, the main area within which the executive is likely to find game theory of some use remains that of oligopoly. Those working in this field stand to benefit greatly from a sound understanding of at least the fundamental principles of the theory of games.

Statistical decision theory

In games played with full information about all firms' profit matrices, each firm knows the probability with which each possible state of nature occurs, since those states of nature are dependent on its rival's pricing decisions. In contrast, where nothing is known about the probabilities which attach to each state of nature, a state of uncertainty is said to exist. There is no one 'correct' way for a firm to deal with uncertainty; maximin, discussed earlier, is one method, This section introduces four additional

Table 9.5 Profit (£) at each location in three weather conditions

	Sunny	Overcast	Rain
Beach	50	45	15
Fairground	50	60	10

methods used by firms to make decisions in an uncertain environment. Since attitudes towards gambling vary from person to person it is inevitable that different decision-makers will employ different statistical decision rules in their work.

We shall begin this section by using a rather stylized example which is none the less useful to fix ideas. A more realistic application follows later. The first example concerns an ice cream vendor who is agonizing over the following decision: should he site his van at the beach or at the fairground? Table 9.5 shows the data about the profit he will make at each location in each of three possible states of nature. It will be assumed that the vendor chooses his location while uncertain of the day's weather prospects, and that once he has chosen a particular site he must stay there for the whole day.

Five decision rules will be considered: maximin, maximax, the Hurwicz criterion, the Bayes-Laplace criterion and the minimax regret criterion.

1. Maximin

This criterion was considered earlier in the context of game theory, but it may also be applied in an environment of uncertainty where statistical decision theory is used. The rule may be described as the 'triumph of pessimism'. The firm starts off by assuming the worst of all possible states of nature, and chooses the strategy which maximizes the return in this state. In the case of the ice cream vendor, the worst possible state is rain, since the profit made when it is raining is less than the profit made in better weather regardless of location. If it rains the better place to be selling ice cream is on the beach. So the pessimistic ice cream vendor sites himself on the beach.

Two points need to be noted about maximin: first, if the three states of nature occurred with equal probability the fairground would be a preferable site. Maximin fails to take into consideration more than a small part of the payoff (or profit) matrix. A second criticism of maximin is the possibility of intractability discussed earlier: for instance, if the vendor knew it wouldn't rain, it is not at all clear whether he should regard 'sunny' or 'overcast' as the worse state of nature.

2. Maximax

This method, in contrast to maximin, may be described as the 'triumph of optimism'. The firm starts off by assuming the best of all possible states of nature, and chooses the strategy which maximizes the return in this state. In the ice cream vendor example the best possible state is either 'sunny' or 'overcast' (we do not know which). In both states the return from siting on the fairground is at least as great as that from siting on the beach. According to maximax the vendor should therefore site at the fairground.

Note that maximax is subject to the same criticisms as maximin: namely that not all the payoff matrix is allowed for in the decision-making process, and that maximax may also be intractable.

3. Hurwicz criterion

The Hurwicz criterion makes use of a crudely determined 'expected' return from pursuing each strategy.

Let P_1 denote the maximum payoff (or profit) from pursuing strategy x, P_2 denote the minimum payoff from pursuing strategy x and a be an index of optimism (a constant between 0 and 1, where the nearer a is to 1 the more optimistic is the decision-maker). The 'expected' payoff from strategy x, according to the Hurwicz formula, is

$$E(P) = aP_1 + (1-a)P_2 \qquad (9.5)$$

The 'expected' payoff is computed for all possible strategies, and the strategy whose 'expected' payoff is highest is chosen.

As an example, consider the ice cream vendor example where $a = 0.5$. The 'expected' payoffs are:

(a) beach: $0.5 \times 50 + 0.5 \times 15 = 32.5$

(b) fairground: $0.5 \times 60 + 0.5 \times 10 = 35$

Therefore the vendor should site at the fairground (since 35 is greater than 32.5). The Hurwicz criterion is always tractable, but, like maximin and maximax, takes only part of the payoff matrix into account. Much also depends on the value of a, the index of optimism: if a falls below $1/3$, the beach becomes the more attractive location.

4. Bayes–Laplace criterion

This method represents an extension of the Hurwicz criterion inasmuch as expected payoffs are again defined and compared across strategies. In this method, however, subjective probabilities are assigned to each of the states of nature. In the absence of any information the states of nature are regarded as equally probable. The expected payoff from each strategy is then calculated and the strategy offering the highest expected profit is chosen. In the ice cream seller's case

(a) beach: $50/3 + 45/3 + 15/3 = 36.6$

(b) fairground: $50/3 + 60/3 + 10/3 = 40$

Hence the fairground is chosen (since $40 > 36.67$).

The Bayes–Laplace criterion takes the entire profit matrix into account and is always tractable. This makes the method particularly attractive and may well explain its widespread popularity amongst practitioners of the art of decision-making under uncertainty. As presented here the method assumes risk neutrality, although this assumption can easily be relaxed by adjusting the subjective probabilities for the degree of risk aversion or risk attraction.

5. Minimax regret criterion

In this method a regret Table 9.6 is constructed as the first step in making the decision. A regret table is the table of the opportunity cost (or sacrifice) involved in making a wrong strategy choice for each state of nature. For instance, if the vendor sites himself at the beach and the weather turns out to be overcast, the regret is what he loses by siting wrongly, that is, $60 - 45 = 15$. The full table of regrets is given in Table 9.6. Once the regret table has been constructed the maximum regret of each row is identified, and the strategy whose maximum regret is lowest is chosen. In the ice cream vendor case, the fairground is chosen, since $5 < 15$.

Table 9.6 Regrets table

	Sunny	Overcast	Rain
Beach	0	15	0
Fairground	0	0	5

As with maximin, maximax and the Hurwicz criterion, minimax regrets takes only some of the payoff matrix into account.

The five methods outlined above all represent slightly different attitudes to decision-making, and slightly different philosophies on the part of the decision-maker. For instance, an eternal optimist would likely attach greater weight to the maximax criterion than would a more conservative strategist, who might accord maximin greater emphasis than the other techniques. A businessman inclined to cry over spilt milk might stress the minimax regret criterion. While the Bayes–Laplace criterion may appear at first sight more rational than the alternative methods, there is no *a priori* reason to suppose that this method performs more satisfactorily than any of the other methods. Most decisions made in real life situations are made using a number of these methods (and probably a good deal of intuition and 'feel' for the market too). Since all but one of these methods would recommend siting at the fairground, this might be considered the best choice.

Example

A further example of the operation of statistical decision analysis can be constructed which serves to focus our attention on the market for oil. The world market for oil is dominated by a group or cartel of oil producers known as OPEC (the Organization of Petroleum Exporting Countries). Oil is a major input into the productive process of many industries, it is also used by households for central heating and as petrol in motor vehicles. As such it is characterized by a very inelastic demand. If the international market for oil were monopolistic, a high price for the product could be supported, and substantial supernormal profits could be earned. Were the market perfectly competitive, the price would be forced down to very low levels, since the *marginal* costs of production are small. The aim of OPEC as a group of producers is to replicate the behaviour of a monopolist, thus enabling high profits to be made by each producer.

All this produces a situation of uncertainty, because members of OPEC are not always able to agree on the level at which they should set the price of oil. A high price is in the best interests of every producer. It is inevitable, however, that any individual producer will try to cheat on the other members of the cartel by secretly lowering its price. If a producer gets caught doing this by other members of the group it is likely that all producers will lower their prices in retaliation. But this lowers the profits of every producer, and so an agreement to raise prices once more is likely to be made.

Figure 9.4 illustrates the fluctuations in the price of Brent blend crude oil during the mid-1980s. The price fell dramatically from $30 to $9 per barrel during the early months of 1986 when disagreements proliferated amongst the OPEC members as they sought to raise the cartel's share of the market. Since then the price has risen once more with the announcement of a production sharing agreement (promoted by Iran) and a price agreement (promoted by Saudi Arabia).

The price of oil has quite substantial effects on the costs of all other industries in the economy. Almost all producers require oil for transportation even if they do not use it directly in the manufacture of their output. For this reason economic forecasters have continued to produce regular predictions of the price of oil in spite of the considerable uncertainty surrounding this figure. Such forecasts are published by the OECD (Organization for Economic Co-operation and Development) in its journal *Economic Outlook* twice yearly. Moreover, the impact of oil prices on the costs faced by firms operating in various sectors of the economy has been investigated by the National Economic Development Office (NEDO) (1974); so changes in the profitability of firms due to oil shocks can (under fairly weak assumptions) be evaluated.

Suppose that, in the light of Figure 9.1, a forecaster believes that by 1990 there is (to the nearest ten dollars) a 0.2 chance of the oil price being $30, a 0.6 chance of it being $20 and a 0.2 probability of the price being $10 per barrel. Suppose, moreover, that the profits matrix of a manufacturer of rubber products is as given in Table 9.7; here profits are recorded for each of two levels of plant capacity (a choice variable for the

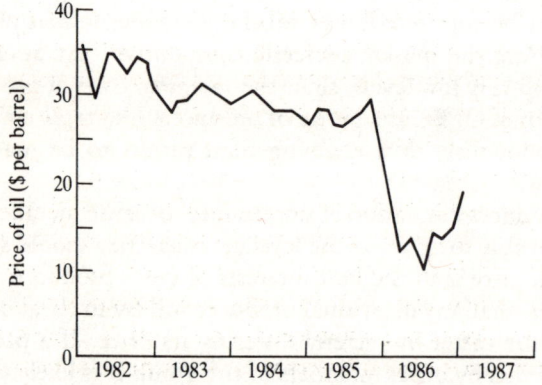

Figure 9.4 Price of Brent blend crude oil
Source: Financial Times, 3 February 1987, pp. 15–17.

Table 9.7 Payoff matrix of a manufacturer of rubber products (profits expressed in £ million)

	Price of oil ($ per barrel)		
Firm's strategy	10	20	30
Cut capacity	94	80	68
Raise capacity	100	80	60

firm) and each of three states of nature (oil prices). In order to keep the problem reasonably straightforward, the decision being considered is that of choosing the direction of change of plant capacity, not the magnitude of such change. This simplification means that the data of Table 9.7 are necessarily hypothetical, but they are none the less perfectly plausible.

In this situation, all criteria bar one (maximax) would advocate that the capacity of the plant should be reduced. It is worth noting, however, that a fairly small change in the forecast of oil prices could lead to a change in the strategy recommended by the Bayes–Laplace criterion. For instance, if the oil price forecast were to change so that the probabilities of prices close to $10, $20 and $30 are now 0.3, 0.6 and 0.1, respectively, then the expected payoff is maximized by raising plant capacity. Moreover, if the assumption that Hurwicz's $a = 0.5$ is amended so that $a = 0.6$, the recommendation of the Hurwicz criterion would also change. Inevitably much therefore depends on both the confidence with which oil price forecasts are made and the degree of optimism or pessimism of the individual manager.

The tools of statistical decision analysis have a variety of applications and are of particular value in situations of limited competition such as oligopoly. Not only can location and plant capacity decisions be taken with reference to these techniques, but – by straightforward extension of the examples given above – the methods can be used to assess the optimal amount of advertising expenditure in an uncertain environment, or to determine the firm's best pricing strategy.

To sum up the foregoing discussion, there is no unique 'correct' way to approach the problems of risk and uncertainty; indeed if there were, the very words 'risk' and 'uncertainty' would lose their meaning. However, the techniques considered above provide objective, consistent and reasonable methods which can and do assist the decision-maker's work. If anything remains certain in an uncertain business environment, it is that a firm basing its decisions on objective, consistent and reasonable criteria in general stands itself in better stead than one which does not.

Exercise: Cattle farming in California

Table 9.8 shows the per period profits which are earned at a ranch for beef cattle in California (Halter and Dean, 1971). A number of states of nature are defined, together with the probability that each state of nature will prevail. Profits are calculated for six different scales of operation. The problem, then, is how to determine the optimal stocking rate of the farm under conditions of uncertainty.

Table 9.8 Payoff matrix for a stocker operation, beef cattle in California (in $)
Source: Halter and Dean (1971)

		Stocking rate (head of cattle)					
State of nature	Probability	841	1009	1177	1345	1513	1681
Very poor	0.045	-3691	-5585	-7575	-9411	-11 395	-13 307
Poor	0.114	-3007	237	-1753	-3589	-5 575	-7 485
Fair	0.182	-2407	969	4147	2311	327	-1 585
Normal	0.318	-1807	1569	4851	8181	6 197	4 285
Good	0.250	-1207	2169	5451	8855	12 067	10 155
Excellent	0.091	-607	2869	6051	9485	12 773	16 015
Expected value		-1879	1254	3670	5274	5 061	3 618

(a) Under fair conditions the profits available first rise and then fall as the size of the herd is increased. Why might this be?

(b) Use the five criteria of statistical decision analysis discussed in this chapter in order to determine the level of stock which the farmer should seek to achieve in order to maximize payoff.

(c) How does the optimal decision depend upon the degree of optimism or pessimism of the decision-maker?

(d) What other methods might be available to help the farmer cope with uncertainty?

Chapter 10
Individuals and the economy

So far the analysis has been confined to a single industry and, in particular, to the way in which a single firm operating in that industry will make decisions about its price, advertising intensity, scale of operation and employment of capital, labour and other inputs. The anatomy of demand functions has been analysed, and the importance to the firm of knowing what level of demand it faces at each price has been discussed. The costs of production are seen to represent only one side of the pricing mechanism: demand for the product matters as well. A profit-maximizing firm, having determined its optimal level of output, will sell that output at as high a price as it can; the price therefore depends not only on the willingness of the firm to supply, but also on the willingness of the customers to buy. The average cost to the firm of producing its output was seen initially to fall and then to rise in the short run with an increase in production levels, as the labour input which best matches the (given) input of capital is approached and then exceeded. The principle of eventually rising average costs (owing to the diminishing marginal product of variable inputs), together with constant or falling average revenues, underlies the existence of a simple profit-maximizing level of output. A change in either the cost structure or the demand faced by a firm will lead to a change in the optimal output level.

While all discussion so far has been in terms of anonymous industries, it is clear that some industries are of greater strategic importance to the macroeconomic performance of a country than are others. This is not to say that other industries are unimportant *per se*; water is a vital commodity, but it would be difficult to conceive of a situation in which fluctuations in water prices drastically affected the state of the British economy as a whole. On the other hand, oil, electricity, steel and financial services are all vital and are major and costly inputs into a large number of industries; large fluctuations in the price of any of these commodities can therefore be expected to generate large fluctuations in the costs of all industries. Consequently the supply curves of firms in all industries will fluctuate, and the prices charged by all industries will vary with the prices of these strategic inputs. The behaviour of firms even in just one industry can therefore bring about macroeconomic changes of some magnitude. The prime example of this in the last couple of decades has been the influence of the price of imported oil on domestic inflation. In 1974, OPEC quadrupled the price of oil sold to Britain; between the years 1973 and 1975 inflation rose from 9.1 per cent to 24.2 per cent. Substantial increases in the price of oil have also occurred in 1979 and 1989. While the rise in inflation was by no means the result of the oil shock alone, there is no doubt that the OPEC price increase had a very severe impact on all Western economies and on Britain in particular.

The effect which some industries (and even some individual firms) can have on the economy as a whole is of little interest to those firms, however. Of considerably greater interest is the fact that macroeconomic fluctuations themselves influence the way in which individual firms behave. While the unemployment rate depends on decisions made by individuals and firms about labour supply and demand at a micro level and the gross domestic product depends on the output of each firm in the economy, it is also the case that certain microeconomic decisions are made on the basis of knowledge about macroeconomic conditions.

In Chapter 3, the income elasticity of demand was defined. For the firm interested in estimating the demand for its product, a knowledge of income elasticities is needed, together with information about the level of income in the economy as a whole. If a firm wants to know what the demand will be for its product in two years' time, it must have some estimate of what the national income will be in two years' time. Similarly, assuming constancy of incomes, both the costs of production and the demand faced by a firm are dependent on the general price level economy-wide: as the general price level rises so do costs, and this shifts the supply curve of the firm upwards and to the left. At the same time demand for the product at any given price will increase if the cross elasticity of demand for the product with respect to a bundle of all other goods is positive, and will fall otherwise. If, then, a firm wants to know what the demand will be for its product in two years' time, it must be able to estimate not only national income, but also the price level two years' ahead.

Macroeconomic forecasts are available which can provide the firm with this information. These forecasts are made by using large scale econometric models on the basis of particular assumptions about the government's future economic policy. Some of these empirical macroeconomic models even make predictions about the performance of each industrial sector in each region. In the next few chapters the types of macroeconomic relationships which such models describe and use for forecasting are described in some detail. It cannot be overemphasized that the individual firm should understand the workings of the macroeconomic system; decision-makers in the firm should not sit back and accept the econometric forecasts of third parties at face value but should themselves understand the economics of broad aggregates. Such an understanding is necessary because forecasts of this kind are meaningful only when comprehended in the context of their basic policy assumptions. Furthermore, a firm will typically want information which is more specific to its particular market than most of the published results provided by the large scale models. Econometric models are becoming increasingly important as a tool of business forecasting, and many large companies have by now developed their own models which enable them independently to predict the macro- and microeconomic variables of greatest interest to themselves. Most large firms, however, continue to purchase econometric forecasts from specialist firms which deal in 'custom built' predictions of a set of variables tailored to the requirements of the individual company. Either way, the management of each firm should know what variables influence its demand and costs, why, and by how much; and to know this they must understand macroeconomic relationships.

In the study of microeconomics it is common practice to hold national income and the general price level constant so as to examine the effect of changes in the price of the commodity the firm produces in isolation from external influences which lie outside the firm's control. In much the same way, it is typically assumed in the study of macroeconomics that relative prices remain constant – that is, if the price of one good doubles, the prices of all other goods also double. By making this assumption it will be possible to talk of 'the' general price level as though all prices vary together; it will not therefore be necessary to worry whether an inflation increases only export prices or only domestic prices – a distinction which could (in the absence of this assumption) have considerable bearing on what type of economic policy can best counter the inflation – since, by assumption, all prices rise by the same proportion. Fortunately, albeit a rule with many exceptions, in general the constancy of relative prices does not seem to be too restrictive an assumption.

Important macroeconomic variables are closely related to important microeconomic variables. For instance, investment is the sum, over all firms, of the acquisition of new capital. This, in turn, is for each firm some function of the gap between existing and desired capital stock; desired capital stock is defined by the point of tangency of the lowest possible isocost line and the isoquant which pertains to the optimal output level. Another example is the relationship between the optimal output of the individual firms in an economy and national output or gross domestic product. The difference between the revenue a firm receives for its output during a year and the cost to the firm of purchasing the materials used in the final product is known as the value added by the firm. The sum of value added across all companies in the economy is the gross domestic product.

The macroeconomy is a complex system; what goes on in one market often has a considerable impact on what goes on in others. For example, an increase in interest rates caused by activity on the money markets has implications for the costs of production incurred by firms supplying goods and services. The money market and the product market and therefore linked together. In order to study a system, it is useful to build up a model in several stages. We therefore start (in Chapter 11) by studying a model which considers the market for goods and services alone, and which does not accommodate the markets for money, labour and foreign trade. This enables some results to be derived which – despite the simplicity of the model and the strength of its assumptions – are useful in a real world context. The assumptions of the model are later relaxed, so that the money market (Chapter 12), the labour market (Chapter 13) and the market for foreign trade (Chapter 14) can be introduced.

Chapter 11
The circular flow of income

The approach to be adopted in this part of the book is as follows: in this chapter a series of simple models of the macroeconomy is presented. While making a number of unrealistic assumptions these models are none the lesss sufficient to illustrate some of the more important concepts and ideas of macroeconomics. Initially the interest rate and prices will be held constant, and foreign trade is assumed negligible, so that the product market may be examined in as simple a framework as possible. In the next chapter the money market is introduced into the analysis, and this enables the assumption of a fixed interest rate to be dropped. In Chapter 13, the labour market is brought into play, thus permitting the variation of prices and wages. Finally, in Chapter 14, foreign trade is brought fully into the picture. The complete macroeconomic model is thus one in which product markets both at home and abroad interact with the money and labour markets. All four sectors have an influence on the national economy. Since the interaction between these four markets is often very complex, however, we shall begin by studying the product market in isolation.

The product market is the set of all communication links between the buyers and sellers of goods and services. In studying the product market alone, without reference to the money and labour markets (which are to be defined later) the following are assumed constant: the money supply, all prices and wages, the interest rate, the exchange rate and the technological relationships between inputs and output. As we progress, these assumptions will be dropped so that the models considered become ever more realistic.

To begin with the following assumptions are also made. There is no foreign trade, no government activity, no savings by households and no investment by firms. In such a world, households will receive income from firms in return for the provision of inputs into the productive process (like labour), and the households will spend all this income on the purchase of the output produced by the firms. In turn, all revenues collected by the business sector are eventually returned to households in the form of income. (Some firms will buy materials from other firms – for instance, a steel works buys coal from the mining companies – but even these expenditures eventually become the incomes of certain households, since it is assumed that no firm retains any of its income for investment purposes.) A diagrammatic presentation of this model appears in Figure 8.1. Firms use all their income to pay for inputs; households use all their income to pay for outputs. Inputs are sold by households to firms in the form of labour, land and finance for the purchase of capital. Outputs are sold by firms to households in the form of goods and services. The sum of all households' incomes and the sum of all firms' incomes (consumers' expenditure) are equal. Income thus flows from firms to households and back again to firms. For this reason, Figure 11.1 is said to represent the circular flow of income.

It is useful to note at this early stage the identity of income, expenditure and output. All three have the same value. The national income – that is, the sum of all payments to factors of production – can therefore be calculated either by summing up all incomes in the economy, or by adding up all final expenditures, or by aggregating the net output of all firms. The results of the first two methods are regularly published for Britain by the Central Statistical Office of Her Majesty's Government. The correspondence between income and output will frequently be referred to in the sequel: although the models adopt greater realism as we progress, the fundamental identity of output and real income remains. Real income and output are one and the same thing.

In the model described above, consumer's expenditure always equals income. Nothing in the structure of the model is capable of explaining the level of income, however. Income, in this model, is fixed at its present value simply because this is what its value has always been. It is as if the economy was created along with the rest of the world, and that the level of income is an unalterable fact of life much as the speed of light is (more or less) an unalterable fact of life. While it is useful for a physicist to assume

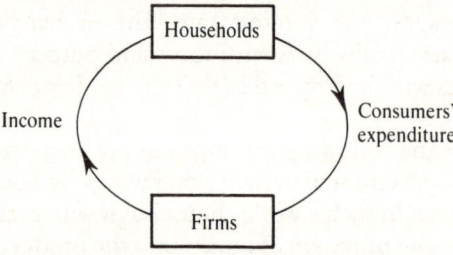

Figure 11.1 The circular flow of income

that the speed of light is constant and given, the same cannot be said for an economist who assumes the level of income is predetermined in this way; fortunately it turns out that by relaxing some of the assumptions made earlier, more can be said about the level of income. The first assumptions we drop are that no savings or investment exist.

Before proceeding further, a few terms must be defined. First, *disposable income* is that part of income which is available for consumption – that is, take-home pay plus unearned income, plus any grants, pensions, benefits or other transfer earnings. *Savings* are defined as that part of disposable income which a consumer does not spend on the consumption of goods and services. They are that portion of disposable income which a consumer prefers to devote to consumption at some time in the future rather than in the present.

Let the consumption of goods and services by individuals vary in proportion to their disposable income, Y_d, according to the formula:

$$C = c_0 + c_1 Y_d \tag{11.1}$$

It seems reasonable to suppose that as the disposable income of all individuals in the economy rises, so will the overall level of consumption. Only if 'present consumption' is an inferior 'good' for consumers in the economy taken as a whole will this not be the case. By the same token, only if 'future consumption' is an inferior 'good' will less be saved as disposable income rises. Thus c_1 will likely lie between 0 and 1; if c_1 were negative, consumption would fall as income rises; if c_1 exceeded 1, then savings would fall as income rises. The coefficient, c_1, on disposable income is known as the marginal propensity to consume out of current disposable income (often referred to as simply the marginal propensity to consume). It is the amount by which consumption rises if disposable income rises by 1. The parameter c_0 is the level of consumption which would persist if disposable income fell to zero; at very low incomes people might be expected to consume out of their past savings and so consumption may exceed income. Thus c_0 is expected to be positive, and is referred to as autonomous consumption.

Given that savings, S, are defined as that part of disposable income which is not spent on consumption, a savings function which corresponds to the consumption function of Equation (11.1) may be derived.

$$Y_d = C + S$$
$$S = Y_d - c_0 - c_1 Y_d \tag{11.2}$$
$$S = -c_0 + (1 - c_1)Y_d$$

The savings function, Equation (11.2), indicates that as disposable income rises, so does savings, since $0 < c_1 < 1$. Further, disposable income must exceed $c_0/(1-c_1)$ for anything to be saved at all, since below this income level people will be dissaving in order to finance their consumption.

Investment – that is, expenditure by firms on capital – will be assumed positive and constant for the time being. Recall that capital is defined as the stock of goods used in production which have themselves been produced. Adjustments made by firms to the size of their capital stock are in general financed either by loans from financial institutions and from the public or by the depletion of the firm's savings. This makes investment, I, responsive to the interest rate, r, and to expected future values of the interest rate: in general, since it costs more to borrow money when interest rates are high and since firms must borrow money in order to augment their capital stock, investment falls as the interest rate rises. Conversely, as the interest rate falls, investment rises.

A number of factors other than the interest rate is likely to influence investment, however. In particular, the growth of national income seems to exert a strong pull. This is not surprising since capital is an input into the productive process: as income rises, demand for final goods rises and so the optimal output and desired capital stock of firms rise; as the growth of income rises, therefore, the magnitude of changes in the capital stock – that is, investment – should rise. This theory, which postulates that investment is positively related to the growth of national income, is known as the accelerator theory.

Business confidence – what Keynes referred to as the 'animal spirits' of investors – is often cited as a determinant of investment. This, though, begs the question: what determines business confidence? The answer would certainly include such factors as interest rates and anticipated future growth of national income. Empirical estimates of the investment function by Jorgenson and Stephenson (1969) and others suggest that over 96 per cent of the variation in investment spending by businesses can be explained by time series of interest rates and income alone. The bulk of economic theory regards the interest rate as the main determinant of investment; while income and the rate of change of income are included as explanatory variables in more advanced studies, it suffices our present purposes to regard the interest rate as the only influence on investment. The simplified investment function may be written:

$$I = \bar{I} - i_0 r \tag{11.3}$$

where $\bar{I}$ and i_0 are constants.

For the moment, however, an even simpler version of the investment function will be employed; investment will be considered as exogenous to the model under consideration. That is, investment is determined by a process which is not considered in the present model and is therefore treated as a given constant. What we are doing then, in effect, is to hold

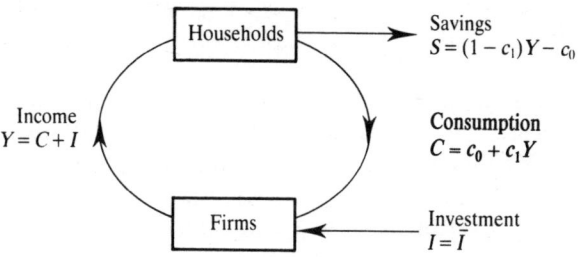

Figure 11.2 Savings and investment in the circular flow

the interest rate constant. This admittedly restrictive assumption will be relaxed in due course. Holding investment constant and letting savings vary with the level of income, the circular flow of income diagram now appears as in Figure 11.2. Note that, since there is no government activity in this system, no taxes exist and so disposable income equals total income. Savings appear as a withdrawal, or leakage, from the circular flow: this indicates that savings are a part of income which was once in the circular flow but is no longer circulating. Investment is an injection into the circular flow: income which was not otherwise circulating around the economy is brought back into action by firms' borrowing activity. The savings and consumption functions are given by Equations (11.2) and (11.1), respectively. Investment, I, is exogenously fixed at a constant $\bar{I}$. Income distributed by the production sector to the households equals the sum of all income received by the firms; that is, the sum of consumption and investment. Hence

$$Y = C + I \qquad (11.4)$$

is described as a national income identity in this simple model. It is also the case, however, as can easily be seen from Figure 11.2, that, as we progress further around the circular flow,

$$Y = C + S \qquad (11.5)$$

and so investment and savings must equal each other if income is to be stable. When investment equals savings, demand equals supply in the product market and so there is no involuntary accumulation of stocks of finished goods; that is, there is no unplanned investment. When income is stable the product market is said to be in equilibrium. The stable, or equilibrium, level of national income can be determined from the parameters and constants of the system by noting that:

$$I = S$$
$$\bar{I} = (1 - c_1)Y^* - c_0 \qquad (11.6)$$

$$Y^* = \frac{c_0 + \bar{I}}{1 - c_1}$$

where the asterisk denotes equilibrium. The equilibrium level of income is no longer an arbitrary constant or an unalterable fact of life. It depends on autonomous consumption, c_0, the marginal propensity to consume, c_1, and investment, I. If investment rises, equilibrium income rises too. For instance, if investment were to rise from $\bar{I}$ to $(\bar{I} + dI)$, the new equilibrium income level would be

$$Y^{**} = \frac{c_0 + \bar{I} + dI}{1 - c_1} \tag{11.7}$$

which is $dI[1/(1 - c_1)]$ more than Y^*. Since c_1 lies in the range $0 < c_1 < 1$, the increase in equilibrium income is greater than the increase in injections which brought it about. *This is a remarkable and vitally important result*: it means that relatively small changes in injections into the circular flow of income (and, by symmetry, in withdrawals from the circular flow) can have a relatively large impact on national income itself. The effect is greater than the cause. In the above example, dI is known as the *multiplicand*, and $1/(1 - c_1)$ is the *multiplier*.

The multiplier is defined as the ratio of the change of equilibrium national income to the change in some variable exogenous to the system whose variation causes disturbance to the product market equilibrium.

Investment is not the only injection into a real world economy, however, and savings is not the only withdrawal. Other injections are government expenditures, G, and exports, X; both introduce into the circular flow of income expenditures in the form of money which was not previously active in the product market. In the case of government expenditure this is done by way of spending on services, grants, subsidies or benefits, while in the case of exports, the payments made by overseas purchasers for goods produced in the domestic economy introduce business revenues originating from abroad into the circular flow of income. Further examples of withdrawals are taxes, T, and imports, M; both take out of the circular flow money which had been circulating between the production and household sectors, by way of deductions from income and payments made to companies based in a foreign economy, respectively. A simple diagram indicating product market flows, injections and withdrawals is shown in Figure 11.3.

Here, all taxes are assumed to be paid by households and are supposed proportional to income. (While it may be objected that firms, too, pay taxes on their profits, this objection can be circumvented by defining the national income so that corporate taxes of this kind are withdrawn from

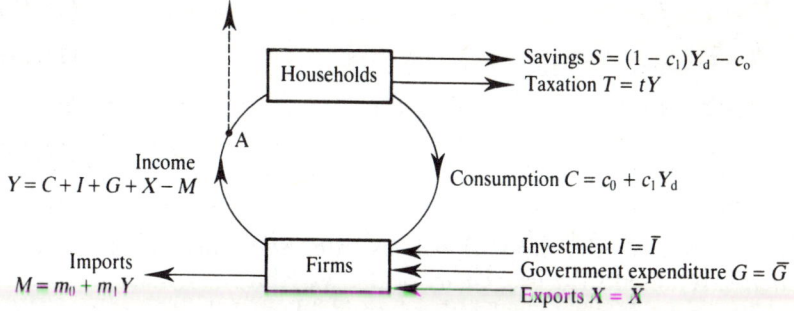

Figure 11.3 Injections and withdrawals: a fuller picture

the circular flow at a point such as A; in other words the income which households receive is less than the national income, Y, not only because of personal taxes but also because of corporate taxes: in this way the definition of national income remains the same regardless of whether separate account is taken of corporate taxation or not.) Imports are almost invariably brought into the country by domestic firms and then sold by these home-based firms to consumers in stores. Thus imports are withdrawn from the circular flow before income is measured. They are positively related to domestic national income; as Britain's national income rises, so does the quantity of goods she imports, other things being equal.

Both the newly introduced injections into the economy – exports and government expenditure – are, for our purposes, to be regarded as exogenously fixed. Exports will depend on the national incomes of overseas countries, and government expenditure, like the tax rate, is controlled by the authorities.

The foreign trade variables, exports and imports, are both likely to vary also with the exchange rate. To keep the analysis simple, the exchange rate will be assumed constant in the sequel; by doing this imports can be seen to vary much as do savings, and exports behave in much the same way as government expenditures. This enables the essential features of an economy to be grasped – albeit at a very basic level – without reference to the complications of foreign trade. For the time being, then, assume $X = M = 0$.

The system which is to be examined in the remainder of this chapter is derived directly from Figure 11.3 and is summarized by Equations (11.8) to (11.14).

$$Y = C + I + G \tag{11.8}$$

$$C = c_0 + c_1 Y_d \tag{11.9}$$

$$Y_d = Y - T \tag{11.10}$$

$$T = tY \tag{11.11}$$

$$S = Y - T - C \tag{11.12}$$

$$I = \bar{I} \tag{11.13}$$

$$G = \bar{G} \tag{11.14}$$

where t denotes the proportional tax rate, and where a bar above a variable represents the exogeneity of that variable.

These equations may look rather formidable as they appear here. They mean nothing more than what we have already said about the economy, however. National income equals the sum of the realized demands of consumers, firms and the government. The consumption which is a part of national income is itself determined by the disposable income of households – in other words consumers base their decisions on how much to spend upon their incomes net of taxes and benefits. Taxes are assumed to be a fixed proportion of the national income. That part of a household's disposable income that is not consumed must (by implication) be saved. Finally, the two injections into the circular flow of income, namely investment and government expenditure, are both assumed to be exogenously determined. Now that an active government has been introduced into the system, the product market equilibrium condition that injections should equal withdrawals becomes somewhat more complicated. In particular, there is a new injection – government spending – and a new withdrawal – taxation. The condition for equilibrium can therefore be redefined as:

$$I + G = S + T \tag{11.15}$$

since it is clearly the case that if consumption (and income) are to remain unchanged from one period to the next, $C + I + G$ must equal $C + S + T$. As was the case in the earlier model with no government, it is again possible in this model to define equilibrium income in terms of the parameters and constants of the model. Substituting from Equations (11.9)–(11.14) into Equation (11.8) we obtain

$$Y = c_0 + c_1(1 - t)Y + \bar{I} + \bar{G}$$
$$Y[1 - c_1(1 - t)] = c_0 + \bar{I} + \bar{G}$$
$$Y^* = \frac{c_0 + \bar{I} + \bar{G}}{1 - c_1(1 - t)} \tag{11.16}$$

If there is no government sector, then $\bar{G} = 0$ and $t = 0$, and Equation (11.16) reduces to Equation (11.6). In the present case, with a government, the multiplier, k, is given by

$$k = \frac{1}{1 - c_1(1-t)} \tag{11.17}$$

It can be seen that as the marginal propensity to consume, c_1, rises, and as the tax rate, t, falls, the value of the multiplier rises. Thus the impact on national income of a change in the level of government expenditure rises with c_1 and falls as t rises. Since the tax rate must lie in the range $0 < t < 1$, it must be the case that the introduction of a government sector reduces the value of the multiplier; nevertheless it is also the case that the multiplier still exceeds unity. Indeed, plausible estimates of the marginal propensities to consume and to be taxed imply a multiplier of around 1.8. If imports are allowed into the model as an extra leakage, the estimate of the multiplier falls somewhat, to around 1.4. Since this is quite significantly greater than unity, an interesting implication is raised by this model. As was demonstrated earlier, a change in injections into the circular flow of income leads to a change in national income which, owing to the multiplier, is larger than the initial change in injections. This makes possible the use of small changes in government spending and taxation as a means of achieving relatively large changes in national income. The government can thereby control the economy in such a way as to meet its macroeconomic objectives.

Before proceeding further, a numerical example will be invoked in order to help fix the ideas hitherto encountered. Let the parameters and constants of the model given in Equations (11.8)–(11.14) take on the following values:

$c_0 = 50$ $c_1 = 0.8$ $t = 0.2$ $\bar{I} = 300$ $\bar{G} = 550$

The units of measurement of c_0, $\bar{I}$ and $\bar{G}$ might be millions of pounds, or some other unit of currency. On the other hand, c_1 and t are proportions or propensities. Inserting these values into the right hand side of Equation (11.16) we obtain

$$Y^* = \frac{50 + 300 + 550}{1 - 0.8(1 - 0.2)} = \frac{900}{0.36} = 2500 \tag{11.16a}$$

as the equilibrium level of income. If the initial position is one of equilibrium, then

$T = 0.2Y = 500$ $C = 50 + 0.8(1 - 0.2)Y = 1650$
$S = 2500 - 1650 - 500 = 350$ $I = 300$ $G = 550$

Note that, since the product market is in equilibrium at this point, injections equal withdrawals; both $T + S$ and $G + I$ equal 850. In other words, Condition (11.15) is satisfied.

Suppose that the authorities now decide to raise the level of government expenditure to 1000 while all other parameters and exogenous

Table 11.1 Endogenous variables for each change in government expenditure

Round	Y	T	C	S	I	G
0	2500	500	1650	350	300	550
1	2500	500	1650	350	300	1000
2	2950	590	1938	422	300	1000
3	3238	648	2122	468	300	1000
4	3422	684	2240	498	300	1000
5	3540	708	2316	516	300	1000
6	3616	723	2364	529	300	1000
...	...	...	...	...	...	...
...	...	...	...	...	...	...
...	...	...	...	...	...	...
Infinity	3750	750	2450	550	300	1000

variables remain unchanged. The economy will be thrown out of equilibrium since injections no longer equal withdrawals. The magnitudes of all variables whose values are determined *within* the model – that is, the *endogenous* variables – will change. New territory must now be explored as the question is begged: how does the economy behave when it is not in equilibrium? To tackle this question the value of the endogenous variables will be calculated for each round of the circular flow of income completed after the change in government expenditure. The results are reported in Table 11.1.

In the first round after the increase in injections, national income immediately rises by the same amount as government expenditure has risen (450). Consequently, consumption rises by $c_1(1-t)450$, that is by 288. As a result of the increased consumption, national income ($Y = C + I + G$) rises further in the second round. This feedback process between consumption and income continues *ad infinitum*, although since $c_1(1-t) < 1$ the increase in income at each round will be smaller than in the previous round. National income therefore converges on its new equilibrium level asymptotically.

As can be seen from Table 11.1 the eventual equilibrium is already fairly close to being reached after only five or six rounds of the multiplier process. The equilibrium level of income is therefore likely to be of considerable interest and importance to policy-makers in charge of controlling the nation's economy. In all but extreme circumstances (such as a full command economy, or situations in which $c_1 > 1$ and t is small) the level of national income will be either at equilibrium or moving towards a new equilibrium after having been disturbed away from its previous equilibrium. Even if the national income never actually arrives at its equilibrium, the equilibrium level of income and output remains a crucially important concept since it characterizes the point to which the economy converges in the long run. If the government wishes to raise income, for instance, it must raise *equilibrium* income, since it is towards this stable level that national income will converge.

This is a convenient point at which to review the progress made so far in this chapter. In so doing a diagrammatic version of the foregoing analysis will be introduced. The crux of the problem lies in the simultaneous relationship between income and consumption. If the sum of all demands, $(C + I + G)$, in one period exceeds national income in the previous period, there is said to be excess demand in the product market: the sum of demands from household, corporate and government sectors exceed the amount which firms are willing and able to supply. In response to this excess demand, firms' stocks of finished goods will be depleted; put another way, there is unplanned disinvestment by firms. In the next round of the circular flow, supply and therefore also national income will increase. This tendency will persist until there is no longer any excess demand. Conversely, where excess supply exists, unplanned investment in the form of stock accumulation takes place and a downward push is exerted on output in subsequent rounds.

In our model, consumption rises with national income, and planned investment and government expenditure are both exogenously fixed. Now let aggregate demand, $(C + I + G)$, be plotted on a graph against national income, Y. Denoting aggregate demand by AD, the graph is illustrated in Figure 11.4. This is commonly referred to as the Keynesian cross diagram. The dotted 45-degree line represents all possible points at which $Y = AD$, that is, where income is stable from one round of the multiplier process to the next. The sloping function, AD, is flatter than the 45-degree line because planned investment and government expenditure are invariate with respect to income, while consumption and savings both rise with income.

At a point like Y_1, $AD > Y$ and so there is excess demand in the product market. Consequently there is a tendency for output to rise as firms attempt to exploit the markets' craving for more commodities. At Y_2, on the other hand, $AD < Y$ and a situation of excess supply exists. Output therefore tends to fall as firms observe unwanted accumulation of inventories. Only at Y^* is $AD = Y$ and so it is only at this point that national income exhibits no inherent tendency to change and is therefore at equilibrium.

Consider now an increase in government expenditure, financed by borrowing from abroad. Government spending thus rises from $\bar{G}$ to $\bar{G} + dG$, this causing a vertically parallel shift in the aggregate demand function. This new function will be dG money units higher than the original function at each level of national income. This is shown in Figure 11.5. As can be seen the parallel shift of AD to AD' causes an increase in

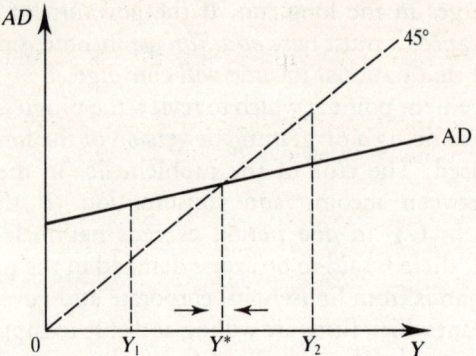

Figure 11.4 The Keynesian cross diagram

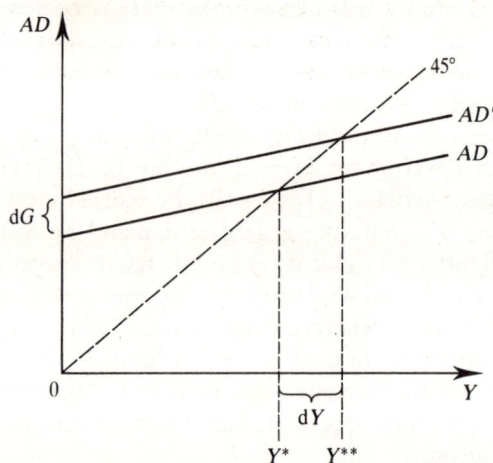

Figure 11.5 The Keynesian cross diagram and the multiplier

the equilibrium level of income at which aggregate demand and output are equal. To be precise, equilibrium national income rises from Y^* to Y^{**}, an increase of dY units. Clearly, since the aggregate demand functions have a slope flatter than the 45-degree line (a fact which follows directly from the assumption that the marginal propensity to consume is less than 1) dY is greater than dG. The ratio of dY to dG is precisely what we have called the multiplier.

It should by now be clear that the slope of the consumption function (and therefore that of the aggregate demand function) plays a crucial role in determining the value of the multiplier, and by way of the multiplier, the effectiveness of government efforts to regulate the level of national income and other key macroeconomic indicators. The slope of the consumption function is given by the marginal propensity to consume, c_1. The higher is c_1, the greater the impact of changes in injections and withdrawals on the national income. Unfortunately, however, empirical evidence would suggest that c_1 is unstable over time. This means that in order for the authorities accurately to predict the impact of their policies on the economy a theory of the consumption function more complete than Equation (11.9) is needed. It is to the development of such a theory that we now turn our attention.

The Kuznets puzzle and Friedman's theory of consumption

The temporal instability of the consumption function was first observed by Simon Kuznets (1946) who used both time series and cross section data to examine the relationship between consumption and disposable income. Interestingly, he found that short run time series (using data over 5–10 years) and cross section studies (using data for various groups of individuals at a given point in time) both imply that the consumption function has a positive intercept and is relatively flat, as in Figure 11.6. Using time series data for a longer period (around 60 years), however, Kuznets found zero autonomous consumption and a relatively steep consumption function, similar to that shown in Figure 11.7. It would appear, then, that what is happening is a series of upward and downward shifts of the short run consumption function, so that for a series of data collected over a short period of time the consumption function is flat, whereas for a longer time series the responsiveness of consumption to changes in disposable income is much more pronounced. This is illustrated in Figure 11.8.

If national income rises, consumption will rise slightly in the short run, by way of a movement along one of the short run consumption functions,

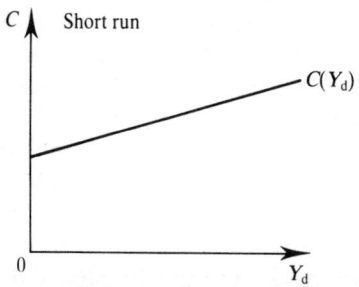

Figure 11.6 The short run consumption function

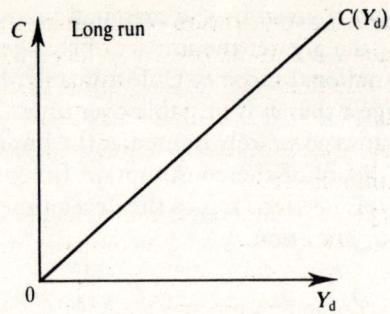

Figure 11.7 The long run consumption function

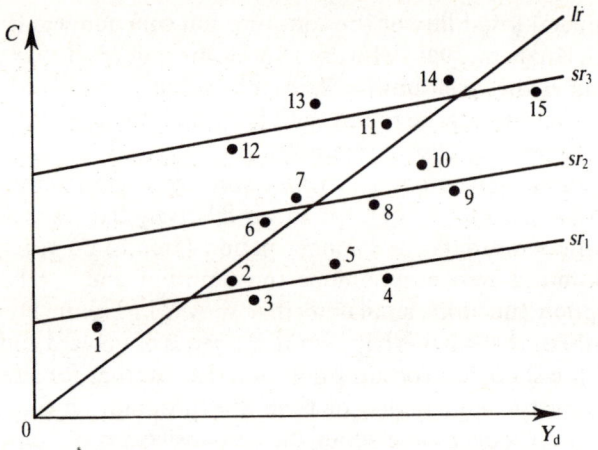

Figure 11.8 The Kuznets puzzle

say sr_1. After a while, however, the short run consumption function shifts up, to sr_2 for example. Thus in the long run the responsiveness of consumption to changes in income is greater than in the short run. This means that the long run marginal propensity to consume is higher than the short run marginal propensity to consume, and so the long run multiplier must be greater than the short run multiplier. Attempts made by the authorities to stimulate or dampen economic activity must therefore take into account the fact that a permanent increase or decrease in injections into the circular flow will take some time to realize its full impact on national income; to achieve a given policy goal quickly, policy must be front-loaded in the sense that new injections must be great to have the desired immediate impact, but should, as the short run consumption function begins to shift, be phased down to their long run level.

Having noted the clear implication of the discrepancy between short and long run consumption functions for policy-making, the question remains: why does the short run consumption function shift? Several theories have been put forward to explain this phenomenon, one of which – the permanent income hypothesis, developed by Milton Friedman (1957) – will be examined here.

Friedman's concept of 'permanent income' enables consumption to be regarded as a function of a measure of income broader than the current income measure which has been used in our discussion up to this point. Permanent income is defined as the average level of income an individual expects to receive over an (unspecified) number of time periods into the future. For instance, if my time horizon is 5 years from now and my income pattern over this period is that given in Table 11.2, my permanent income will be £7,000 per annum (£35,000/5). (This assumes, for simplicity, a zero interest rate, so that there is no time preference.) The difference between total income and permanent income is known as transitory income. Transitory income is essentially random and cannot be predicted by the consumer. The value of transitory income in a single period or year may be positive or negative; if a series of several years is taken, however, the variations in transitory income above and below trend income balance each other so that the expected value of transitory income is zero.

Consumers' incomes seldom fluctuate in tandem with their needs. Consumers' needs will rise as more children are born into the household, but while the size of the family is growing the income earners in the household will experience many fluctuations in their incomes which are totally unrelated to their family circumstances. For this reason consumers tend to want to 'smooth out' their consumption over long periods of time. A young family may borrow money to consume now on the strength of future income; senior citizens may also consume more than they earn if they consume out of wealth which they accumulated during their working

Table 11.2 Permanent income over a five-year period compared with the actual annual income

Year		Annual income (£)	Permanent income (£)	Transitory income (£)
1	Unemployment spell early in year	4 500	7 000	– 2 500
2	Steady work	5 500	7 000	– 1 500
3	Promotion at beginning of year	7 500	7 000	500
4	Extra overtime opportunities	10 000	7 000	3 000
5	Steady work	7 500	7 000	500
	Total	35 000	35 000	0

lives. A household whose head is temporarily out of work will consume out of past savings and/or money borrowed on the strength of future income. While consumption remains more or less constant over time, income fluctuates. While households consume a steady proportion of permanent income, the relationship between consumption and total income (permanent and transitory) is not so clear.

Suppose consumption is a steady £5,000 per annum. Then the long run consumption function may be written

$$C = \frac{5}{7} Y \qquad (11.18)$$

since on average in the long run total income and permanent income are equal. In the short run, however, the difference between total income and permanent income will in general be non-zero. For this particular example the short run consumption function is horizontal, and so the short run marginal propensity to consume is zero while the long run marginal propensity to consume is 5/7. Clearly, then, the permanent income hypothesis – that consumption is dependent on the long run trend level of income rather than on current period income alone – is capable of explaining the Kuznets puzzle.

Friedman's consumption function may be written:

$$C_t = c_1 Y_t + c_2 E(Y_{t+1}) + c_3 E(Y_{t+2}) + \ldots + c_{n+1} E(Y_n) \qquad (11.19)$$

where the operator $E(\ )$ denotes expected values. That is, consumption in period t is dependent on income in period t, expected income in period $(t+1)$, expected income in period $(t+2)$ and expected income in all future time periods until the nth period, where n denotes the time horizon. It is very difficult to measure people's expectations of future income, however, and so most empirical models settle for a version of the consumption function which captures the spirit of the permanent income hypothesis – that is they estimate consumption as a function of income over a span of several periods rather than income in the current period alone. Typically this is done by including past as well as current income in the consumption equation.

The concept of permanent income becomes particularly important in the dynamic macroeconomic models of Chapter 15, however. In that chapter, it will become clear that the optimal response of a firm to changes in government policy depends crucially on whether or not the firm allows for the dynamic behaviour of the consumption function in its calculations of the effects of policy changes.

Fiscal policy and monetary policy

Manipulation of government expenditures and taxation which is carried out in order that the national income be controlled is known as fiscal policy. Fiscal policy was at the forefront of macroeconomic strategy in the Western economies during the thirty years following the second world war, and this period is still considered by many to represent a time when economic policies were notably successful in stimulating employment and limiting the severity of macroeconomic fluctuations. After a short spell out of favour (in the United Kingdom at least) fiscal policy has in recent years been restored to a position of central importance. It is not the only type of policy tool available to the authorities, however, and since the relatively low value of the short run multiplier casts doubt on the short run effectiveness of fiscal policy increasing emphasis has been laid on the role of monetary policy. Monetary policy deals with the influence on national income and other macroeconomic variables of the quantity (or stock) of money in existence in the economy.

In order to discuss properly the combined roles of fiscal and monetary policies in controlling the economy it is necessary first to examine the money market. This will be the subject of the next chapter.

Exercise: Multiplier effects over time

Tables 11.3 and 11.4 below show the multipliers associated with increases of exogenous expenditures in an economy at various time periods after the initial injection. Since the multiplier effect is calculated separately in each of several years, these are known as dynamic multipliers. Table 11.3 details the impact on the local economy of an additional unit of tourism expenditure in Malaga. Because this region of Spain is small, much of the expenditure is leaked out of the local economy as soon as it is spent; that is why the multipliers are all less than one. Moreover, it can be seen from this table that expenditure by tourists

Table 11.3 Multipliers for tourism expenditure in Malaga 1970–75
Source: Sinclair and Sutcliffe (1982).

Types of tourism expenditure	Year 1	Year 2	Year 3	Year 4	Long run
Hotels, etc.	0.39	0.44	0.48	0.50	0.50
Food, drink, entertainment	0.32	0.36	0.38	0.40	0.40
Flats and villas	0.28	0.32	0.34	0.36	0.36
Miscellaneous	0.59	0.66	0.71	0.74	0.75
Total	0.43	0.48	0.51	0.54	0.54

Table 11.4 Government expenditure multipliers estimated by two models assuming fixed interest rates
Source: Wallis (1985) p. 34.

Year	NIESR	LBS
1	1.07	0.86
2	1.20	1.06
3	1.26	1.32
4	1.28	1.53

staying in hotels, for instance, has a greater local impact than does spending by those staying in apartments. This is likely to be because hotel accommodation generates more local employment than other types of lodging, and so the impact of tourism is felt in a particularly direct manner as the total income of hotel workers rises. Notice that the multipliers are particularly low during the early years after the injection of exogenous expenditure, but rise over time. This is characteristic of the behaviour of many dynamic multipliers.

Table 11.4 shows the dynamic multipliers which emerge from an analysis of two macroeconomic models of the UK economy when an increase in government expenditure is considered. This injection is assumed to be financed partly by increasing the money supply and partly by borrowing, since interest rates are supposed fixed. The models considered are those of the National Institute of Economic and Social Research (NIESR) and the London Business School (LBS).

(a) Explain the relative magnitude of the multipliers which attach to food, drink and entertainment and those relating to flats and villas.

(b) Explain the relative magnitude of the multipliers which attach to food, drink and entertainment and those relating to hotels, etc.

(c) The 'miscellaneous' category in Table 11.3 has the highest multipliers. What types of commodity are likely to fall into this category? Why, then, are the multipliers high?

(d) Why do the dynamic multipliers all rise over time?

(e) What implications do the time profiles of the dynamic multipliers in Table 11.4 have for the implementation of government policy?

(f) The multipliers shown in the above tables do not show the full effect of the extra injections. It is likely that economies other than those referred to will benefit as well. For instance, more tourism in Malaga means higher incomes elsewhere in Spain as the increasingly wealthy citizens of Malaga import goods produced in other areas. Bearing this in mind, explain why the leaders of Western governments often call for greater co-ordination in the formulation of economic policy.

Chapter 12
The money market

Money is the set of all assets which can be (and are) used for making immediate payment. The types of assets which fall in this category vary from time to time and place to place, and this makes the whole concept of 'money' rather chimeric. For instance, a dollar note is clearly money in the United States of America, but it is not at all clear whether it is money in Britain. In the Second World War prisoner-of-war camps cigarettes were used as money (Radford, 1945), but one would hardly call them money today. To avoid confusion, then, a working definition of money will be used in all that follows. Whenever we refer to 'money' we shall mean cash (notes and coins). This (if we add the relatively small amounts held by banks as till money and as deposits at the Bank of England) corresponds to the narrow M0 definition of money used by the British authorities.

Several alternative definitions of money, in widespread use, include also assets which are held in current accounts, interest bearing sight accounts, time deposits (such as 90-day accounts), and even Treasury Bills. Indeed, the main instrument of British monetary policy during the late 1970s and early 1980s was the relatively broad (M3) definition of money, which includes (in addition to notes and coins) all sterling deposits held (in both public and private sectors) by UK residents, plus deposits of foreign currency held by UK (non-bank) residents. These alternative definitions of money are, however, rather technical and are of limited relevance to the argument of the present chapter. For our purposes it will be sufficient to think of money simply as cash.

The money market is the set of all communication links between buyers and sellers of money. People and firms buy money in the sense that in order to hold money they must forgo or sacrifice the utility they get from holding other assets. In particular, if the choice faced by individuals is one between holding money and holding interest bearing assets (perhaps in the form of a deposit account at a bank, or a building society account, or as company shares or bonds), the cost to them of holding money is the interest which they forgo by 'selling' their interest bearing assets for cash (or current account holdings). The authorities are the sellers of money: they control (to a large extent) the quantity of money in the economy.

Having identified the demand and supply sides of the money-market, the nature of the price in this market will now be considered. The price of money is the percentage interest rate, r, divided by 100 so that it is expressed as a proportion. If £1 is held as money over a year, then the price of holding that asset in the form of money is r pence, that is the amount of interest forgone. For instance, an individual who holds on average £500 of his assets in the form of money throughout the year will pay £500($r/100$) in interest; if the interest rate is 10 per cent, then $r = 10$ and the cost to the individual of holding money will be £50.

For the time being, the supply of money will be considered perfectly interest inelastic; the authorities can control the quantity of money in the economy precisely. Demand for money is defined by the liquidity preference function. (Liquidity preference is simply another term for money demand.) The demand for money is dependent on national income, the interest rate and the rate of inflation. Each of these will now be examined in turn.

As income rises so does the demand for money; since consumption rises with income then so must the need for money, since money is used in transactions made by the consumer.

There are two reasons why the interest rate affects the demand for money. First, as the rate of interest rises so the cost to the consumer of holding money (as opposed to holding interest yielding assets) rises; it follows that as the interest rate rises the demand for money will fall, all other things being equal. The second reason relates to the purchase and sale of bonds. Bonds are fixed yield securities; for instance, a £5 *per annum* interest bond always yields £5 *per annum* interest. If the interest rate is 5 per cent then the price of the bond must be £100. If the interest rate falls to 1 per cent, the price of the bond must have risen to £500. The rate of interest is thus inversely related to the price of the bond. As the interest rate falls people sell their bonds for money, hoping to make a capital gain as the price of bonds reaches a peak. Conversely as the interest rate rises people dispose of money by purchasing bonds in an attempt to make capital gains in the future. The demand for money is thus negatively related to the demand for bonds, and it rises as the interest rate falls.

An example might help illustrate this point. In October 1987, stockmarkets around the world crashed. This followed a lengthy period of gradual appreciation of share (equity) prices. As prices of equity rose, the dividends available on a typical share fell in relation to the share price. In other words, the returns (or interest rate) obtainable from equity fell. The crash was therefore in part the result of a large number of savers deciding that the return available on certain kinds of asset (shares) had fallen too low. A stage was reached when they preferred to hold their assets in another form (perhaps as cash or Treasury Bills). Consequently the demand for money rose as a result of a sudden decision on the part of many savers to sell their stock. The low interest rate therefore led to a rise in the demand for money.

The above discussion can be summarized very briefly. The demand for money is positively related to national income and inversely related to the rate of interest.

Inflation is defined as the percentage rate of change of prices. In the present chapter prices are still being held constant and so no inflation can exist. In the more sophisticated model of Chapter 13, however, prices are allowed to change and inflation can become an important determinant of the demand for money. As people expect prices to rise in the future, they hold less money as they buy more goods in an attempt to hedge against future inflation. If I want to buy a TV satellite dish sometime during the next year, then the higher the rate of inflation the less likely I am to delay my purchase (other things being equal) since delay becomes more costly as inflation rises. For the remainder of the present chapter, however, inflation must be assumed zero.

The liquidity preference function may be summarized as

$$M_D/p = L(Y, r, \dot{p}) \tag{12.1}$$

where M_D is the demand for nominal money balances, p is the general price level, Y is income and r is the interest rate. A dotted variable indicates the rate of change of that variable with respect to time, so the $\dot{p}$ represents price inflation. It will be convenient in the sequel to adopt the following specific form for the liquidity preference function:

$$M_D/p = \bar{M} + l_0 Y - l_1 r \tag{12.2}$$

Note that M_D/p represents the demand for real money balances and that liquidity preference concerns *real* balances, not nominal balances. The important distinction here is that people want to hold money not so much for its own sake but for what it can do; the face value (or nominal value) of the money stock is not so important as its real value. That is, with given values of output, interest rate and inflation, the demand for the services of money (the number of typical transactions undertaken per week) remains constant, although as the general price level rises, the nominal money supply will also need to rise simply in order to accommodate the higher prices. Again, since prices are held constant in the present chapter, real and nominal balances will always be equal to one another in the

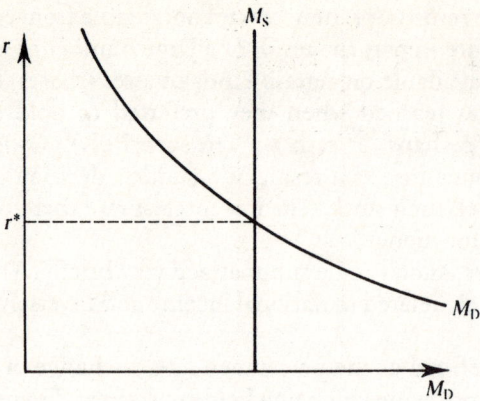

Figure 12.1 The money market

model currently under consideration. In Chapter 13, however, the distinction becomes important.

In order to examine the effects on the economy of changes in the supply of money, consider the way in which money demand varies with the interest rate. Figure 12.1 shows the liquidity preference function with the demand for money inversely related to the interest rate at any given level of income. The equilibrium interest rate is that rate of interest at which the demand for real balances equals the supply of real balances. This is indicated by r^* in Figure 12.1 Nothing in the discussion so far, however, guarantees that the money-market will tend to equilibrium, and so the next question to be answered is: will it?

Suppose the authorities raise the real money supply to M'_S as in Figure 12.2. Initially the interest rate will remain at the previous equilibrium level, r_1. Shortly, however, people will realize that there is more money available in the economy. This does not necessarily mean that the national income has risen; it is perfectly possible for more money to exist in the economy while national income remains constant or even falls. It does mean, however, that if the number of typical transactions occurring in the economy remains unchanged, the money in circulation is circulating slower than before. That is, if output is constant and the money stock doubles, then each pound coin is being used only half as often as it was before. Banks play an important role in the circulation of the money stock, and when they perceive that the velocity of circulation has decreased and that pound coins are lying idle they will use the surplus pound coins to buy bonds. Thus the excess supply of money created by the increase in the money supply leads to an increase in the demand for bonds. This in turn raises the price of bonds and, since the price of bonds is inversely related to the interest rate, the rate of interest falls. The

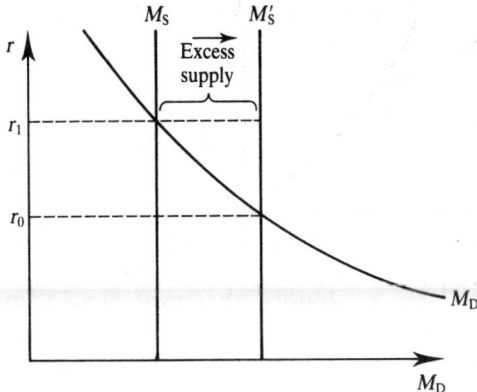

Figure 12.2 Shifting money supply

interest rate continues to fall until the money market clears once more, at r_0.

By symmetry, a reduction of the money supply induces an increase in the rate of interest. The interest rate thus acts as a price which moves up and down in response to market forces in such a way as to clear the money market of any surplus or shortage.

For much of the last chapter, investment and interest rates were assumed constant, but it was noted that a more realistic assumption would allow investment to vary inversely with the rate of interest. It has been established above that an increase in the real money supply brings about a reduction in the interest rate, other things being equal. Thus by increasing the size of the real money stock the authorities can stimulate investment. The increase in investment expenditures by firms constitute a new injection into the circular flow of income and, via the mutliplier process, national income rises. An increase in the real money supply is therefore expansionary since it tends to raise the level of real national income. Conversely, a decrease in the real money supply would be contractionary. This, in a nutshell, is the crux of monetary policy.

This would be an opportune moment at which to pause and reflect on the progress made so far in this chapter. The macroeconomic model of Chapter 11 concentrated on the product market. The money market was present only in the most skeletal form, since it implicitly underlay the fixed interest rate assumption. In that simple model the government was able to influence the level of the national income by varying government expenditure and taxation. In this chapter the relaxation of the fixed interest rate assumption has enabled a second type of policy instrument to be identified, namely monetary policy. Monetary policy and fiscal policy are generically different in that the former works through a change in the money market equilibrium position while the latter directly causes a change in product market equilibrium.

That both fiscal and monetary measures are capable of influencing national income begs the question: given one type of policy, what need is there for another which appears to perform the same task? The answer lies in the influence each policy tool has on the equilibrium interest rate: expansionary fiscal policy increases the interest rate while expansionary monetary policy reduces it. To prove this assertion further analysis is required.

It has already been established that expansionary monetary policy reduces the equilibrium interest rate, but what of expansionary fiscal policy? Increasing the level of national income by fiscal means shifts the liquidity preference function to the right, since the demand for real balances is positively related to the level of real income. In Figure 12.3, this shift is represented by the shift from M_D to M_D'. With a given money stock, M_S, the equilibrium rate of interest rises from r_0 to r_1. Consequently expansionary fiscal policy raises the interest rate through its influence on the liquidity preference function.

If the government wishes to control both national income and the interest rate, both fiscal and monetary policies must be used. It could control either one of the two variables by using one policy measure alone, but if it wants to control both it must use both policy tools. As is the rule in engineering, so it is in economics: for each variable you want to control you must have at least one separate means of controlling it. A truck driver who wants to control his vehicle's speed and direction must use both the accelerator and the steering wheel; it would be impossible to satisfy both objectives using only the accelerator or only the steering wheel. So it is

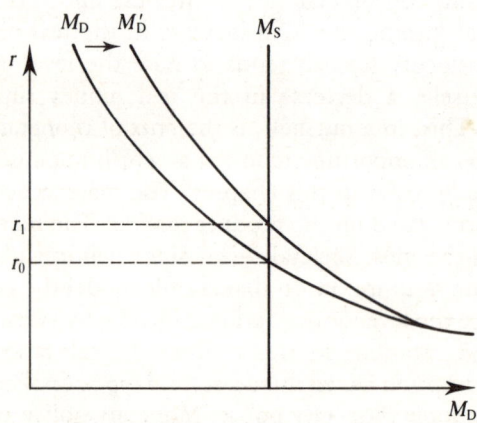

Figure 12.3 Shifting money demand

with economic policy. Two objectives require (at least) two policy tools; two such tools are fiscal and monetary policy.

A useful system of diagrammatic analysis has been developed which illustrates very effectively the roles of fiscal and monetary policy. The system, known as ISLM analysis, is based on two curves. One represents product market equilibria and the other represents money market equilibria. The variables whose values are targeted by the authorities are stable only when both curves coincide. The ISLM system is described in some detail below.

ISLM analysis

So far, the following economic relationships have been established

$S = (1 - c_1)Y_d - c_0$	savings function (11.2)
$T = tY$	tax function (11.11)
$Y_d = Y - T$	disposable income (11.10)
$I = \bar{I} - i_0 r$	investment function (11.3)
$G = \bar{G}$	government expenditure (11.14)
$I + G = S + T$	product market equilibrium condition (11.15)
$M_D/p = \bar{M} + l_0 Y - l_1 r$	liquidity preference function (12.2)
$M_D/p = M_S/p = \bar{M}_S/p$	money market equilibrium condition (12.3)

It has also been established that if the product market is out of equilibrium, output will change in the direction of equilibrium output, and moreover when the money market is out of equilibrium the interest rate will change in the direction of the equilibrium interest rate. There will thus be a tendency for the economy to converge towards the point at which both the product and money markets are in equilibrium.

Routine substitution of Equations (11.2), (11.3), (11.10), (11.11) and (11.14) into Equation (11.15) gives

$$\bar{G} + \bar{I} - i_0 r = (1 - c_1)(1 - t)Y - c_0 + tY$$

$$Y = \frac{c_0 + \bar{I} + \bar{G} - i_0 r}{1 - c_1(1 - t)} \quad (12.4)$$

This is a single equation in two unknowns, Y and r. It defines all pairs of output, Y, and interest rate, r, which satisfy Condition (11.15), the product market equilibrium condition. Any time this equality holds,

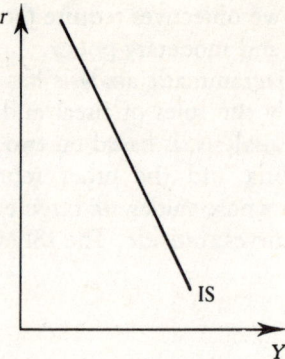

Figure 12.4 The IS curve

injections equal withdrawals and national income is stable. Note that Equation (12.4) is very similar to Equation (11.16), the only difference being that in Chapter 11 i_0 was implicitly held at zero since no variation of the interest rate was allowed. As can be seen from Equation (12.4), as the interest rate rises the level of real income compatible with product market equilibrium falls. Conversely, as the interest rate falls the level of income compatible with product market equilibrium rises. The pairings of real income and interest rate which satisfy Equation (12.4) can be plotted on a graph as in Figure 12.4. The line which results is known as an IS (investment – savings) curve.

The IS curve is the locus of points in (r, Y) space consistent with product market equilibrium. The IS curve alone cannot define the equilibrium level of income; it can only say 'if the interest rate is so-and-so then equilibrium income must be this'. In order to solve for two unknowns, interest rate and income, there must be two equations. The second equation in this case is derived by examining the condition for money market equilibrium. Substituting Equation (12.2) into Equation (12.3) gives

$$\bar{M} + l_0 Y - l_1 r = \bar{M}_S / p$$

$$Y = \frac{(\bar{M}_S / p) - \bar{M} + l_1 r}{l_0} \qquad (12.5)$$

Once more, a single equation in two unknowns has been derived, and again the two unknowns are output and the interest rate. Equation (12.5) defines all pairs of output, Y, and the interest rate, r, which satisfy Condition (12.3), the money market equilibrium condition. Any time this equality holds the demand for real balances equals the real money supply and so the interest rate is stable. Equation (12.5) indicates that as

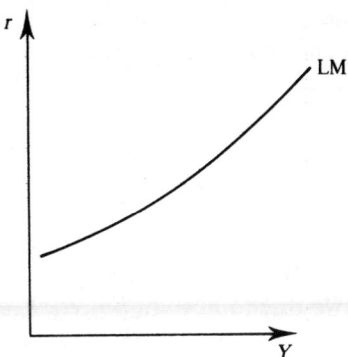

Figure 12.5 The LM curve

the interest rate rises, so does the level of real national income compatible with money market equilibrium. The pairings of interest rate and output which satisfy Equation (12.5) are plotted in Figure 12.5. The resultant line is known as the LM (liquidity preference – money supply) curve.

The LM curve is the locus of all points in (r, Y) space consistent with money market equilibrium.

Together, the IS and LM curves define overall macroeconomic equilibrium in the model currently being developed. Product market equilibrium exists anywhere along IS, and money market equilibrium exists anywhere along LM. Only at the point of intersection of the IS and LM curves are both the product and money markets in equilibrium. This point is illustrated in Figure 12.6, where both the equilibrium interest rate, r^*, and equilibrium real national income, Y^*, are shown.

If the economy is not on the IS curve there is disequilibrium in the

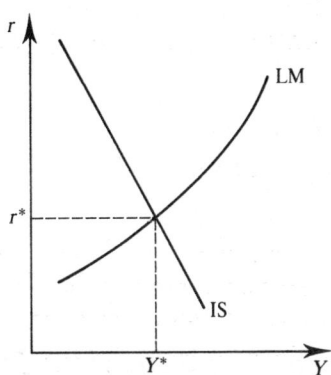

Figure 12.6 The ISLM model

product market: to the north-east of the IS curve there is excess supply $(S + T > I + G)$ and so income tends to fall via the multiplier process. To the south-west of the IS curve, on the other hand, there is excess demand, and income tends to rise.

If the economy is not on the LM curve there is disequilibrium in the money market: to the south-east of the LM curve there is excess demand $(M_D > M_S)$ and so the interest rate rises to encourage people to reduce their holdings of money. To the north-west of the LM curve, on the other hand, there is excess supply, and the interest rate tends to fall.

Combining these two disequilibrium processes, the phase diagram of Figure 12.7 is derived. The arrows show the direction of movement of the interest rate and of national income in each of the four segments of (r, Y) space. If the initial position is one of disequilibrium, at C say, the economy converges on equilibrium along a spiral path similar to that indicated by the dotted line.

Further examination of Equations (12.4) and (12.5) reveals the following:

1. An increase in government expenditure shifts the IS curve away from the origin.
2. A decrease in government expenditure shifts the IS curve in towards the origin.
3. An increase in the tax rate shifts the IS curve in towards the origin.
4. A decrease in the tax rate shifts the IS curve away from the origin.

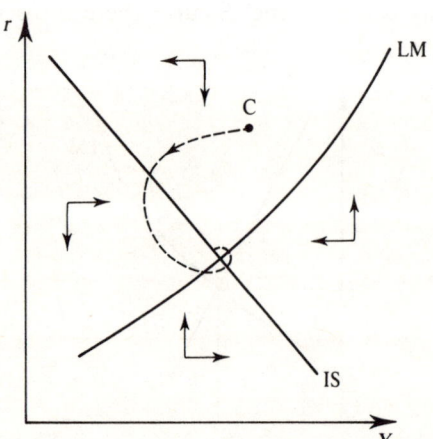

Figure 12.7 Dynamics of the ISLM system: a phase diagram

5. An increase in the money supply shifts the LM curve to the right.
6. A decrease in the money supply shifts the LM curve to the left.

Given these rules, some statements can be made about the effects on the economy of various government policy packages.

1. Fiscal expansion, constant real money stock (Figure 12.8). The IS curve shifts out; there is no change in the LM curve. The new equilibrium is at a higher level of output and a higher interest rate than the old.

2. Monetary expansion, no change in fiscal policy (Figure 12.9). The LM curve shifts out; there is no change in the IS curve. The new equilibrium is at a higher output and lower interest rate than the old. Policy packages 1 and 2 confirm the assertion made earlier that expansionary fiscal policies tend to raise the interest rate while a fall in the interest rate is usually associated with an expansionary monetary policy.

3. Contractionary monetary and fiscal policies (Figure 12.10). Such a policy mix was attempted in Britain during the early 1980s in order to reduce inflation. While the ISLM model is still too simple to allow the effects of this policy on prices to be ascertained, such a package will unambiguously reduce national income. The effect of the policy package on the interest rate is uncertain.

4. Contractionary monetary policy with an expansionary fiscal policy

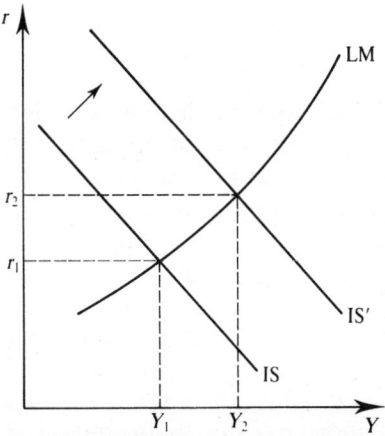

Figure 12.8 Fiscal expansion with a constant real money stock

172 · ECONOMICS FOR MANAGERS

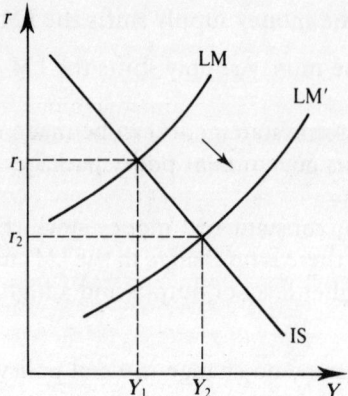

Figure 12.9 Monetary expansion with no change in fiscal policy

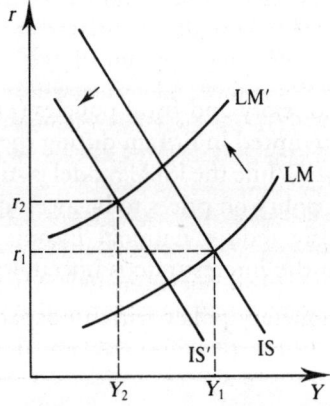

Figure 12.10 Contractionary fiscal and monetary policies

(Figure 12.11). This type of policy mix was tried in the United States during the Reagan presidency of the early 1980s, when a tight grip on the money supply was maintained during a period of extensive rearmament. Theory alone cannot predict the effect of such a policy package on output, but it is clear that the equilibrium interest rate will rise as the government budget deficit increases.

The above statements should suffice to convince the reader that ISLM analysis can be of considerable value in analysing the effects of policy. The model is still too simple to tell us anything about prices and therefore about inflation, but this shortcoming will be rectified in the next chapter.

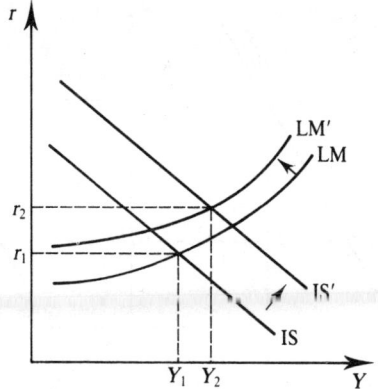

Figure 12.11 Contractionary monetary policy with an expansionary fiscal policy

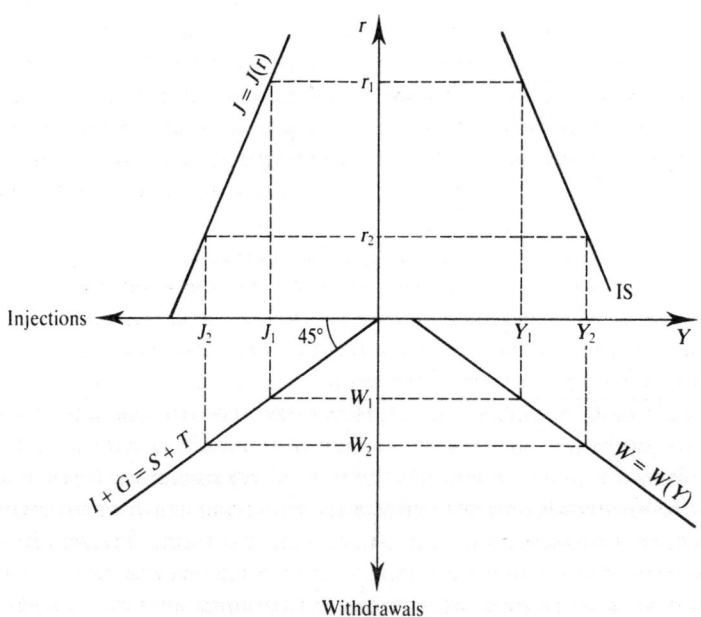

Figure 12.12 Derivation of the IS curve

Diagrammatic derivation of IS and LM curves

Figures 12.12 and 12.13 show, respectively, the derivation of the IS and LM curves. Consider first the IS curve. Injections (investment and

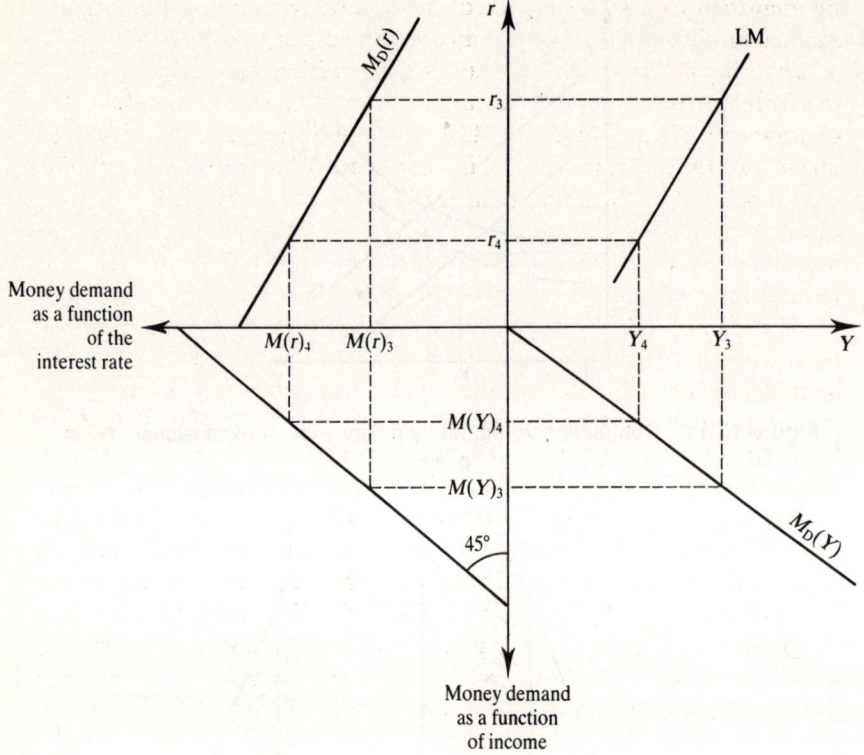

Figure 12.13 Derivation of the LM curve

government spending) vary only with the interest rate, while withdrawals (savings and taxation) vary only with national income. The IS curve defines all pairs of interest rate and income which satisfy the product market equilibrium condition that injections should equal withdrawals. If the interest rate is known then the level of injections can be calculated using the negatively-sloped injections function in Quadrant II; for instance, if the interest rate is r_1, injections must be J_1. Given product market equilibrium, injections equal withdrawals. This is represented in the third quadrant by a 45-degree line along which $I + G = S + T$. Hence the level of withdrawals which would guarantee equilibrium in the product market is $W_1 = J_1$. Since both of the withdrawals considered in the model are increasing functions of income, there must exist just one level of income at which the sum of savings and taxation is equal to W_1. The withdrawals function in Quadrant IV enables this level of income to be identified as Y_1. In sum, then, if the interest rate is r_1, the product market equilibrium level of real income (or output) is Y_1.

Choosing a different interest rate to begin with would, of course, result in a different answer for equilibrium income. By tracking around the four quadrant diagram of Figure 12.12 in a manner similar to that described above, one finds that the level of income compatible with product market equilibrium when the interest rate is r_2, say, would be Y_2. This procedure can be repeated for any number of different interest rates so that a large number of equilibrium (r, Y) pairs can be plotted in Quadrant I. The line joining these (r, Y) pairs is the IS curve.

Turning now to the LM curve and Figure 12.13, the demand for real balances is dependent on both real income and the interest rate. The demand for real balances is negatively related to the interest rate (as shown in Quadrant II) and positively related to real income (Quadrant IV). The equilibrium condition in the money market is that the demand for real money balances should equal the real money supply. The money supply is an exogenously determined variable; prices are fixed in the present model and the nominal money stock is assumed to be precisely controlled by the authorities. There is therefore a limited amount of real balances available in the economy to satisfy whatever demand exists. Given the supply of money and given that along the LM curve the money market equilibrium condition is satisfied, the problem reduces to one of finding the pairs of r and Y which equate the demand for real balances to the fixed supply. The demand for money in Figure 12.13 is found by adding $(\bar{M} - l_1 r)$, the horizontal distance from the origin in Quadrant II, to $l_0 Y$, the vertical distance from the origin in Quadrant IV. Given real money supply, the higher is $(\bar{M} - l_1 r)$ the lower $l_0 Y$ must be if the money market is in equilibrium. The equilibrium condition is therefore given by the 45-degree constraint in Quadrant III; anywhere along this line the demand for real balances equals supply.

Choosing an arbitrary interest rate, say r_3, the value of $(\bar{M} - l_1 r)$ can be calculated. This represents the level of money demand when real income is zero, and for the case in which the interest rate is r_3, will equal $M(r)_3$. From the constraint in the third quadrant it can be seen that the amount of money demanded to accomodate the real income level must be $M(Y)_3$ if the money market is to be in equilibrium. The constant interest rate demand for money function in Quadrant IV indicates that only at one level of real income, namely Y_3, can the total demand for real balances equal supply, given the interest rate, r_3.

If the interest rate selected to begin with had not been r_3, the income level which guarantees money market equilibrium would not have been

Y_3. By tracking round the four-quadrant diagram in the manner described above, starting with various interest rates, a set of (r, Y) pairs compatible with money market clearing can be derived. For instance, the level of income which clears the money market when the interest rate is r_4 would be Y_4. The line joining all these (r, Y) pairs is the LM curve.

NUMERICAL EXAMPLE

At this stage much is to be gained from working through a numerical example of the ISLM model. The equations below refer to a hypothetical economy. (They do, however, bear some resemblance to a highly simplified model of the US economy around the beginning of the 1980s (money amounts being measured in $ billions). The parameters of the model may have been estimated using regression analysis.)

$$Y = C + I + G \tag{12.6}$$

$$C = 50 + 0.7 Y_d \tag{12.7}$$

$$Y_d = Y - T \tag{12.8}$$

$$T = 0.3Y \tag{12.9}$$

$$I = 500 - 4r \tag{12.10}$$

$$G = 1000 \tag{12.11}$$

$$M_D/p = 0.8Y - 100r \tag{12.12}$$

$$M_D/p = M_S/p \tag{12.13}$$

$$M_S/p = 500 \tag{12.14}$$

Using this information the IS equation, the LM equation and the equilibrium values of national income and the interest rate will be calculated. Consider first the IS equation. Substituting from Equations (12.7) – (12.11) into Equation (12.6),

$$Y = 50 + 0.7(1 - 0.3)Y + 500 - 4r + 1000$$

$$= 1550 + 0.49Y - 4r$$

$$0.51Y = 1550 - 4r$$

$$Y = 3040 - 8r \tag{12.15}$$

Equation (12.15) is the expression for the IS curve. Since Equation (12.6) is satisfied, income is stable from one period to the next and so the product market is in equilibrium whenever Equation (12.15) holds.

Next, to estimate the LM curve Equations (12.13) and (12.14) are substituted into Equation (12.12) to give

$$0.8Y = 500 + 100r$$

$$Y = 625 + 125r \qquad (12.16)$$

Equation (12.16) describes the LM curve. Note that the sign of the coefficient on the interest rate in Equation (12.15) is negative, whereas it is positive in Equation (12.16); this indicates that the IS curve is downward sloping while the LM curve slopes upwards. With Equations (12.15) and (12.16), we have two equations with two unknowns, namely Y and r. Solving these equations simultaneously, equilibrium income is found to be 2,895, and the equilibrium interest rate is around 18 per cent. The reader might wish to experiment a little at this stage to see what would happen if government expenditure rose to say 1,200, or if the tax rate rose to say 0.33, or if the real money supply fell to 450.

Real and nominal balances

Up till now prices have been held constant and the distinction between real and nominal values has therefore been unimportant. In the next chapter, however, the assumption of constant, exogenously determined prices will be relaxed, and so the real and nominal values of variables become distinct.

The introduction of endogenously determined prices is an important step, particularly since changes in the nominal supply of money are, in themselves, likely to generate similar changes in the general price level in the long run, thereby leaving the *real* supply of money (and so other real magnitudes in the economy) unchanged. The reason for this is that a change in the nominal amount of money in circulation cannot, in the long run, affect real magnitudes such as the amount of goods and services being produced. This being so, firms respond to the rise in demand consequent upon an increase in the supply of money to the economy by raising prices. In the long run, therefore, the position of the LM curve is beyond the control of government. This observation has made a large group of monetarist economists very pessimistic about the scope for demand management policies. Since monetary policy cannot influence national income (in the long run) these economists argue that attempts to control output and unemployment are futile, and that consequently the thrust of macroeconomic policy should be directed towards an attack on inflation. Such ideas were clearly influential in the formation of UK government policy in the early 1980s.

The variables of greatest interest to the economist are real variables. Consumers decide how many commodities to buy on the basis of their

178 · ECONOMICS FOR MANAGERS

purchasing power – that is, their real disposable income – and do not buy more goods just because their incomes rise when prices are perceived also to be rising. When the French redefined the value of the franc in 1962, people did not suddenly cut their consumption to one hundredth of what it had been before; there was no change in real consumption because there was no change in real income. Similarly, British consumers did not change their real consumption patterns in 1971 when, with decimalization of the currency, the penny was redefined at 2.4 times its old value. For the same reason, government expenditure, investment, savings and taxation are all properly dealt with as real variables. The demand for money is similarly a demand for real balances. By way of contrast, the money supply is controlled by the authorities with reference to the nominal value of the money stock. Consequently a price increase will reduce the real money supply (the buying power of the pound coins already in circulation) unless the nominal money supply is increased in tandem with prices. Hence as prices rise, the IS curve remains unchanged, while the LM curve shifts to the left unless the authorities change the money supply. Conversely, as prices fall, the IS curve again remains unchanged and the LM curve shifts to the right. These are important results.

In Chapter 13 prices and wages are allowed to vary. The levels of wages and prices are shown to be closely related to one another, and the central role of the labour market in determining two of the most frequently talked about macroeconomic variables is discussed. These variables are inflation and unemployment.

Exercise: Product and money markets in the United Kingdom

The demand for currency (as for other definitions of 'money') depends on national income and on the rate of interest. Smith (1978) estimates that the income elasticity of the demand for currency is 1.20 and the interest elasticity of the demand for currency is – 0.68. Hence a rise of 10 per cent in gross domestic product would raise the demand for currency by 12 per cent. A similar change in the demand for currency could be realized if the interest rate were to fall by around one-sixth of its current value.

Over the years 1980–1985, the UK gross domestic product (measured at current prices) rose from £230.6 billion to £351.9 billion. Meanwhile, Smith's measure of the interest rate fell from 11.9 per cent to 10.1 per cent. For the purposes of the present exercise it is useful to ignore changes in the general price level over the period in question.

(a) If the currency in circulation in 1980 was worth £10.2 billion, how much currency would have been in circulation in 1985 if the money market were constantly in equilibrium?

(b) Use the above information to draw the LM curve which describes the United Kingdom money market in 1980.

(c) Recall the estimate of the Keynesian income multiplier provided in the last chapter (that is, $k = 1.8$). Assume realistically that for the United Kingdom in 1980 the IS curve could be represented by the equation $Y = 237 - 0.54r$, where national income, Y, is measured in billions of pounds, and the interest rate, r, is measured as a percentage. Draw the IS curve.

(d) What were the equilibrium levels of national income and the interest rate in 1980?

(e) In 1981 the amount of currency in circulation rose to £10.8 billion. Draw the new LM curve.

(f) Government expenditure in 1981 rose by £6.5 billion. Draw the new IS curve.

(g) What are the new equilibrium levels of the national income and interest rate?

(h) The actual levels of national income and the interest rate observed in 1981 were £254 billion and 13.0 per cent, respectively. Compare these out-turns with the answer to question (g) above.

(i) How might the answers to the above questions have changed if the ISLM model could accommodate changes in the level of prices?

Chapter 13
The labour market

Labour is an input into the productive process which is hired by firms. Labour is supplied by individuals or groups of individuals who, in return for a wage, put at the disposal of the firm their physical and mental capabilities. The labour market is the set of all communication links between those who hire labour and those who are hired. It is a market whose operation is greatly complicated by the existence of wage floors, employers' associations, trade unions, contracts and imperfect information. As a result macroeconomic disequilibria are frequently perpetuated by a labour market which might itself be chronically out of equilibrium.

The cost to the firm of its labour input is a major determinant of price; indeed in an economy without foreign trade and with constant relative prices (like that of our models) there is a direct correspondence between the wage and total costs: even the cost of purchasing new capital eventually ends up as a wage payment to labour albeit the labour hired by another company. Given the demand curve in the product market, there will be a positive relation between the general wage level and the general price level.

The task of this chapter is to relax the constant price assumption made hitherto. Implicit in the analysis of the last two chapters has been the supposition of a constant price and wage level, as though the supply of labour were perfectly elastic. While this may indeed be the case in certain situations (during severe recessions, for instance) such an assumption does not permit sufficient generality to let it be retained in a complete model.

Aggregate demand and aggregate supply

Aggregate demand was encountered at an elementary level in Chapter 11. There it referred to the sum of consumption, investment and government expenditure in the product market, and was seen to vary with income. In

Chapter 12 a further condition for product market stability – namely money market stability – was derived. For aggregate demand, and therefore real national income, to be stable, both product and money markets must be in equilibrium. As was seen at the end of the last chapter, the general price level influences the position of the LM curve and therefore influences also the level of income which clears both the product and money markets. The equilibrium level of aggregate demand is therefore a function of price, p. The aggregate demand curve is defined as the locus of points in (p, Y) space at which both product and money markets are in equilibrium.

With the IS curve

$$Y = \frac{c_0 + \bar{I} + \bar{G} - i_0 r}{1 - c_1(1-t)} \qquad (12.4)$$

and the LM curve

$$Y = \frac{(\bar{M}_S/p) - \bar{M} + l_1 r}{l_0} \qquad (12.5)$$

the unique level of income compatible with both product and money-market equilibrium is found by solving Equations (12.4) and (12.5) simultaneously to give:

$$Y^* = \frac{(\bar{M}_S/p) - \bar{M} + l_1(c_0 + \bar{I} + \bar{G})/i_0}{l_0 + l_1[1 - c_1(1-t)]/i_0} \qquad (13.1)$$

As the general price level, p, rises, so the equilibrium level of income, Y^*, falls (unless the price rise is accommodated by a change in the nominal money supply). The aggregate demand curve is therefore downward sloping.

The reasoning which underlies this derivation of the aggregate demand curve might be understood more clearly with the aid of a diagrammatic analysis. Such analysis is made by reference to Figure 13.1. As the general price level rises from p_1 to p_2 so the real money supply, $\bar{M}_S/p$, falls, as is shown in Quadrant III of Figure 13.1a. The effect of this is to shift the LM curve to the left, from LM to LM'. The point of intersection of the IS and LM curves, where the product and money-markets are both stable, consequently moves so that the equilibrium level of real national income declines from Y_1 to Y_2. Figure 13.1b directly plots price, p, against real income, Y, as derived in Figure 13.1a. As can be seen from the diagram, the aggregate demand curve, AD, is downward sloping: as price rises product and money market equilibrium is given by a fall in national output, and vice versa.

The labour market has no part in the derivation of the aggregate demand schedule. However, it is an important component of aggregate

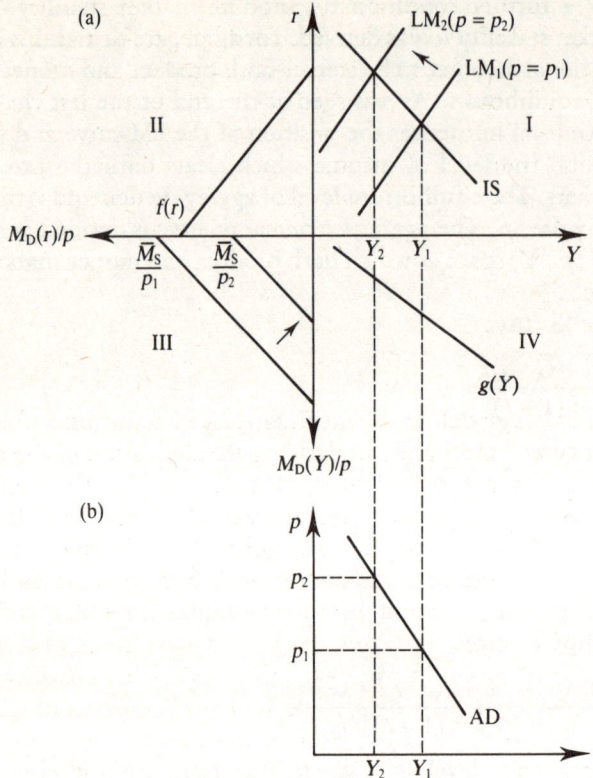

Figure 13.1 Derivation of the aggregate demand curve. (a) ISLM with price changes, (b) Aggregate demand

supply analysis. While the aggregate demand curve indicates the level of output which clears the two macroeconomic markets in which tradeables (commodities or assets) are produced for final demand, the aggregate supply curve is concerned with the clearing of markets on which inputs into the productive process are traded. Recall that the demand for labour is a derived demand; at the level of the perfectly competitive firm it depends on the shape of the marginal product curve which in turn is the dual of the firm's supply curve. The demand for labour is therefore very closely related to the supply of goods to the product market. The labour market therefore underlies aggregate supply. In order to understand the operation of this process it is first necessary formally to define aggregate supply.

The aggregate supply curve is the locus of points in (p, Y) space which shows, for each price level, the amount of output that firms are willing to supply, given the state of the labour market. In simple models the aggregate supply curve is constructed so that the labour market is kept in equilibrium. A model like this is discussed below. More realistic models, on the other hand, go further than this by modelling the behaviour of the labour market when it is in disequilibrium; such a model is considered later in the present chapter. Although necessarily increasing the complexity of the models, it is crucial to incorporate sluggish adjustments to labour market equilibrium since it is only by doing so that many of the most important macroeconomic phenomena can be properly understood.

The labour market is in equilibrium when the wage is such that the demand and supply of labour are equal. When this is so all those who are able and willing to work at the existing (equilibrium) wage rate are in employment; the only unemployment that can exist when the labour market is in equilibrium is voluntary, in the sense that, simply by reducing their wage demands, the unemployed could find work.

To describe the mechanics underlying the derivation of the aggregate supply curve it is necessary first of all to examine the response of the labour market to changes in the general price level. The demand for labour rises as the nominal wage falls, other things being equal, and the supply curve of labour rises with the wage, as shown in Figure 13.2. The initial equilibrium obtains when the price level is set at p_1, and so the nominal wage is w_1 and the labour input is L_1. As the price level rises to p_2, so the labour demand curve shifts out to $D(p_2)$. This happens because the revenue of each firm rises while its costs remain constant; consequently the optimal output of each firm in the economy rises (see Figure 8.9), and more labour is employed to produce the additional output. Therefore the quantity of labour demanded at each nominal wage level rises as the price of the product rises.

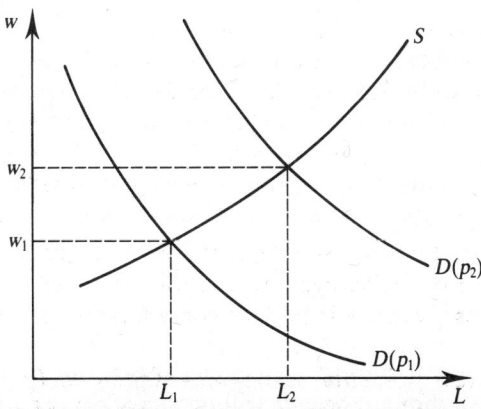

Figure 13.2 The labour market

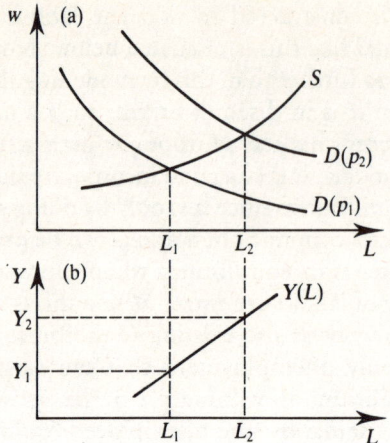

Figure 13.3 The production function. (a) The labour market, (b) the production function

Figure 13.3 shows the labour market response to a general price increase, together with a single production function which relates output, Y, to labour input, L. When the general price level is set at its initial level, p_1, the labour input is L_1 and firms are able to produce Y_1 units of output. Increasing the price level to p_2 leads to increased employment of labour and subsequently to a greater level of output, Y_2. The pairings of price and output thus derived reflect labour market equilibrium (Figure 13.3a) and the willingness and ability of firms to supply output to the product market at the equilibrium levels of labour input (Figure 13.3b). Plotting the price–output pairs derived in this manner yields the aggregate supply curve, AS of Figure 13.4. Note that AS slopes upwards.

There are two problems with the approach just outlined above. First it supposes wage bargains to be struck according to the nominal wage, implying that unions do not consider the price level (and so the purchasing power of their members) when bargaining with employers. It is, however, clearly the case in the real world that the general price level is accounted for in bargaining procedures and that present price changes influence future nominal wage demands. Secondly the above approach does not permit periods of involuntary unemployment; the labour market always clears in the model of the last few pages. A more realistic model, on the other hand, should allow for periods of labour market disequilibrium during which the supply of labour at the existing wage exceeds the demand; during such periods some individuals would be unemployed even though they are willing to work at the going wage rate.

To overcome these problems an approach which is somewhat more

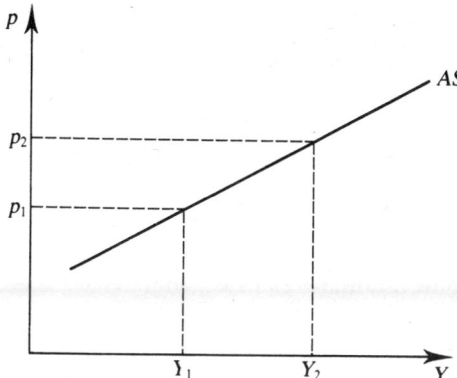

Figure 13.4 Aggregate supply

sophisticated than that adopted up till now will be taken. While the mathematics used to convey the ideas of this method may at first sight appear rather complicated, they do not consist of anything more than simple algebraic manipulation. Moreover the returns to a thorough understanding of this section are considerable.

Suppose now that wages adjust slowly to their new equilibrium level. This may be because of the institution of labour contracts, or because of the inflexibility introduced into the wage-setting process by the existence of unions and employers' associations. Let the adjustment of wages towards the equilibrium level be given by

$$w = w_{-1}\{1 + \epsilon[(L/\bar{L}) - 1]\} + f(\Delta p^e) \tag{13.2}$$

Here w represents the current period wage; w_{-1} is the last period's wage; $\bar{L}$ is the labour market equilibrium level of labour input; p^e is the expected price level; ϵ is a positive constant; and Δ denotes 'change in'.

Equation (13.2) states that the wage is a function of past wages, of the expected change in the general price level and of how far the labour market is from equilibrium. In particular, suppose that the labour market is already in equilibrium; hence $L = \bar{L}$ and so the wage is equal to the last period's wage plus some function of the expected change in prices. If current employment is below equilibrium, $L < \bar{L}$, and there is unemployment of labour; the expected real wage rate will be falling in such a situation in order to entice firms to take on more labour. (In these circumstances some of the unemployed may be induced to withdraw from the labour force.) Conversely, if there is overemployment, the expected real wage will be rising. Noting that prices and wages are positively related to one another by the function

$$p = p(w) \tag{13.3}$$

and substituting this into Equation (13.2) a price function can be derived:

$$p = p\{w_{-1}[1 + \epsilon(L/\bar{L}) - 1)]\} + \Delta p^e \tag{13.4}$$

since $f(\ )$ is, by assumption, identically equal to $p^{-1}(\ )$. Assuming a linear production function of the form

$$Y = aL \tag{13.5}$$

and substituting into Equation (13.4), then

$$p = p\{w_{-1}[1 + \epsilon((Y/\bar{Y}) - 1)]\} + \Delta p^e \tag{13.6}$$

where $\bar{Y}$ is the full employment level of income. Further substitution from Equation (13.3) yields

$$p = p_{-1}\{1 + \epsilon[(Y/\bar{Y}) - 1]\} + \Delta p^e \tag{13.7}$$

which is an aggregate supply curve, explaining price, p, as an increasing function of real output, Y. (Note that this analysis assumes a proportional relationship exists between national income and employment. To the extent that productivity improves over time the value of $\bar{Y}$ will increase, since the level of output needed to guarantee full employment rises as each worker becomes increasingly productive. Hence even if employment is constant over time, national income is expected to grow owing to productivity improvements. In order to maintain simplicity such considerations are abstracted from in the text.)

Equation (13.7) is properly regarded as an adjustment mechanism in which prices adjust slowly to their new equilibrium level. It differs from the aggregate supply curve of Figure 13.4 in that Equation (13.7) includes a dynamic element; if the labour market is thrown out of equilibrium it reverts to equilibrium, but does so only gradually, and so prices in one period will equal those in the next only if the level of income compatible with labour market equilibrium has been arrived at. In other words, Equation (13.7) defines not only the shape and position of the aggregate supply curve but also describes the way in which the curve shifts over time as labour market equilibrium is approached. Note that this AS equation therefore incorporates labour market disequilibrium behaviour as well as the steady state behaviour covered by the earlier, simpler model.

The Phillips curve

A close relative of the aggregate supply curve which has gained the status of a key economic relationship is the Phillips curve. The Phillips curve shows the relationship between inflation and unemployment. Subtracting p_{-1} from both sides of Equation (13.7) and then dividing through by p_{-1} gives

$$(p - p_{-1})/p_{-1} = \epsilon[(Y/\bar{Y}) - 1] + \Delta p^e/p_{-1} \tag{13.8}$$

This is the equation for the rate of inflation, $(p - p_{-1})/p_{-1}$, which for convenience will henceforth be denoted by $\dot{p}$. Inflation is defined as a process of steadily rising prices and wages that persists over time. The price inflation rate, $\dot{p}$, is the percentage change in the general price level from one period to the next. The wage inflation rate, $\dot{w}$, is the percentage change in the general wage level from one period to the next. Note that at $\bar{Y}$, the rate of unemployment is at its equilibrium level, $\bar{u}$ (and so only voluntary unemployment exists). Since the labour market clears, every worker who wants to work at the going wage rate is able to do so. Letting the unemployment rate, u, be a linear function of real income, so that

$$u - \bar{u} = [1 - (Y/\bar{Y})]/k \qquad 0 < k \tag{13.9}$$

and substituting Equation (13.9) into Equation (13.8) gives

$$\dot{p} = \epsilon k(\bar{u} - u) + \Delta p^e/p_{-1} \tag{13.10}$$

Thus inflation is positively related to the equilibrium rate of unemployment and to the expected inflation rate, but negatively related to the unemployment rate itself. This is the famous Phillips curve equation.

We have progressed a long way in this chapter, and have done so at a deliberately fast pace so that the major point of the chapter can be arrived at quickly. In sum the major point is this: other things being equal, the Phillips curve equation shows that there exists a trade-off between inflation and unemployment. As the inflation rate rises, the unemployment rate falls and vice versa.

The potential importance of the inflation–unemployment trade-off was first pointed out by Phillips (1958) using British data for unemployment and wage inflation for the years 1861–1957. In doing so he implicitly assumed expectations of inflation to be zero; for the years considered by Phillips this was not an unreasonable assumption, because actual inflation was typically low, rarely rising above 10 per cent. The curve estimated by Phillips is illustrated in Figure 13.5. The line of best fit through the observations of $\dot{w}$ and u forms a curve, convex to the origin, indicating that neither negative unemployment nor rapidly declining wages is possible.

While expectations of price inflation remain stable, the authorities are presented with a menu of choices along the Phillips curve: if they want to reduce inflation they can do so provided they accept higher

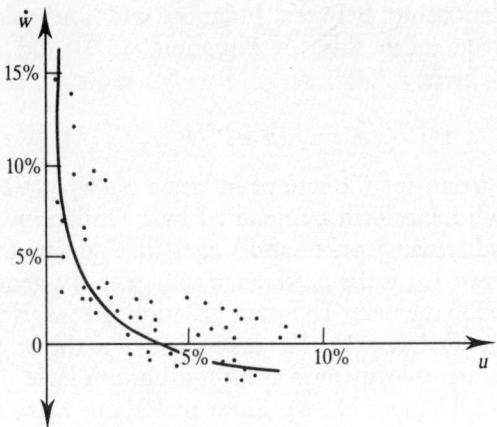

Figure 13.5 The Phillips curve

unemployment as the consequence. Conversely, if the authorities want to reduce unemployment they can do so at the cost of higher inflation. The Phillips curve thus tells the government what combinations of inflation and unemployment are feasible.

Suppose the authorities decide to reduce unemployment (or increase inflation). From Equation (13.9) it can be seen that to do this they must raise the real national income, Y. The only types of government policy considered so far have been fiscal and monetary policies, both of which influence the position of the aggregate demand curve and therefore may be labelled (aggregate) demand management policies. Increasing government spending or the money supply, or reducing taxes would achieve an outward shift of the aggregate demand curve (see Figure 13.6). This would raise the price level at which the product, money and labour markets are all in equilibrium from p_1 to p_2, and would therefore cause inflation during the periods over which the labour market adjusts to its new equilibrium. Furthermore, the equilibrium level of real output would rise from Y_1 to Y_2, thus bringing about the desired fall in unemployment. Expansionary fiscal and/or monetary policy therefore increases inflation and reduces unemployment, so long as expectations of price inflation remain unchanged. For given inflation expectations, then, the expansion of aggregate demand moves the economy up and leftwards along the Phillips curve of Figure 13.5. Conversely, contractionary or restrictive demand management policies move the economy down and rightwards along the Phillips curve, thus reducing inflation and increasing unemployment.

The Phillips curve story outlined above has considerable appeal because of its simplicity: all it says is that there is a trade-off between

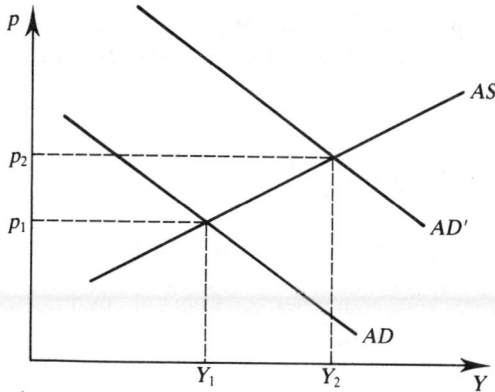

Figure 13.6 Shifting aggregate demand

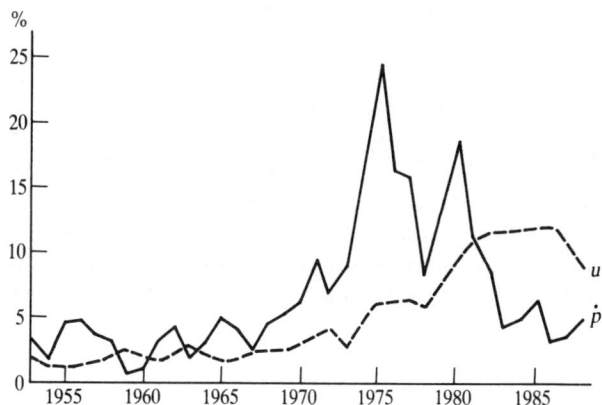

Figure 13.7 Unemployment and inflation in the United Kingdom, 1953–1988

inflation and unemployment and that the authorities can select any level of the inflation rate they please so long as they accept the consequences for unemployment. Particularly attractive is the fact that the simple Phillips curve usually works – an important exception being the 1970s. The history of inflation and unemployment in Britain up till that decade had been a stable pattern of trade cycles at the peaks of which inflation was high and unemployment low, and at the troughs inflation was low and unemployment high. This pattern is illustrated in Figure 13.7. Also apparent in Figure 13.7 is the way in which the simple Phillips curve relationship appeared to break down during the 1970s; over this period both unemployment and inflation consistently rose – a phenomenon which is termed 'stagflation'. This apparent breakdown of the Phillips curve called for explanation, and it is to this we now turn our attention.

Stagflation and expectations

The analysis of the last section assumed throughout that expectations of price inflation were constant. In the present section we shall relax this assumption and, in so doing, show how the Phillips relationship of Equation (13.10) can explain stagflation.

Equation (13.10) implies that as expected price inflation rises, so does the actual level of inflation at any given level of unemployment. In diagrammatic terms, an increase in the expected rate of inflation produces an outward shift of the entire Phillips curve as shown in Figure 13.8. At a given unemployment rate, say u_1, inflation is only $\dot{p}_1$ if no inflation is expected, while if expectations of inflation are positive and the relevant Phillips curve shifts out, inflation is $\dot{p}_2$.

Suppose the initial position is A on Figure 13.8. If the government decided to engage in restrictive monetary policies, unemployment would rise. Provided that inflationary expectations remain at 0, inflation should fall to $\dot{p}_4$. However, the facts that the initial position was A, and that at A actual inflation is $\dot{p}_1 > 0$, may lead people to expect inflation to continue into the future. As people's expectations of inflation rise in this way, the entire Phillips curve shifts outwards, say to $PC(\dot{p}^e > 0)$. While the aim of

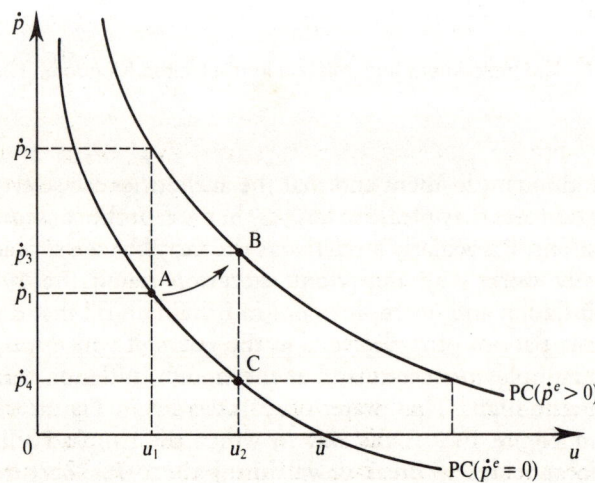

Figure 13.8 The expectations augmented Phillips curve

government policy may have been to allow an increase in the unemployment rate to u_2 so that inflation would fall to $\dot{p}_4$, then, such a move is no longer possible. This is because the relevant Phillips curve has shifted out, and the rate of inflation which is now compatible with u_2 is $\dot{p}_3$. This point, $(\dot{p}_3, u_2)$ is labelled B.

If the rate of inflation expected by the public rises then, and if the policy target is set without allowing for such a rise (or if the policy target is unemployment rather than inflation), the economy will move from A to B (rather than from A to C). It is therefore perfectly possible to experience simultaneously rising inflation and unemployment in the Phillips curve model; the move from A to B is an example of stagflation of this kind. The stagflation occurs because the existence of price inflation at point A raises the expected level of price inflation thus shifting the Phillips curve outwards; since some co-ordinates on the new Phillips curve lie to the north-east of A (point B is an example of such a point) it must be possible for inflation and unemployment to rise simultaneously.

What is the intuition behind this result? When inflation is zero and no inflation is expected, and where markets operate perfectly, there can be no jobless workers whose unemployment is 'involuntary'. By this it is meant that, in such a perfect world, anyone who is out of work can immediately find a new job simply by reducing their asking wage. The only unemployment which remains in this instance, then, is 'voluntary'. This may mean that workers remain unemployed because they are not able or willing to move or retrain to find work; alternatively, jobless workers may be willing and able to work only at a higher wage than is currently available. Such workers will enter employment only if they believe that the real wage has risen. If they misperceive inflation their decisions about whether or not to work will be based on expected inflation, not actual inflation. For instance, if they underestimate the rate of price inflation, they will overestimate the real value of the wage offers they receive; they will thus be more likely to enter employment as a result of their mistakes. Unemployment would then fall as a result of the misperception of the inflation rate – so-called money illusion. Whenever the unemployment rate lies below $\bar{u}$, some workers must be suffering from money illusion in that they believe their real wage is higher than it actually is; the expected inflation rate is below the actual inflation rate.

People do not stay fooled forever, though. As soon as workers once more correctly estimate the rate of inflation they will also be estimating their real wage offers correctly. This means that they will no longer make mistakes in the labour market, and eventually the unemployment rate will rise back to $\bar{u}$. Whenever expected inflation equals actual inflation, therefore, there is no money illusion, and because there is no money illusion the unemployment rate is $\bar{u}$. Since expectations should be reasonably accurate when averaged out over a very long period of time, the unemployment rate compatible with accurate expectations must be one around which the economy oscillates. For this reason, $\bar{u}$ is sometimes referred to as the 'natural rate' of unemployment. It is the rate of unemployment which pertains when the labour market is at equilibrium. In the short run the level of unemployment compatible with any given rate of price inflation rises as expectations of inflation rise; this happens simply because as expectations of inflation rise workers' estimates of the real wage fall and so the supply of labour falls. In the long run there is, according to the above theory, no trade-off between inflation and unemployment, since unemployment will average out at the natural rate. Since it might vary over time in response to shifts of the labour demand and supply curves some economists have argued that there is nothing particularly 'natural' about the 'natural rate'; they have invented a plethora of alternative terms, including the non-accelerating inflation rate of unemployment (NAIRU) and the full employment unemployment rate (FEUR).

It should be stressed at this stage that the theoretical result of a vertical long run Phillips curve relies crucially on the assumption of perfect markets. If the labour market is not perfect then firms can earn supernormal profits, and workers will attempt to bargain with firms in order to secure wage increases financed out of these profits. In such a scenario, high profits – and so high wage demands – would coincide with periods of high demand in the product market. Since unemployment is low when product market demand is high, this implies that a downward-sloping Phillips curve may exist even in the long run when markets are imperfect.

The above discussion begs the following question. The expectations-augmented Phillips curve is fine in theory and might indeed explain the stagflation of the 1970s. But if macroeconomics is to be of practical value it should be able accurately to predict the future as well as explain the past. To do this, economic forecasters must have empirical estimates of past values of expected inflation so that an empirically applicable theory of expectations formation can be constructed. Without a theory of how expectations are formed the Phillips curve is useless as a predictive tool (albeit indispensable for *ex post* rationalizations). Unfortunately, the evidence on this problem has not yet led to a consensus among economists about the manner in which expectations are formed. This is likely due to the paucity of data about what expectations people actually hold. The two most widely accepted theories are the rational expectations hypothesis and the adaptive expectations hypothesis.

Put simply, the rational expectations hypothesis supposes that each consumer and producer uses all available information together with an intuitive and perfect knowledge of how the economy works in forming their expectations. No *systematic* errors can ever be made by economic agents who are attempting to forecast the future behaviour of economic variables; random mistakes can occur, however. On the other hand, the adaptive expectations hypothesis assumes that economic agents' expectations of a variable in future periods are based on past observations of that variable alone. In order to fix the ideas encountered in our discussion of macroeconomics it will henceforth be assumed that expectations of price inflation are formed adaptively according to the rule

$$\dot{p}^e_t = b\dot{p}_t + (1-b)\dot{p}^e_{t-1} \qquad (13.11)$$

where b is a constant in the range $0 \leqslant b \leqslant 1$. Thus if $b = 0$ expected inflation is a constant (and so the Phillips curve never shifts owing to changes in expectations) and if $b = 1$ expectations of inflation are always perfectly accurate. Non-extreme values of b indicate more moderate adjustment of expectations.

Empirical estimates of the Phillips curve

The most common formulations of the Phillips curve in the literature of applied economics posit that the rate of change of nominal wages depends in some way on the rate of unemployment. There are some rather interesting exceptions to this general rule (see, for instance, McCallum, 1986), but most studies build on the work of Phillips himself by focusing attention on the nominal wage. Phillips' own estimate of the curve which bears his name is given by the equation

$$\dot{w}_t = 9.64\, U_t^{-1.4} - 0.9 \qquad (13.12)$$

where $\dot{w}$ represents the rate of nominal wage inflation, U is the unemployment rate, and the subscript, t, denotes the tth time period.

This representation of the inflation–unemployment trade-off is deficient in one important respect, however. Equation (13.12) assumes that a nominal value (inflation) depends on a real value (unemployment). To correct for this it is necessary to introduce price expectations into the analysis. As has been seen above, economists are not yet fully agreed on how expectations of price inflation are formed in the real world. While the arguments in favour of the rational expectations hypothesis are compelling (the alternative is to assume irrational behaviour, and this would be extremely difficult both to justify philosophically and to model satisfactorily), the costly acquisition of full information may mean that the adaptive expectations mechanism (or some other alternative) might serve as a good approximation. The empirical estimates of an expectations–augmented Phillips curve which are reproduced below were made by Parkin (1970); they are based upon British data for years between 1948 and 1969 when no incomes policy operated, and assume an adaptive expectations mechanism.

Suppose that the equation to be estimated is

$$\dot{w}_t = a_1 + a_2 U_t + a_3 \dot{p}_t^e \qquad (13.13)$$

where

$$\dot{p}_t^e = b\dot{p}_t + (1-b)\dot{p}_{t-1}^e \qquad (13.14)$$

That is, the rate of nominal wage inflation is hypothesized to depend (negatively) on the unemployment rate and (positively) on the expected rate of price inflation. This latter variable in turn depends in part on the actual rate of inflation, but in part also on its own past values. Rearranging Equation (13.13) and lagging by one period gives

$$\dot{p}_{t-1}^e = (\dot{w}_{t-1} - a_1 - a_2 U_{t-1})/a_3 \qquad (13.15)$$

Straightforward substitution of Equation (13.15) into Equation (13.14) gives

$$\dot{p}_t^e = b\dot{p} + (1-b)(\dot{w}_{t-1} - a_1 - a_2 U_{t-1})/a_3 \qquad (13.16)$$

and substituting Equation (13.16) into Equation (13.13) yields

$$\dot{w}_t = c_0 + c_1 U_t + c_2 U_{t-1} + c_3 \dot{p}_t + c_4 \dot{w}_{t-1} \qquad (13.17)$$

where the coefficients c_0, c_1, c_2 and c_3 are constructed so that

$$a_1 = c_0/(1-c_3) \qquad a_2 = c_1 \qquad \text{and} \qquad a_3 = c_2/(1-c_3)$$

Since all variables in Equation (13.17) are observable, the coefficients of Equation (13.13) can now be estimated even though the variable which represents expectations of price inflation is *not* directly observable. The Phillips curve thus obtained is given by the equation

$$\dot{w}_t = 6.967 - 2.542\, U_t + 0.472\, \dot{p}_t^e \qquad (13.18)$$

Since the coefficient on the expected rate of change of price inflation is not equal to one, this equation does not fully support the natural rate hypothesis. There remains scope for active government intervention to change unemployment as well as inflation because even in the long run there appears to exist a trade-off (though the Phillips curve does appear to be steeper in the long run than in the short run). This result may be due to Parkin's use of adaptive rather than rational expectations. Alternatively it may be the case that the assumptions underlying the natural rate hypothesis are not fully met.

Equation (13.18) nevertheless enables some interesting inferences to be made about the nature of the relationship between inflation and unemployment. Other things being equal, an increase of five percentage points in the rate of wage inflation should be accompanied by a reduction in the unemployment rate of around 12 percentage points (2.542 × 5). British experience of the 1970s suggests that all else is not equal, however. At that time, wage increases were largely the consequence of high inflationary expectations. So if the rate of price inflation expected by economic agents rises by the same amount as does the rate of change of nominal wages (5 per cent), the unemployment rate might be expected to *rise* by some 1.7 percentage points. Thus the introduction of price expectations into the model has enabled the phenomenon of stagflation to be explained.

Tying it all together

A considerable amount of ground has been covered in the last three chapters. Even so, this is the minimum amount of macroeconomics which must be mastered in order to understand the value of economic modelling to the individual firm. Having come this far, this would be an appropriate time to summarize the arguments made in this part of the book. This is best accomplished by reproducing the system of equations which lies at the heart of the macroeconomic model which has been developed.

Table 13.1 consists of eleven equations and three identities which together summarize this part of the book. Table 13.2 lists the parameters and exogenous variables of the model whose values must be known in order to calculate the values of endogenous variables. In addition, starting values of Y, w and p^e must be known. Given the values of the exogenous and predetermined variables, the values of the endogenous variables can be forecasted for any number of periods into the future.

To provide a quick overview of the macroeconomic models covered in the last three chapters, note the following progression. In Chapter 11 only the product market was considered, and both the interest rate and the general price level were assumed constant and exogenous. In Chapter 12, the fixed interest rate assumption was relaxed by introducing the money market into the analysis; this endogenized the interest rate but prices remained fixed. Finally in the present chapter the labour market was introduced thus enabling both prices and interest rates to vary. The

Table 13.1 Elements of a macroeconomic model

$Y = C + I + G$	In equilibrium, national income equals the sum of planned expenditures; that is, consumption, investment and government spending.
$C = c_0 + c_1 Y_d + c_2 Y_{d-1}$	Consumption is positively related to the permanent value of disposable income; permanent disposable income is a weighted average of present and past values of disposable income.
$I = \bar{I} - i_0 r + i_1(Y - Y_{-1})$	Investment varies negatively with the interest rate, since a higher interest rate implies a higher cost of borrowing funds with which to make investment expenditures. It also varies positively with national income growth, according to the accelerator relationship.
$G = \bar{G}$	Government expenditure is an exogenous variable under the control of the authorities.
$Y_d = Y - T$	Disposable income is defined as total income less taxes.
$T = tY$	A fixed proportion of income is taxed.
$M_D/p = \bar{M} + l_0 Y - l_1 r$	The demand for real money balances increases with income but falls with the interest rate. As income rises the number of transactions involving money rises. As the interest rate rises the opportunity cost of holding money rises and so demand for real balances falls.
$M_D/p = \bar{M}_S/p$	The money market clears when the demand for money equals the (exogenously determined) supply of money.
$w = w_{-1} + w_{-1}\epsilon[(L/\bar{L}) - 1] + f(\Delta p^e)$	The wage adjusts sluggishly towards labour market equilibrium. Expectations of the price level positively influence the wage.
$p = w(1 + k)$	The price is related to the wage via a simple mark-up pricing rule.
$p^e = p_{-1}(1 + b\dot{p}^e_{-1})$	Price expectations change adaptively on the basis of past expectations of prices.
$L = Y/ap$	The production function is linear in labour.
$\dot{p} \equiv (p - p_{-1})/p_{-1}$	Inflation is defined as the rate of change of prices.
$\dot{p}^e \equiv (p^e - p^e_{-1})/p^e_{-1}$	Expected inflation is defined as the rate of change of price expectations.

Table 13.2 Variables, parameters and end points

Parameters and exogenous variables

$c_0\ c_1\ c_2\ \bar{I}\ i_0\ \bar{G}\ t\ \bar{M}\ l_0\ l_1\ \bar{M}_s\ k\ a\ \epsilon$

Endogenous variables

$Y\ C\ I\ G\ Y_d\ T\ M_D\ p\ r\ w\ p^e\ L\ \dot{p}\ \dot{p}^e$

Initial values

$Y\ w\ p^e$

resultant macroeconomic model is the one summarized in Table 13.1. It is capable of explaining phenomena such as inflation, unemployment and stagflation. Moreover, two variables of critical interest to the firm, namely wages and interest rates (the prices of labour and capital, respectively), emerge from the model as endogenous variables and can be forecasted by applying the model to empirical data. The model of Table 13.1 is one with which we shall become more familiar in due course.

Exercise: The trade-off between inflation and unemployment in the United Kingdom

Two estimates of the Phillips curve relationship were reproduced earlier in this chapter. These were

$$\dot{w}_t = 9.64\ U_t^{-1.4} - 0.9 \qquad (13.12)$$

and

$$\dot{w}_t = 6.967 - 2.542\ U_t + 0.472\ \dot{p}_t^e \qquad (13.18)$$

These equations are needed in order to answer the following questions.

(a) Use Equation (13.12) to draw the naive Phillips curve for the United Kingdom. Label this curve PC.

(b) Use Equation (13.18) to draw the Phillips curve when expected price inflation is zero. Label this line SRPC. It is the short run Phillips curve estimated by Parkin. Note that this line approximates PC.

(c) Use Equation (13.18) to draw the Phillips curve which pertains when nominal wage inflation equals expected price inflation. Label this line LRPC. It is the long run Phillips curve estimated by Parkin.

(d) Why is LRPC steeper than SRPC?

(e) Draw the Phillips curve for the United Kingdom when the expected rate of price inflation is 4.5 per cent. Label this curve PCE.

(f) Use PCE to estimate the level of unemployment when wage inflation is 4.5 per cent per annum.

(g) During the latter half of the 1980s price inflation has been fairly constant at around 4.5 per cent per annum. Expectations have therefore had time to adjust so that they are fairly accurate. Unemployment, however, has been higher than the answer to question (f) above might lead one to expect. What factors might explain this?

(h) What might cause the equilibrium rate of unemployment to vary over time?

Chapter 14
Foreign trade

Hitherto it has been assumed that the economy is totally self-contained, and so no trade occurs across national boundaries. While this assumption is useful in allowing us to learn much about the way in which the economy works, it is none the less one which we must now leave behind. While many small firms (especially in the services sector) compete only with firms based in their own locality, many others must compete in a worldwide market. Moreover, a large number of firms import at least some of their inputs from abroad. To these firms, export prospects and the prices of imports are crucial determinants of success.

In each of the last three chapters a new market has been introduced, and this has led in turn to the construction of three tools of analysis (the Keynesian cross diagram, ISLM analysis, and aggregate demand and aggregate supply methods). In this way, the macroeconomy can be viewed as a series of simultaneous relationships. At the end of the last chapter, there were three markets (product, money and labour) and three equations (IS, LM and AS) in three unknown variables (national income, the interest rate, and the general price level). This chapter continues that trend. By introducing a fourth market – that for foreign exchange – a fourth endogenous variable, namely the exchange rate, can be determined.

When importing goods from abroad, firms or consumers must, in general, first convert their domestic currency into foreign currency. Often, the goods will be priced in terms of the currency of their country of origin. This is not always the case, however – oil, for example, is typically priced in US dollars, regardless of whether or not it is American oil. Usually, however, foreign trade will require an exchange of currencies at a bank. An example of this is the exchange of currencies made by holiday-makers before they travel abroad to enjoy (and so import) the recreational services offered by other countries. Over the long term the domestic banking system must be selling domestic currency to overseas institutions while at the same time domestic firms are demanding an equivalent amount of foreign currency. If the value of imports equals that of exports the above will clearly be the case (other things being equal); firms abroad will, in general, require an amount of domestic currency which is equal to the amount of foreign currency demanded by domestic firms. If imports are not equal to exports in value, however, a period of adjustment follows.

Consider the following, highly simplified, example. Suppose imports into the United Kingdom exceed exports from the United Kingdom. This means that there will be an excess demand for foreign currency and an excess supply of pounds sterling. This pushes down the price of sterling (in terms of the foreign currency) – that is, the *exchange rate* falls. (This assumes that perturbations in the domestic economy have negligible effect on prices and other variables in the rest of the world; a sufficient condition for this is that the domestic economy should be small relative to the world economy.) Hence the sterling price of imports rises, thus choking off the demand for imports. At the same time the prices which foreign firms must pay (in terms of foreign currency) for UK exports go down, thereby increasing the international demand for UK firms' output. The quantities of imports and exports demanded are sure to fall and rise, respectively, in response to a fall in the exchange rate. This may or may not mean that the *value* of all imports necessarily falls in relation to that of all exports, since the higher price of imports after the fall in the exchange rate may lead to an *increase* in the value of imports despite a fall in their quantity; at the same time the lower price of exports may lead to a *decrease* in their value even though they are increasing in quantity. The outcome clearly depends on the demand elasticities of imports and exports, and is neatly summarized in the 'Marshall–Lerner' condition: if the exchange rate falls in response to a situation where the value of imports exceeds that of exports, the gap between the value of imports and that of exports will fall if the sum of the price elasticities of demand for imports and exports exceeds unity. (In the following discussion it is (realistically) assumed that the Marshall–Lerner condition is satisfied.) Eventually, then, the gap between imports and exports is closed, and the situation is resumed where the demand for domestic currency equals its supply.

Spot markets, futures markets and options

In the above discussion, it has been assumed that the exchange rate is free to move in response to demand and supply fluctuations. This is a useful simplifying assumption, but it should be borne in mind that the operation of foreign exchange markets is rarely free of distorting influences. These distortions include speculative behaviour and government intervention. The value of one currency (measured in terms of others) may rise more than is warranted by the foreign trade position of the economy if speculators view the currency as a 'good bet'; this may be the case if the long term prospects of the economy concerned are regarded as being favourable, thus increasing speculators' demand for the currency. Governments may at times choose to bolster or dampen a currency if it is in danger of reaching levels which are considered detrimental to the domestic economy. The government may even borrow from other countries in order to support a currency in this manner.

During the post-war decades the extent to which market forces were allowed to operate in the determination of exchange rates was negligible. The governments of the main Western economies had agreed, at Bretton Woods in New Hampshire, that the values of their currencies should remain stable. This was agreed in order to avoid the problems of the interwar years, during which exchange rate instability had apparently aggravated the severe cyclical behaviour of the major macroeconomic variables. The Bretton Woods agreement established the International Monetary Fund (IMF) which had powers to supervise the maintenance of fixed exchange rates. The IMF was also given lending rights in order to support countries experiencing difficulties in maintaining their exchange rate at its target level. Although the principle of fixed exchange rates was abandoned during the early 1970s, governments have continued to exercise influence over their currencies' exchange rates.

The various distortions which impinge upon the free movement of exchange rates can cause severe problems for firms which do not successfully hedge their bets when predicting future trends. It has, for instance, been contended that a sustained overvaluation of the dollar in 1982 contributed to the demise of Sir Freddie Laker's airline (*The Economist*, 1987). Having borrowed money from the United States, the rise in the value of the dollar against sterling left Laker exposed to exceptionally high costs. Other companies which trade extensively abroad are in similar fashion vulnerable to unpredictable movements of the exchange rate. Indeed, many – including Eastman-Kodak, Cable and Wireless, Cadbury-Schweppes and Volkswagen – have publicly attributed variations in their own performance during the last decade to exchange rate fluctuations.

It is possible for firms to protect themselves, at least to a limited extent, against adverse exchange rate movements. Firms are now able to make agreements to purchase or sell foreign currency in twelve months' time at an exchange rate agreed today. The 'forward market', in which such arrangements take place, thus enables firms to enjoy a degree of stability over the year whatever the actual (or 'spot') exchange rate does in the meantime. By planning ahead on the forward market, firms such as Jaguar (which sells most of its products in the United States) can set a dollar price for their output which can remain stable over a twelve-month period while truly reflecting the (sterling) costs of production in the United Kingdom.

A further refinement to the currency market which grew considerably in importance during the 1980s is that of 'options'. Options give traders in currency the right, but not the obligation, to trade in currency at a pre-set rate of exchange twelve months hence. They therefore enable firms to bet on future exchange rate movements while providing a fall-back position which precludes particularly expensive mistakes. Suppose that a British firm buys an option today which would allow it to sell $100 million at the current spot exchange rate of $1.60 to the pound in one year's time. Suppose further that the spot exchange rate rises (say to $1.65) over the coming year. Pounds become more expensive in terms of dollars and so the firm will benefit by exercising its right to sell dollars at the agreed rate of $1.60. The $100 million is therefore traded for £62.5 million (rather than, say, £60.6 million). If, on the other hand, the spot exchange rate falls over the year, the firm will forgo its right to sell dollars at the agreed price, and will opt to trade on the spot market instead. By following this course of action, the company could save £2 million if the exchange rate were to fall to $1.55.

From the above example it is clear that even quite small changes in the exchange rate can severely affect the profitability of a firm. It is crucial, therefore, that firms be aware of the need to hedge against fluctuations in the price of foreign currency. For the purpose of simplicity the discussion which follows concentrates upon spot exchange rates. The insights so gained certainly compensate for any loss of realism.

The economics of the Dutch disease

As has been seen above, the exchange rate provides an example of a price which is not generally allowed to vary freely in response to the movements of demand and supply. The adjustment of the exchange rate in response to a gap between the values of exports and imports, albeit imperfect, nevertheless represents an important feature which distinguishes foreign trade from that which occurs within the boundaries of a single economy. Within a single economy an excess supply of a good leads to a fall in its price. When the exchange rate falls in response to an excess supply of domestic currency, the (foreign currency) price of *all* exports falls and the (domestic currency) price of *all* imports rises. Conversely a rise in the exchange rate raises the (foreign currency) price of all exports and lowers the (domestic currency) price of all imports. This means that exporters in one sector of the domestic economy who are already struggling to compete in overseas markets may suffer from an increase in the exchange rate caused by a high demand for the exports of another (domestic) industrial sector. British manufacturing suffered in this manner in the early 1980s, as the export of North Sea oil pushed up the sterling exchange rate. Manufacturing firms in the Netherlands suffered similarly in the 1960s as a consequence of the export of natural gas. For this reason, a situation in which the buoyancy of one sector of a national economy raises the exchange rate and damages the export prospects of other industries is known as the Dutch disease.

There are, however, alternative explanations of the Dutch disease and deindustrialization. Corden and Neary (1982) and Corden (1984) have argued that a booming sector (oil, say) can lead to a transfer of resources from a less buoyant tradeable goods sector (like manufacturing) to a sector in which non-tradeable outputs (such as services) are produced; this is the outcome of the following mechanism. Both oil and manufacturing industries face foreign competition and so are price-takers. The exploitation of new oil discoveries therefore cannot raise the prices of tradeable commodities, but it does raise the demand for services (through the multiplier effect) and so also raises the price of services. (Any increase in demand for manufacturing goods can be met by a rise in manufacturing imports.) The higher prices now available in the services sector attract resources into that sector from manufacturing. At the same time, wages in the services sector must rise in order to compete with the higher wages now available in the booming oil sector (while responding to the higher demand for services generated by the oil boom itself). Labour therefore moves out of manufacturing into both oil and services. The end result, then, is that manufacturing gets squeezed out by oil on the one hand and services on the other, even without changes in the (nominal) exchange rate.

The balance of payments

Having briefly considered the behaviour of the exchange rate in response to fluctuations in imports and exports, it is appropriate now to turn to a discussion of the factors which determine the quantities of imports and exports demanded. First, though, some terminology needs to be defined.

The *balance of payments* is a summary of all international economic transactions between residents of one country and those of other countries. It is usual to divide the balance of payments into two main components; these are the current account and the capital account, respectively. The *current account* records trade in goods and services. Imports and exports of food, clothing and all other goods are detailed in the current account, as is trade in less 'visible' products such as financial services, holidays or satellite (pay-TV) broadcasts. The *balance of payments on current account*, which we shall denote by F, is the difference between the values of exports and imports of goods and services. If the balance of payments on current account is negative, then imports of goods and services exceed exports in value, and a current account *deficit* is said to exist; conversely, a positive balance of payments on current account implies a current account *surplus*.

The *capital account* records trade in assets. Imports and exports of equity, bonds and rights to land are therefore detailed in the capital account. The capital account *must* offset exactly any surplus or deficit on the current account. This is because current account surpluses or deficits must be financed somehow, and financial transactions are recorded on the capital account. For instance, a current account deficit might be financed by the sale of government bonds to overseas purchasers; this represents an export of IOUs which is recorded as a positive item on the capital account and which pushes that account into surplus. The US current account deficit of the 1980s was largely financed in this way. Alternatively, suppose that the current account deficit is financed by a running down of domestic bank reserves of foreign currency. In this case the value of the claims which domestic banks have on foreign countries is diminished; foreign currency held by our banks is equivalent to IOUs payable by countries overseas, and so the depletion of foreign reserves is tantamount to a sale of these IOUs back to the foreign country. A current account deficit which is financed by a running down of foreign currency reserves, therefore, results in the capital account moving into surplus.

It is clear from the above discussion that any surplus or deficit on the current account must be exactly offset by a deficit or surplus on the current account. Readers who are familiar with the basic principles of accounting will recognize this as an example of double-entry bookkeeping. Since the balance of payments consists of the sum of the current account and capital account balances, it immediately follows that *the balance of payments must always balance* – in other words it *must* sum to zero. As such, the balance of payments is rather uninteresting. Of considerably greater interest and importance are the individual components of that balance.

The balance of payments on current account is important because it determines the values of imports and exports which respectively leave and enter the circular flow of income. It is also important because the capital flows required to finance a current account deficit or surplus have implications for domestic monetary policy and interest rates. The nature of these implications will become clear later.

One of the most important determinants of imports is the level of the *national income*, Y. As national income rises, the demand for goods and services, be they produced at home or abroad, rises too. In the short run, the ability of domestic producers to increase their output by an amount sufficient to meet the rise in demand may be limited. This might occur if the rise in national income is demand-induced, say by a relaxation of monetary and fiscal policy, or by an easing in the availability of credit. In this instance the rise in domestic demand can be met fully only by way of an increase in imports. So domestic national income is expected positively to influence the level of imports into an economy. Following the same line of reasoning, exports from an economy are likely to depend, in part, on the level of world income (excluding domestic income).

The second major factor which influences imports and exports of goods and services is the *competitiveness* of the domestic economy's output. This measures the price of a given domestically produced product relative to that of its imported equivalent. The more competitive a country's output, the more firms from that country can expect to sell, both at home and abroad. A measure of competitiveness which is in common use is (p_w/pe), where p_w denotes an appropriately weighted average of prices in the countries with which the domestic economy trades, p measures the general domestic price level, and e is the exchange rate. From this definition it is easily seen that a rise in world prices or a fall in domestic prices improves the domestic country's competitiveness. Moreover, a fall in the exchange rate improves competitiveness, since it becomes easier to sell exports abroad as the exchange rate falls (that is, as more units of the domestic currency can be bought for a given outlay of foreign currency).

Data on the UK current account balance, national income growth and competitiveness are given in Table 14.1. As can be seen, the current account deficit of the late 1980s can be associated both with a sustained period of rapid national income growth and with a decline in competitiveness. The earlier period of current account surpluses originated in 1980 when real gross domestic product (GDP) was falling so rapidly that (even with uncompetitively priced output) export growth outstripped that of imports.

It is useful at this stage to summarize the above discussion by expressing the current balance function as a behavioural equation of the form:

$$F = f_0 - f_1 Y + f_2(p_w/pe) \tag{14.1}$$

This function says that the balance of payments on current account, F,

Table 14.1 The UK current account balance and its determinants
Source: Economic Trends (various issues), Bank of England Quarterly Bulletin (various issues).

Year	Current account balance (£ million)	Growth of real GDP at factor cost (%)	Competitiveness
1978	964	3.0	108
1979	−496	2.6	100
1980	3,122	−2.2	91
1981	6,936	−1.1	91
1982	4,685	1.8	99
1983	3,829	3.6	100
1984	2,021	1.8	93
1985	3,336	3.8	100
1986	149	3.0	100
1987	−2,906	4.4	100
1988	−14,665	3.8	91

Note: The measure of competitiveness shown here is $10\,000/k$ where k is the Bank of England's index of price competitiveness in export markets. (This is preferred to the Bank of England's measure since the latter index has the potentially confusing property that 'a fall in the index represents an improvement in UK competitiveness'.)

deteriorates as national income increases, and as the economy's output becomes less competitive.

The introduction of foreign trade into a model of the macroeconomy such as that of Table 13.1 requires that the product market equilibrium condition be amended to take into account the possibility that net exports are non-zero. This implies that the condition becomes

$$Y = C + I + G + F \qquad (14.2)$$

In addition to this amendment, Equation (14.1) must be introduced into the system of Table 13.1. The extra equation introduces into the model a number of new variables, namely F (which is endogenously determined), p_w, which is clearly determined outside the system, and the exchange rate, e. This last variable may be exogenous or endogenous, depending upon the exchange rate regime in operation.

If a substantial group of countries which trade extensively with each other agree to maintain a fixed exchange rate regime (such as the Bretton Woods agreement which operated from 1944 to 1971) then e is exogenous, and the system is complete. If, on the other hand, exchange rates are allowed to vary in response to changes in the values of other variables within the system (F, say), then e is endogenous. In this latter case one further equation is needed to close the model, since any model must have as many equations as it has endogenous variables. This final equation may take the form of an exchange rate adjustment function, such as

$$e = e_{-1} + g(F) \tag{14.3}$$

where e_{-1}, the lagged exchange rate, is predetermined, and where g is an increasing function of F. Equation (14.3) therefore says that the exchange rate moves gradually in the direction which helps clear the foreign trade market. If net exports are positive the exchange rate will rise in order to make imports cheaper for domestic consumers and exports more expensive for foreign buyers. Provided that the Marshall–Lerner condition is satisfied this will reduce the current account surplus, other things being equal.

Conversely, the exchange rate will fall in response to a current account deficit, thereby tending to reduce the deficit. Such movements in the exchange rate are to be expected because a current account deficit creates an excess supply of the domestic currency which pushes its price down in terms of the foreign currency; meanwhile a current account surplus creates a shortage of the domestic currency which tends to raise its price in terms of other currencies.

Consider now how the economy might adjust in response to a persistent current account deficit or surplus. From Equation (14.1) it is easily seen that a deficit can be reduced by one of several means. First, Y could be reduced. Secondly, p could be allowed to fall (relative to world prices). Thirdly, e could be allowed to fall.

When the current account is in deficit, net imports must be paid for by depleting reserves of foreign currency or by otherwise running a capital account surplus. Domestic currency is withdrawn from circulation as it is exchanged for foreign currency. This puts downward pressure on the money supply, other things being equal, and the causes a monetary deflation. The growth of national income is therefore *automatically* dampened during periods of current account deficit, and this dampening itself tends to reduce imports relative to exports. At the same time, the monetary deflation allows domestic prices to fall relative to the world price level. Conversely, during times of current account surplus, the domestic money supply rises thereby pushing domestic income and prices up.

When there is a deficit on the current account, the excess demand for foreign currency and excess supply of domestic currency pushes the exchange rate down, other things being equal. A current account surplus, on the other hand, leads to an appreciation of the exchange rate. These movements help to restore current account balance. There exist, therefore, several *automatic* mechanisms which come into operation when the current account is out of balance and which serve to reduce the severity of that imbalance. Taken together, these mechanisms guarantee that the current account cannot indefinitely remain either in surplus or deficit.

Purchasing power parity

Suppose now that the costs of transporting goods and services from one country to another are negligible, and that the market in which firms specializing in import–export activity compete is perfectly competitive. Suppose, further, that initially p is less than p_w/e. In this case traders could earn supernormal profits simply by moving goods and services from the domestic economy to other countries. This would tend to raise p and e while lowering p_w, since the supply of goods is falling at home and rising abroad. Entry of new firms into the import–export industry would continue until the supernormal profits have been eroded away – that is until $p = p_w/e$. In the long run, therefore, given our (admittedly restrictive) assumptions about the nature of competition and of transport costs, domestic prices and world prices will tend towards equality. This result is known as *purchasing power parity* (PPP) and has drawn a great deal of attention in the literature on international economics. Of course, as every holiday-maker knows, PPP does not at all times occur in the real world – the long run nature of the theory and the extreme nature of the assumptions preclude that. Despite this, it is worth persevering with the PPP theory a little longer in order to establish some 'benchmark' results.

For the domestic economy, the above analysis implies that (to the extent that the assumptions underlying PPP are satisfied) one of the right hand variables of Equation (14.1) is given. This reduces Equation (14.1) to

$$F = f_0 + f_2 - f_1 Y \tag{14.4}$$

As has been observed earlier, F cannot over an indefinite period remain either positive or negative. A persistent current account deficit is removed by depreciation of the exchange rate or monetary deflation; a persistent surplus is removed by a rise in the exchange rate or a monetary reflation. So the long run value of F must be zero. This implies that, in the long run and assuming that the conditions required for PPP are met,

$$Y = (f_0 + f_2)/f_1 \tag{14.5}$$

In other words, the long run value of Y is fixed. Note that this analysis assumes that the short term changes in Y which cause variations in imports are not determined by productivity fluctuations; to the extent that productivity improves over time, the long run value of Y follows an upward trend. For simplicity such considerations are abstracted from here. In addition, the result implied by Equation (14.5) will hold true only to the extent that the assumptions underlying PPP are satisfied.

This last result echoes a result which was obtained in the last chapter – that of the vertical long run Phillips curve. This begs the question: is the level of national income which guarantees labour market clearing the same as that which guarantees a balance of payments on the current account in the long run? In the short run the exchange rate can move to ensure that both markets can clear at once. The PPP requirement precludes this in the long run, though. Since the national income level, Y, at which the labour market clears was introduced into the last chapter as an exogenous variable, it should be clear that it will coincide with the value implied by Equation (14.5) merely by chance.

If the values of national income which produce, respectively, labour market and foreign trade market equilibrium do not coincide the authorities will persistently by faced with a policy dilemma. They can either achieve current account balance of payments equilibrium or labour market equilibrium, but not both. This is because only one policy tool – demand management – would be available to try to cope with two policy objectives (labour market clearing and foreign trade balance). This is somewhat akin to a car driver who tries to control both the speed and direction of his vehicle by using only the brakes. To alleviate this policy dilemma a further kind of policy would need to be introduced which could change the equilibrium level of national income in either the labour market or the foreign trade market. This might involve changing incentives to work in the labour market in an attempt to move the vertical long run aggregate supply curve. Alternatively the price and income elasticities of demand for imports and exports might be changed by way of tariffs or subsidies in order to change the level of income which is compatible with current account balance in the long run.

It should be noted that the long term referred to in the above discussion is likely to be beyond the planning horizons of most organizations. The experience of national economies during the period covered by the Bretton Woods agreement demonstrated the extent to which foreign reserves are able to cover all but the most chronic balance of payments problems. While an interesting piece of theory, therefore, the concept of PPP applies in a long term which is, in the main, simply too long to be of concern to many organizations.

Graphical analysis

It is appropriate at this stage to pause for a while to review the progress made hitherto in this chapter. This offers an opportunity to express the arguments presented above in diagrammatic fashion.

Consider Figure 14.1. The vertical axis measures the competitiveness of the domestic economy's output, and the horizontal axis measures

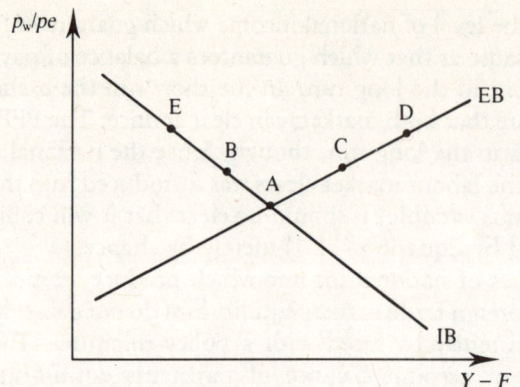

Figure 14.1 Internal and external balance: the Swan diagram

domestic demand. The current account will balance at a variety of combinations of demand and competitiveness. Such a point is given by C, and is said to be a point of external balance. A rise in domestic demand above the level indicated by C, given constant competitiveness, would suck in imports and would therefore throw the current account into deficit. At this higher level of domestic demand, external balance could be achieved only by way of an improvement in the competitiveness of the domestic economy's output. This would entail a movement to a point such as D. The line joining C and D therefore describes combinations of domestic demand and competitiveness which are compatible with current account balance. For this reason it is labelled EB (external balance).

As we have seen in previous chapters, the coincidence of aggregate demand and aggregate supply occurs when the product, money and labour markets are all in equilibrium. These three markets are those which operate entirely within the domestic economy, so when aggregate demand and aggregate supply are equal, internal balance is said to exist. Since the exchange rate has introduced a new dimension into our analysis, there is a variety of points in Figure 14.1 which are compatible with internal balance. One such point might be B. Starting at B, then, suppose the level of domestic demand falls, so that unemployment occurs. Internal balance can be restored, and the unemployment removed, only if the domestic economy becomes more competitive. This entails a move to a point such as E. The line joining B and E therefore forms a locus of points which are compatible with internal balance, and the locus is for this reason labelled IB.

It is clear from the above discussion that external and internal balance can simultaneously be achieved only when EB and IB intersect one another – that is, at point A. In the neighbourhood of A, $F = 0$ and p is constant (at the level determined by the intersection of the aggregate demand and aggregate supply curves). Consequently Figure 14.1 shows, in effect, the pairing of the exchange rate and national income which is compatible with simultaneous equilibrium in the product, money, labour and foreign trade markets. The price level which is compatible with this equilibrium may be found by reference back to the aggregate demand (or aggregate supply) curve. The equilibrium interest rate can be found by referring back to the IS (or LM) curve.

In the long run, owing to the absence of money illusion, there is (theoretically at least) a possibility that IB is vertical, say at Y_1. Moreover, owing to purchasing power parity, there is a theoretical possibility that external balance can be achieved only when income is Y_2 (and $p = p_w/e$). This extreme case has generated much interest. By fluke it may be the case that Y_1 and Y_2 coincide. In practice this is most unlikely. More common would be a situation where the level of national income consistent with long run current account balance differs from that which guarantees stability in the 'internal' markets – product, money and labour. This is where the authorities face a policy dilemma. An example of such a policy dilemma is shown in Figure 14.2. Faced by such a scenario, the authorities might choose to use demand management policies to aim for internal balance during some periods and external balance during others, while recognizing that both cannot simultaneously be achieved. Alternatively, they might consider introducing a new arm of government policy – for example, tariffs – which aims to reconcile the aims of internal and external balance; such a new policy would shift either IB or EB until the two coincide, giving full internal and external equilibrium.

Much ground has been covered in this chapter so far, and it is appropriate at this stage to summarize the main points. First, trade in goods

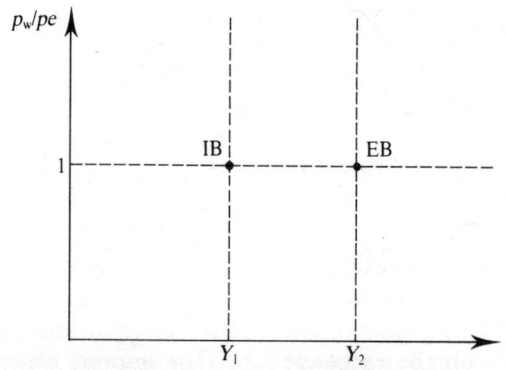

Figure 14.2 A policy dilemma

and services is mirrored by exchange of currency and other assets. Consequently imbalances on the current account of the balance of payments are perfectly offset by imbalances on the capital account. This implies that temporary imbalances in the foreign trade market can be maintained by transfers of assets between countries. A current account deficit, for instance, can be financed by running down foreign currency reserves; hence, importing firms would buy foreign currency from the banks in order to pay for their imports, but the banks' reserves of foreign currency would not fully be replenished. This creates an excess demand for foreign currency and an excess supply of domestic currency, so the exchange rate will tend to fall. (This assumes that the authorities are not bolstering the exchange rate in an attempt to use it as a separate instrument of economic policy. Such a policy would be reminiscent of a fixed exchange rate regime, or (if more lightly applied) of a dirty float.) As they run down their reserves of foreign currency, banks accumulate stocks of domestic currency which are withdrawn from the domestic economy. This represents a reduction in the money supply which (in the short run) causes a deflation. So both the exchange rate and the money supply automatically move in the direction which removes the foreign trade imbalance.

In the long run the exchange rate will depend on the relative levels of domestic and foreign prices. Hence the competitiveness of an economy cannot be improved *in the long run* simply by inducing a fall in the exchange rate. Abstracting from growth due to productivity gains, the level of national income compatible with current account balance in the long run can be changed only by introducing policy tools other than demand management. This last point may be of limited relevance in practice, however, since exchange rate policies can, over quite lengthy periods, be used to vary the foreign trade market clearing level of national income.

Empirical studies

The empirical estimation of demand functions for imports and exports has been a topic of considerable interest to applied economists (see, for example, papers by Arize, 1987; Houthakker and Magee, 1969). Studies on this topic typically posit that the demand for imports depends on their price (relative to that of home produced goods) and on the domestic economy's national income. The relative price of imports depends in part, of course, on the exchange rate. The imports function therefore enables income and own price elasticities of demand to be estimated.

An example of an empirical imports function is that estimated by

Houthakker and Magee (1969) for the United States of America. They found that the own price elasticity of demand for imports was − 0.54, and the income elasticity of demand was 1.51 (over the period 1951–66). Thus the demand curve for imports into the United States was inelastic, while the corresponding Engel curve was highly elastic. This indicates that imports vary relatively little with respect to price, but are very sensitive to changes in the national income. Similar results were obtained for the United Kingdom, where the income elasticity was 1.66 and the own price elasticity could not be distinguished from zero (at standard levels of statistical significance).

Since one country's exports are another country's imports it is not surprising to find empirical support for specifications of the export function which are mirror images of the import function. Hence, exports, like imports, depend on relative prices and on income. Now, though, the price elasticity refers to the price of a country's *exports* relative to prices elsewhere in the world, and the income elasticity is defined with reference to the (weighted) sum of national incomes of all trading partners. For the United States, Houthakker and Magee found that the income elasticity of demand for exports was 0.99, while the own price elasticity of demand was − 1.51. The corresponding figures for the United Kingdom were 0.86 and − 0.44, respectively. Broadly similar results have since been obtained by other researchers (see, for instance, Deppler and Ripley, 1978).

The astute reader will have noticed that the Houthakker and Magee estimates imply that while the Marshall–Lerner condition is satisfied for the United States, it is not met in the case of the United Kingdom. It should be noted, however, that the Houthakker and Magee estimates concern the *short run* effects of income and price changes, since no lagged terms in income or relative prices appear in their regressions. The effect on the demand for traded goods may, however, not be fully realized in the short run; domestic firms producing cheap substitutes for (now expensive) imports will need time to expand their output. Only in the long run, therefore, can they satisfy the increased demand for their products caused by depreciation. Moreover, while the elasticity estimates are those which define the 'line of best fit', the scatter diagram through which such a line may be drawn indicates that many observations lie far away from this 'line of best fit'. This means that − while they represent the best available estimates − some of the price elasticity values reported above may well not be accurate. Put another way, they are not statistically significant.

Movement of the exchange rate over time has also been a subject of much empirical research. In the remainder of this section we shall concentrate on results derived from a model developed by Branson *et al.* (1977) and also on the work of Sachs (1981); several other studies are surveyed by Levich (1985). Branson *et al.* investigate the variation in the dollar–Deutschmark exchange rate (the number of dollars that can be bought for one Deutschmark), and use regression methods to estimate the equation

$$e = -94.3 - 0.10M_g + 0.14M_a + 0.25F_g - 0.29F_a \qquad (14.6)$$

where M_g and M_a denote, respectively, the money stock in Germany and America, and F_g and F_a are measures, respectively, of the current account balance in Germany and America. (Strictly speaking, these measures are the stock of foreign assets held by Germany and America, respectively.) The signs on the coefficients estimated in Equation (14.6) indicate that the exchange rate varies with money stock and current account balances according to the following rules. The Deutschmark depreciates in response to an increase in the German money stock and in response to a deficit on the German current account. It appreciates in response to an increase in the American money stock and in response to a deficit on the American current account. These results agree with the predictions of the economic theory presented earlier in this chapter.

Further evidence is provided by Sachs (1981), in an analysis of exchange rate movements during the 1970s. The UK current account was in surplus during three years over the period 1973-79. In all three years, the exchange rate was appreciating. The remaining four years were characterized by current account deficits, and in two of these years, the pound was depreciating. While not providing overwhelming support for the theory, this evidence – which is reproduced for many other countries – does suggest that economic theory offers much by way of explanation of exchange rate fluctuations.

The relevance of exchange rate movements to the individual business cannot be overstated. Many firms rely crucially on foreign trade – they either import many of their inputs from overseas or they export their output. A depreciation of the exchange rate will be bad news for the former and good news for the latter. An idea of the likely future behaviour of the exchange rate is therefore essential for firms when making plans concerning output, investment, labour employment and pricing.

Assuming that the authorities allow it to move freely, the exchange rate will tend to depreciate when the current account of the balance of payments is in deficit, and it will appreciate during times of current account surplus. (It should be noted, however, that the exchange rate is *not* always allowed to move freely. For instance, if the government wishes to reduce inflation by operating a tight monetary policy, the LM curve will shift to the left and interest rates will rise. This will attract 'hot money' (footloose and fancy free funds, which are induced by the high interest rate) from abroad. This is turn pushes *up* the exchange rate as the current account must move further into deficit in order to finance the capital account surplus.) The exchange rate also tends to move in response to changes in the level of prices in the domestic economy (compared to those charged elsewhere). If the balance of payments on current account is in deficit, then (other things being equal) a firm should expect the exchange rate to fall. If a burst of inflation is expected, then (other things being equal) a firm should again expect the exchange rate to fall. Conversely, a current account surplus or a spell of inflation which is low by world standards should (other things being equal) lead planners to expect an appreciation of the exchange rate. Either way, managers need to look ahead and anticipate fluctuations in the exchange rate. Only thus can they make informed decisions and plans concerning import costs and export prospects.

Exercise: Internal and external balance in the United Kingdom 1970-83

The following equation explains the current account balance (measured in 1980 £million) of the United Kingdom over the period 1970-83. The data for the current account balance are taken from the Annual Abstract of Statistics, and all other data have been constructed from variables used by Layard and Nickell (1986).

The variables used in the equation are defined as follows: F is the current account balance. Positive values of F represent surpluses, and negative values represent deficits. YGAP is the difference between actual output and potential output. Potential output is the national income level consistent with a natural rate of unemployment. Thus as YGAP rises the economy is expanding. A positive value of YGAP implies overheating of the economy. Finally, COMP is a measure of the competitiveness of the United Kingdom economy. If COMP exceeds unity then UK goods in general sell at prices below those of goods produced elsewhere. If, on other hand, COMP is less than 1, then UK products are not competitively priced.

The general form of the equation to be estimated is:

$$F = a - b\,YGAP + c\,COMP \qquad (14.7)$$

(a) Express, in terms of the parameters of this algebraic equation (a, b and c) the value of YGAP which guarantees external balance in the long run, where purchasing power parity applies.

The regression estimate of the equation is:

$$F = -41942 - 1.16\,YGAP + 52996\,COMP \qquad (14.8)$$

(b) What value of YGAP guarantees external balance in the long run, where purchasing power parity applies?

(c) Your answer to (b) should be non-zero. What does this imply for government policy?

Chapter 15
A macroeconomic model and its usefulness to the firm

In this chapter the material of the preceding chapters is synthesized in a manner which shows the usefulness of economic analysis to the firm. Important ideas from each chapter will be combined as a specific numerical problem, typical of problems facing modern day firms, is tackled. Before starting this exercise, however, some important preliminary observations must be made.

First, the techniques used in this chapter have all been described in earlier chapters. While it is true that regression techniques more advanced than those used here might be more appropriate, these are not used because only the ordinary least squares method was discussed earlier. For the same reason, tests of statistical significance are not reported.

Secondly, the model is static in the sense that the firm is assumed to want to maximize its short run profit during the next period. The firm is not, therefore, interested in subsequent periods, as it is supposed to make all its decisions on a period-by-period basis. The static nature of the model presented in the sequel is due to the fact that dynamic techniques lie beyond the scope of this book; thus theories of optimal capital accumulation, the maximum principle and dynamic games are omitted.

Thirdly, the example considered below is a simplified version of the real world equivalent in that, for the sake of generality, we abstract from any idiosyncracies of the industry under consideration. Furthermore, the macroeconometric model is small and simple (many models used in the real world employ hundreds of simultaneous equations), the production function is similarly simplified (most real world firms employ more than two distinct factors of production), as is the demand function. Finally, it should be remembered that no problem of this type has a unique correct answer; there is no rule that governs the 'right' form of a consumption function or a price expectations function, for instance. While a useful rule of thumb is to choose the economically meaningful function which best fits the data, it is by no means always clear which function provides the best fit. While this fact contributes to the intensity and longevity of academic debates amongst economists, businessmen can simply shrug their shoulders and argue that if several functions provide a good fit then for practical purposes any one of them is likely to do the job as well as any other.

In spite of these qualifications, the example on which this chapter concentrates serves as a forceful illustration of the potential of economic analysis – both macro and micro – for the modern firm. While such techniques were – until recently – worthwhile only for the larger firms, the computer revolution has made their applicability and use much more accessible and widespread. While not all firms will want to employ all the techniques described here, most can benefit from the use of at least some of these methods.

The problem

Given the data in Table 15.1, advise the management of Firm A on its best pricing, output, employment and investment policies during the coming period.

Firm B is Firm A's closest competitor. Each unit of capital is assumed to be worth £30,000. (The data specific to Firms A and B are hypothetical, but the macroeconomic variables refer to the United Kingdom during the period 1971–1981.) The study uses figures defined on an annual basis. The macroeconomic data are all available on a regular (monthly or quarterly) basis and are published by the HMSO in *Economic Trends*, the *Monthly Digest of Statistics* and the *Annual Abstract of Statistics*. Newspaper reports and government statements suggest that in the next year the money stock and government expenditure will rise to £92 billion and £60 billion, respectively. There is assumed to be no change planned in the basic tax rate.

Solution

The approach chosen here is to proceed through the following steps:

1. Construct a macroeconomic model.
2. Use the given information about exogenous and predetermined variables to forecast the national income, interest rates, inflation, prices and wages in the next period.

218 · ECONOMICS FOR MANAGERS

Table 15.1 A macroeconomic model and its usefulness to the firm

Time period	1	2	3	4	5	6	7	8	9	10	11
Consumer's expenditure (£ billion)	36	40	46	53	65	75	86	99	117	135	151
Business fixed investment (£ billion)	11	12	14	17	20	24	26	29	34	39	39
Government expenditure (£ billion)	10	12	13	17	23	27	29	33	38	48	55
Taxation (£ billion)	9	10	9	11	13	18	24	25	25	36	44
Money stock (£ billion)	20	25	32	35	37	41	45	52	58	69	86
Interest rate (per cent)	6.7	4.3	8.2	12.1	10.6	9.9	12.7	5.8	11.8	15.7	12.8
Consumer price index	77	82	90	108	134	157	182	197	223	263	295
Average wage (£/week)	30	35	40	49	59	67	73	83	97	113	125
Employment (millions)	24.4	24.4	25.0	25.1	25.0	24.8	24.8	24.9	25.1	24.7	23.4
Labour force (million)	25.1	25.2	25.5	25.6	25.8	26.1	26.3	26.4	26.4	26.4	26.1
Basic rate of income tax	38.75	38.75	30	33	35	35	34	33	30	30	30
Wage, Firm A (£/week)	27	32	36	44	53	60	66	75	88	103	115
Output, Firm A (million units/year)	74	87	98	100	110	115	118	115	112	116	120
Employment, Firm A (no.)	730	930	1109	1145	1330	1410	1468	1412	1362	1421	1499
Capital stock, Firm A (units)	1978	2523	3082	3107	3576	3823	3983	3832	3628	3882	4087
Price, Firm A (pence)	15	16	17	20	22	26	29	27	27	31	35
Price, Firm B (pence)	12	15	18	22	25	29	33	22	18	25	30

3. Estimate the firm's production function.
4. Use the estimated production function to calculate the firm's total cost function.
5. Estimate the firm's demand function.
6. Use the estimated demand function to calculate the firm's total revenue function
7. Use the total revenue and total cost functions to derive Firm A's profit matrix, where profits depend on the price charged by Firm A and the price charged by Firm B
8. Statistical decision analysis can be employed to determine 'best' price, output, employment and capital accumulation.

These steps will now be described in turn.

1. *The macroeconomic model*

This is based on the model developed in Chapters 11 to 13. The consumption, investment and tax functions are all cost in real terms. The consumption function has as explanatory variables the real value of current disposable income and of lagged real consumption; the latter term appears so as to capture the idea that current consumption depends on long run trend income rather than just current income – a simple version of the permanent income hypothesis. The investment function embodies the negative relationship between investment and interest rates, and also contains an accelerator. Tax revenues to the government rise as incomes rise and also as the basic rate of income tax increases.

The liquidity preference function is the standard Keynesian function with a time trend included. A mark-up pricing rule is assumed, and wages are assumed sluggish; to be specific, the Phillips curve of the model has wages varying positively with the lagged wage, employment rate and inflationary expectations. Employment also adjusts sluggishly, the number of workers employed being determined by lagged employment and the deviation of real income from its long run trend level. Expectations of inflation are assumed to be dependent on past changes in the money supply. (This is an approximation to 'rational' expectations; accurately to model expectations of inflation in a rational manner would require many more years' data than are available in the present example.) Finally the labour force (that is, those in employment plus those looking for employment) is assumed to grow linearly over time. Foreign trade is not included in this example in order to maintain simplicity. It could be added to the model by including net exports as a component of product market demand, and by augmenting the system with some additional behavioural equations. For instance, a real imports function and a real exports function (with real income and a measure of competitiveness as right hand variables) could be introduced. The exchange rate itself could be endogenized, for example, by allowing it to vary with net exports (lagged by up to two years).

The least squares regression results and identities which define the macroeconomic model derived from the data of Table 15.1 are reported in Table 15.2. All coefficients have the expected sign, and experimentation with the model (which is not reported here) reveals that it is robust with respect to changes in the specification of the equations and to the omission of data for certain periods. Moreover a variety of statistical significance tests (such as the t-test, F-test and the r-squared statistic) can also be used to test the power of the model. Detailed examination of these methods lies beyond the scope of the present text, but it is worth noting that in the example under consideration the tests all indicate satisfactory performance of the estimated equations.

Four exogenous variables, namely *TIME*, *TR*, *GOVEX*, and *M*, must be given before the model can be used for forecasting purposes. Together with the predetermined variables described above, these can be fed into the model to provide the required predictions of future national income (Y), interest rate (R), inflation (*INF*), prices (*PRICE*), and wages (W). This is the next step in the solution.

2. Forecasting values of macro variables

Given the values of all the exogenous and predetermined variables, it is a straightforward matter to solve the system of Equations (15.1)–(15.10) to find the estimated predictions of the required variables in Period 12 (and, for that matter, any future periods). The list of exogenous and predetermined variables is:

$TIME = 12$ $\qquad$ $TR = 30$

$GOVEX = 60$ $\qquad$ $PRICE_{-1} = 295$

$M = 92$ $\qquad$ $W_{-1} = 125$

$YREAL_{-1} = 245/295 = 0.83$ $\qquad$ $L_{-1} = 23.4$

$PE = 18.13$ per cent $\qquad$ $C_{-1} = 151$

Once these values have been substituted into the equations of Table 15.2,

Table 15.2 The macroeconomic model

Equations

$$\frac{CONS}{PRICE} = 0.455 \frac{YD}{PRICE} + 0.370 \frac{C_{-1}}{PRICE_{-1}} \quad (15.1)$$

$$\frac{INV}{PRICE} = 0.143 - 0.001\, RREAL + 0.102\, YRDOT \quad (15.2)$$

$$\frac{TAX}{PRICE} = 0.441 \frac{Y*TR}{PRICE*100} \quad (15.3)$$

$$\frac{M}{PRICE} = -0.476 + 1.065 \frac{Y}{PRICE} + \frac{0.027}{RREAL} - 0.015\, TIME \quad (15.4)$$

$$PRICE = -0.029 + 2.345\, W \quad (15.5)$$

$$W = -209.090 + 1.296\, WLAG + 203.650\, EMP + 0.282\, PE \quad (15.6)$$

$$L = 8.580 + 0.649\, LLAG + 11.360\, YGAP \quad (15.7)$$

$$CLF = 25.104 + 0.133\, TIME \quad (15.8)$$

Identities

$LLAG = L_{-1}$ $\qquad$ $YREAL = Y/PRICE$
$EMP = L/CLF$ $\qquad$ $RREAL = R - INF$
$Y = CONS + INV + GOVEX$ $\qquad$ $WLAG = W_{-1}$
$YD = Y - TAX$ $\qquad$ $MDOTL = (M_{-2} - M_{-3})/M_{-3}$
$INF = 100(PRICE - PRICE_{-1})/PRICE_{-1}$
$YRDOT = (YREAL - YREAL_{-1})/YREAL_{-1}$

PE is the vector of fitted values from the regression of the percentage change in prices against the twice-lagged percentage change in the money supply. This yields:

$$PE = 9.500 + 0.455\, MDOTL \quad (15.9)$$

YGAP is the vector of residuals from the regression of Y/PRICE against TIME. It is therefore a measure of the difference between actual national income and trend national income — the 'output gap'. The regression estimate is:

$$(Y/PRICE) = 0.761 + 0.007\, TIME \quad (15.10)$$

CONS represents consumer's expenditure
INV is business fixed investment
GOVEX is government current expenditure
TAX is taxation (measured as GOVEX minus the PSBR)
M is money stock (sterling M3)
R is the interest rate (annual average bank rate)
PRICE is the consumer price index
W is the average weekly wage of manual workers
L is employment
CLF is the labour force
TIME is the time period
Any variable followed by the subscript -1 is lagged one period.
Any variable followed by an integer x is parentheses refers to the value of that variable in the xth time period.
All variables are measured in the units of measurement given in Table 15.1.

some simple but rather tedious algebraic manipulation of the equations must be undertaken. This yields a rather cumbersome polynomial in just one of the variables of the system. Numerical methods (or systematic trial and error) must be used to solve this polynomial. This task is facilitated by the widespread availability of appropriate computer software.

Once the system of regression estimates has been solved for this one variable, it is a relatively easy task to substitute through the system to find the forecast values of the other variables of interest. Hence, given the assumed values of the exogenous variables, $PRICE = 325$, $W = 137$, $Y = 270$, $L = 23.7$ and $CLF = 26.7$. The solution for the interest rate, R, is 12.2 per cent. These results imply that unemployment is forecast to rise from 10.3 per cent in Period 11 to 11.2 per cent in Period 12, while price inflation falls from 12.2 per cent to 10.2 per cent.

It is interesting to note that the economy is expected to slide down the Phillips curve in spite of the apparently reflationary nature of government policies. This is so for two main reasons. First, the lags in the model ensure that fiscal and monetary policies need time to take full effect. Secondly, while there is some growth in real income as a result of the increases in government spending and money supply, this growth in output is insufficient to match the underlying trend; this is evidenced by the increase in the output gap, $YGAP$. Consequently deflation persists.

3. The production function

The production function of the firm will be assumed Cobb–Douglas. The goodness of fit of the regression reported below supports the fairness of this assumption. Recall that a Cobb–Douglas production function has the form

$$Q = AK^a L^b \tag{15.11}$$

where A, a and b are the parameters to be fitted by the regression, and K and L denote capital and labour, respectively. Such a function is linear in natural logarithms, that is

$$\ln Q = \ln A + a\ln K + b\ln L \tag{15.12}$$

To perform the least squares regression, therefore, the logged values of Q, K and L must be used. The OLS estimates of the parameters are given in the equation

$$\ln Q = 13.5481 + 0.1536 \ln K + 0.5164 \ln L \tag{15.13}$$

$$Q = e^{13.5481} K^{0.1536} L^{0.5164} \tag{15.14}$$

$$Q = 765\,359\, K^{0.1536} L^{0.5164} \tag{15.15}$$

Thus the firm experiences diminishing marginal returns to both labour and capital. Returns to scale must be decreasing if the sum of the elasticities of a Cobb–Douglas production function are less than 1, and so Firm A must also be experiencing decreasing returns to scale, since $1 > 0.1536 + 0.5164$.

4. *The total cost function*

The annual cost of each unit of capital equals the interest rate multiplied by the value of the capital itself. That is, the cost of capital is the cost of borrowing the money with which to buy the capital. This assumes, for simplicity's sake, negligible depreciation of the resale value of capital over the period considered. In Period 12 the interest rate is expected to be 12.2 per cent and so the cost of each unit of capital is $30,000 \times 0.122 = £3,660$.

The annual cost of labour equals the weekly wage rate times the number of weeks in a year. (For simplicity we assume non-wage labour costs to be negligible.) Wages in Firm A are generally about 92 per cent of the average weekly wage in all industries and so in Period 12 the weekly wage offered by Firm A might be expected to rise to $137 \times 0.92 = 126$. Thus the annual cost of labour is expected to be £6,552 per person employed. It should be noted that an *ad hoc* wage determination process is being postulated here. That is, the wage predicted to pertain in Period 12 is not forecast on the basis of anticipated demand and supply movements but rather on the basis of an established relationship between Firm A's wage and economy-wide wages. While it is not determined from the first principles of economics, the accuracy of this procedure is likely to be sufficient for present purposes.

The next step is to calculate the firm's total cost function. Recall that the total cost function, TC, is defined as the relationship between the output level and the costs of efficient production. It is derived by solving the following optimization problem:

minimize $\quad TC = 3660K + 6552L \quad$ (15.16)

subject to the production function,

$$Q = 765\,359\,K^{0.1536} L^{0.5164} \quad (15.17)$$

The Lagrangian function is given by

$$\mathcal{L} = 3660K + 6552L - \lambda(765\,359 K^{0.1536} L^{0.5164} - Q) \quad (15.18)$$

For the optimal use of capital and labour inputs the following three conditions must be satisfied:

$$\frac{d\mathcal{L}}{dK} = 3660 - 117\,559\,K^{-0.8464}L^{0.5164}\lambda = 0 \tag{15.19}$$

$$\frac{d\mathcal{L}}{dL} = 6552 - 395\,231\,K^{0.1536}L^{-0.4836}\lambda = 0 \tag{15.20}$$

$$\frac{d\mathcal{L}}{d\lambda} = 765\,359\,K^{0.1536}L^{0.5164} - Q = 0 \tag{15.21}$$

The Conditions (15.19)–(15.21) provide three equations in three unknowns – namely, K, L and λ – and a given variable, Q. Simultaneous solution of Equations (15.19) and (15.20) reveals that

$$K = 1.878\,L \tag{15.22}$$

Substituting for K in Equation (15.21), and solving for L gives

$$L = Q^{1.5}/774\,207\,285 \tag{15.23}$$

Finally, substituting from Equations (15.22) and (15.23) into Equation (15.16) gives the total cost function in which total cost is seen to vary positively with output

$$TC = Q^{1.5}/57\,667 \tag{15.24}$$

As output rises, total cost rises at an increasing rate.

5. The demand function

No information is provided about changes in inventories or stocks, and so it will be assumed that they remain constant. Consequently the output variable used in the production and cost functions above can also be used as the sales variable in the demand function. Like the production function, the estimated demand function is linear in natural logarithms. The estimated equation is

$$\ln Q = 13.6405 - 1.3695 \ln(p_f/p) + 0.5963 \ln(p_t/p)$$
$$+ 0.5958 \ln(Y/p) \tag{15.25}$$

where p_f is Firm A's price measured in £, p_t is Firm B's price measured in £, p is the consumer price index and Y is national income. Noting that, in Period 12, Y is forecast to equal 270 and p is expected to be 325, the implied expected demand function is

$$Q = 65\,835\,773\,p_f^{-1.3695}p_t^{0.5963} \tag{15.26}$$

where Q is measured in units produced per year. Thus demand for the good being produced by Firm A varies inversely with Firm A's price, but positively with its competitor's price. The own price elasticity of demand is -1.3695. That this elasticity should (in absolute terms) exceed unity is important in the present model in order to guarantee tractability. Had it turned out to be less than one it would have been necessary to choose an alternative specification of either the demand function or the production function; otherwise the model would recommend that Firm A should set a spuriously high price.

6. *The total revenue function*

Total revenue equals the product of average revenue and price. This is found by multiplying the demand function by p_f. Hence

$$TR = 65\,835\,773\, p_f^{-0.3695} p_r^{0.5963} \tag{15.27}$$

7. *The profits function*

Profits, π, are defined as the surplus of revenue over costs, that is

$\pi = TR - TC$

$$= 65\,835\,773\, p_f^{-0.3695} p_r^{0.5963} - Q^{1.5}/57\,667 \tag{15.28}$$

Substituting for Q from Equation (15.26) the profits function can be expressed in terms of p_f and p_r alone. Hence

$$\pi = 65\,835\,773\, p_f^{-0.3695} p_r^{0.3148} - 9\,263\,296\, p_f^{-2.0543} p_r^{0.8945} \tag{15.29}$$

As before the prices are measured in £.

Once the profits function has been constructed it can be used to build a payoff matrix. Firm A will be uncertain about Firm B's strategy in the coming period and must therefore take into consideration all values which p_r could possibly take. For the purpose of this example we shall consider all values of the rival's price which lie in the range from 30 to 35 pence (this being a range within which it is considered reasonable for the rival to set its price, given the forecast 10.2 per cent inflation rate). Equation (15.29) can then be used to compute, for each plausible value of rival's price, the profit which Firm A can expect to make at any price, p_f. The resulting payoff matrix is shown in Table 15.3; the element in row i and column j represents the profit expected if Firm B charges the price indicated by i and Firm A charges the price indicated by j.

Table 15.3 Payoff matrix profit to Firm A (in £000s)

Firm B price (p)	Firm A price (p)					
	69	70	71	72	73	74
30	30 069	30 070	30 067	30 060	30 049	30 034
31	30 595	30 598	30 597	30 592	30 582	30 568
32	31 112	31 118	31 118	31 114	31 106	31 094
33	31 621	31 628	31 631	31 629	31 622	31 612
34	32 122	32 131	32 136	32 136	32 131	32 121
35	32 615	32 627	32 633	32 635	32 631	32 624

8. Statistical decision analysis

In order to keep things as simple as possible, only one of the rules of statistical decision analysis will be employed here: the Bayes–Laplace criterion. Assume that Firm B is as likely to charge any one price in the plausible range as it is to charge any other. In this instance the expected profits of Firm A at each price between 69 pence and 74 pence are given in Table 15.4. It is easily seen from this table that Firm A should set its price equal to 71 pence in order to maximize expected profits.

Given then that the price to be charged by Firm A is 71 pence, the expected level of sales (and so too the output level) is found by substituting $p_f = 0.71$ and $p_r = E(p_r)$ $p_r = 0.325$ into the demand function, Equation (15.26):

$$Q = 65\,835\,773 \times 0.71^{-1.3695} \times 0.325^{0.5963} \qquad (15.30)$$
$$= 54 \times 10^6$$

This established, it remains to calculate the optimal levels of the inputs, capital and labour. From Equation (15.23) we know that

$$L = Q^{1.5}/774\,207\,285 = 513 \qquad (15.31)$$

Table 15.4 Expected Period 12 profits of Firm A at various prices

Price (pence)	Expected profits (£'000s)
69	31 356
70	31 362
71	31 364
72	31 361
73	31 354
74	31 342

and from Equation (15.22)

$$K = 1.878 L = 963 \tag{15.32}$$

These results, of course, imply that the firm should severely cut production. This would entail substantial job losses and scrapping of capital. (The firm would by no means have been alone in realizing this in 1982.) It is important to appreciate, however, that the economic model being used here is, in some critical respects, amoral. It does not care for the workers who might have to be laid off, nor does it care for the consumers who might have to face a substantial price increase. All the model does is to calculate (under various assumptions) the strategy which is most likely to maximize the firm's profits. If there are constraints which the firm wishes to (or is compelled to) impose on the allowable extent of job loss or price rise, then these should be incorporated in a more advanced model. Otherwise such constraints must be dealt with by managers in an *ad hoc* way. The model outlined in the foregoing pages is – like any other economic system – *only* a model. That means that the results which it produces should be regarded as potentially useful, but they are not cast in stone. Inevitably much is left to the manager's discretion.

Summary of results

The study recommends that Firm A should aim to produce 54 million units of output in Period 12. These should be sold at a price of 71 pence each. In order to cut output to this level, both capital and labour inputs should be decreased, to 513 and 963 units, respectively. Using this set of choices, the firm can expect to make a profit in Period 12 of around £31.4 million.

Conclusion

As was stated earlier, no problem of the type tackled in the foregoing pages has a unique correct answer, or indeed even a unique correct method of solution. A different macroeconomic model (for instance, one with an alternative expectations mechanism) or a different production function (say, a constant elasticity of substitution production function) might well lead to different policy prescriptions. Readers interested in various empirical macro models are referred to Coutts and Cripps (1982),

Renton (1975), Scott (1987) and Wallis (1985). Those interested in alternative forms of production or cost functions are referred to Fuss and McFadden (1978), Heathfield and Wibe (1987), and Johnston (1960). Various types of demand function are discussed in Houthakker and Taylor (1966).

While results may be somewhat sensitive to method, however, it remains the case that alternative models will – if they are all statistically sound and provide good fits to the data – in general yield broadly similar results. One football reporter may say 'United hammered City two nil today', while another may say 'United squeezed two goals past hapless, goalless City'. The same event is being described from different perspectives, but the important conclusion is the same. Exactly the same is true of alternative economic models which fit the real world data well.

Many large firms now have their own models of the macroeconomy which can provide them with special forecasts about the incomes of certain groups of consumers of particular interest to the firm. Many other firms, however, rely on the macroeconomic forecasts generated by the large scale macroeconometric models. Several of these exist in Britain at present; many of these are constructed and operated at universities – Liverpool, Cambridge, Southampton, the London Business School – although some, like the Treasury model, are not. The forecasts of these models are published regularly by the institution at which the model is operated and are often reported in the press. The existence of a number of different models is testimony to the fact that economists cannot always agree about the best way in which to simplify the complexity of the real world into a set of equations. Although the broad similarity of the models is impressive and indicates a considerable degree of consensus amongst economists, the differences which remain lead to different models predicting different events. Hence one could argue, for example, that the Cambridge model predicted the 1981–82 recession better than did the London Business School model because it takes better account of inventory changes. Typically the large scale models consist of several hundred equations, and delving into their anatomies in order to try and explain their performance is a fascinating activity.

It is worth noting that the track record of economic forecasting models has improved markedly over time. Until recently, an alternative technique – time series analysis – tended to compare favourably with economic models in terms of forecasting performance. This was so even though time series models are essentially a special case of the econometric models, and do not have the advantage of being grounded in economic theory. As Wallis (1989) notes, it was said in the early 1970s that the sparring partner (the time series forecast) is consistently out-pointing the potential champion (the econometric model) but the potential champion quickly reached match fitness.... Published model forecasts generally outperform their time series competitors.

The level of detail at which results are published varies from model to model; of particular interest is the Cambridge model which ambitiously publishes forecasts up to eight years ahead at the industry and region levels of disaggregation. An example of the Cambridge forecasts is given in Table 15.5. More recent series have been produced which forecast in detail the fortunes of regional economies up to the Year 2000 (Gudgin, 1988). These predict that GDP and employment will, between 1988 and 2000, grow faster than the UK average in East Anglia, the East Midlands and the South West, but slower than the UK average elsewhere. The recent predictions also include forecasts on employment and output by region and industry, as well as rates of migration and economic activity. With such detailed long term forecasts available, the firm can use economic models in its long term planning decisions as well as for short term objective optimization.

Table 15.5 Forecasts of the Cambridge model (1982 policies, with constant 1975 prices assumed)
Source: Cambridge Economic Policy Review, 1982.

(Constant 1975 prices)	1984	1986	1990
Consumer's expenditure (£ billion)	72.7	75.6	81.3
Public consumption (£ billion)	24.7	25.7	25.8
Private fixed investment (£ billion)	11.8	10.9	10.7
Public fixed investment (£ billion)	6.0	6.2	6.2
Stockbuilding (£ billion)	0.4	0.7	0.6
Exports of goods and services (£ billion)	32.8	35.5	41.4
Imports of goods and services (£ billion)	37.2	40.5	47.8
Gross domestic product (£ billion)	111.1	114.0	118.1
Unemployment (millions)	3.6	3.9	4.5
Price inflation (per cent)	7.9	5.5	3.7
North-West region:			
Employment in agriculture, mining ('000s)	45	43	41
Employment in manufacturing ('000s)	735	698	628
Employment in services ('000s)	1716	1707	1650
Total unemployment (per cent)	16.7	17.6	20.0

Summary

In this chapter the material of the foregoing chapters has been synthesized to provide an example of the way in which economic analysis can help firms solve their decision-making problems. Macroeconomic techniques have been combined with the microeconomic analysis of demand, production and costs, all within the structure of the theory of the firm, by way of the techniques of regression, mathematical programming and statistical decision analysis.

Exercise: Forecasting the UK Economy

The macroeconomic data of Table 15.1 refer to the United Kingdom between 1971 and 1981. Consequently the equations of Table 15.2 represent a complete working model of the UK economy. While naive in many respects (most particularly in the absence of a foreign trade sector), this model does enable tolerably accurate economic forecasts to be made for one or two years ahead, given information about the planned changes in tax rates, government spending and the money supply.

(a) Assume that in Period 13 government spending rises to £66 billion and the money stock increases to £102 billion, while tax rates again remain unchanged. What would the model forecast for Period 13 inflation and unemployment?

(b) Suppose that, instead of rising by £5 billion and £6 billion, respectively, government expenditure and money supply rose by £10 billion and £12 billion in Period 12. What then would the model forecast for Period 12 inflation and unemployment?

(c) It was seen in Chapter 15 that the model forecast unemployment of 11.2 per cent and inflation of 10.2 per cent in the United Kingdom in 1982. The interest rate was expected to be 12.2 per cent, and nominal income was forecast at £270 billion. The actual values of these variables (the 'out-turn' values) were somewhat different. Unemployment was 11.2 per cent; inflation was 8.5 per cent; the average rate of interest was 11.9 per cent and nominal income (as measured here) was £269 billion. Explain these differences. Would it be true to say that the forecasts are none the less sufficiently accurate to help firms in their decision-making?

Chapter 16
Behavioural theories

In this chapter two alternatives to the standard profit maximization model (around which much of the analysis of the earlier parts of this book revolved) are outlined. First, Baumol's (1959) model of sales revenue maximization is considered. Then Cyert and March's (1963) behavioural theory is discussed. Both these theories – and others like them – react against the idea that the large firms which presently dominate many industries set out to maximize their profits. Once a firm becomes so big that ownership and management are divorced, the incentive for those who administer the business to try and maximize its profits becomes much less clear. Certainly some minimum level of profit must be made, but there is no *a priori* reason why profits should be maximized in this type of firm. Managers might be 'hassle minimizers' subject to a minimum profits constraint. Or, as Baumol argues, they might try to maximize whatever it is that determines their own salaries.

While the balance of empirical evidence suggests that, by and large, firms behave as if trying to maximize their profits (see, for instance, Shipley, 1981), it remains the case that many firms do not. Even if we confine our analysis to the private sector, some very obvious cases exist of businesses which would never even dream of maximizing their profits – Oxfam, the Co-op, the Conservative Party and Manchester United are examples. Each is none the less a commercial enterprise which needs its own administration and methods of solving what remain economic problems. The models discussed in the present chapter will serve to show how versatile the tools of analysis presented earlier are, and how the analysis can be adapted to suit a variety of company objectives.

Baumol's sales revenue maximization model

One objective which firms may pursue as an alternative to profit maximization is the maximization of sales revenue, subject to some minimum profit constraint. Managerial salaries appear to be more closely correlated with sales performance than with profits in large firms; to the extent that this is true it would be natural for the top managers to adopt sales revenue maximization as their goal. Sales are frequently used to measure growth and such expansion adds to the prestige of the firm and the reputation of its managers. It becomes easier to secure finance if sales are growing rapidly, since financial institutions require data on sales when evaluating investment projects. With the emphasis on revenue rather than on costs, higher wages can be paid to labour without reducing the optimal value of the maximand; this makes it easier for the firm to handle labour relations. Finally, as Peston (1959) points out, short run sales revenue maximization may be a rule of thumb used by the firm trying to maximize its profits in the long run; high sales revenues in the short run promise a favourable market share in the future, which in turn results in high long run profits.

While Baumol's model concerns large firms, he abstracts from the problems of oligopolistic interdependence by assuming that the firm does not usually consider such interdependence in its plans and that, even when it does, the internal bureaucracy of its rivals results in a very slow reaction to changes in the first firm's behaviour.

Two versions of the sales revenue maximization model will be discussed here: first, a static single product model, and secondly, a dynamic version of the model.

1. The static model

Assume the following: the firm aims at maximizing single period sales revenue subject to a minimum profits constraint. No consideration is given to the effects of current period decisions on sales or profits in any future period. The minimum profit constraint is determined exogenously by the requirements of the firm's creditors, namely the shareholders, banks and financial institutions which have invested money in the firm. The cost curves of the firm are assumed to be well behaved, as defined in Chapter 7.

To illustrate this model, consider Figure 16.1. The short run total revenue and total cost curves appear just as in Chapter 7, and a supernormal profit curve, defined as the vertical distance between total revenue and total cost, is also illustrated. Large firms of the type accommodated by this theory are not price-takers and so the TR schedule peaks at a finite level of output. This is crucial for the theory. Since TC is positively sloped at all levels of output the profit maximizing output

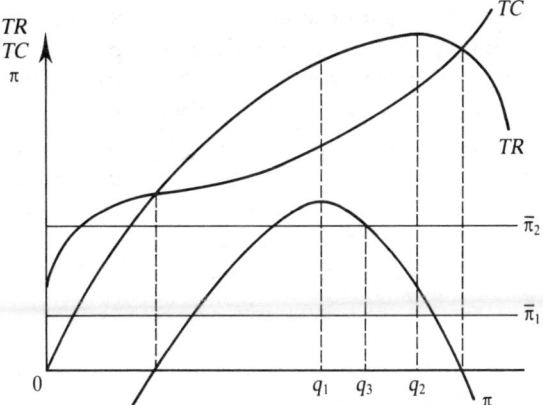

Figure 16.1 The static sales revenue maximization model

level, q_1 (where the slopes of the TR and TC curves are equal), must be lower than the level of output at which total revenue peaks, q_2. A firm which wishes to and is able to maximize its sales revenue will generally, therefore, produce more output than one which wishes to maximize its profits. If, for instance, the firm makes sufficient profits at q_2 to cover its minimum profit requirement, the firm will indeed produce at q_2. This would be the case if the minimum profit constraint stated that profits had to equal or exceed $\bar{\pi}_1$, for example.

If, on the other hand, the minimum profit constraint specified that the firm must earn at least $\bar{\pi}_2$ in profits during the current period, the argument is not quite so simple. The firm now wants to maximize its sales revenue, TR, subject to an effective constraint. Ideally the firm would like to produce at q_2, but the constraint that it must earn profits of (at least) $\bar{\pi}_2$ forces the firm to produce at $q_3 < q_2$. Apart from the extreme case in which the profit constraint is tangent to the profits function, it remains the case that a sales revenue maximizer produces more than does a profit maximizer.

In order to sell more output than its profit-maximizing counterpart, the revenue-maximizing firm must sell at a lower price. This follows from the downward slope of the demand function implied by the (twice differentiable) total revenue function.

By definition of profit maximization, the sales maximizer makes lower profits than the profit maximizer (except for the extreme case where the profit constraint is tangential to the profits function).

An interesting implication of the static sales revenue maximization theory is that an increase in fixed costs can reduce optimal output. This contrasts with the profit maximization case, where marginal costs – and

234 · ECONOMICS FOR MANAGERS

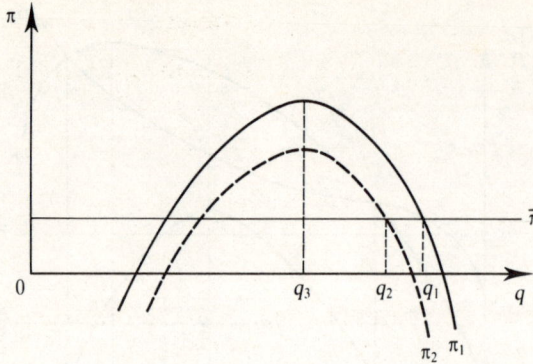

Figure 16.2 Fixed costs and optimal output under revenue maximization

so the point of intersection of MC and MR – remain unchanged. With reference to Figure 16.2 point q_3 characterizes profit maximization, and a change in fixed costs does not affect the level of output at which profits peak. In the sales revenue maximizing case, where the profit constraint is effective, optimal output falls from q_1 to q_2 with the increase in fixed costs. While an increase in fixed costs is of no interest to a profit maximizer when making price and output decisions, such a change is of crucial interest to a sales maximizer.

So much for the static model of sales revenue maximization. While leading to some predictions which clearly differ from the profit maximization case studied earlier, the model is nothing more than a simple application of the tools of cost and revenue schedules with which we are by now familiar. The dynamic model of sales revenue maximization, which is examined below, extends the static analysis and introduces some new ideas.

2. The dynamic model

First of all, let us consider what need there is for a dynamic model. In the simple theory of the firm presented in earlier chapters dynamic considerations were given only the most superficial consideration. A perfectly competitive firm must maximize instantaneous profits (which, in equilibrium implies zero supernormal profit) otherwise it will go out of business. In the case of a monopoly, the profit-maximizing rule that marginal cost should in each period equal marginal revenue holds true in a dynamic context, where the firm aims to maximize the (net present value of the) stream of future profits (see Appendix 4). The same is true of oligopoly. This similarity between the results of static and dynamic analysis does not, however, occur when sales revenue is the optimand.

The following assumptions are made in Baumol's dynamic model. First, the firm is assumed to maximize the present value of the stream of sales revenue over its lifetime. It does this by selecting the best values of the choice variables, namely current sales, S, and the rate of growth of sales revenue, g. Secondly, the growth of sales revenue over time is governed solely by the level of profits. There is no exogenous minimum profit constraint like the one in the static model, but the need to make profits in the current period in order to fuel future sales potential enables a minimum profit requirement *endogenously* to be determined; that is, a profits constraint is implied by the model itself, not by assumption. Thirdly, cost and revenue curves are well-behaved, just as in the static model.

Sales revenues in the current period are S. Next period they will be $S(1+g)$. In two periods' time they will be $S(1+g)^2$ and after n periods revenues will have risen to $S(1+g)^n$. However, the present money value of the utility which the firm gets from the $S(1+g)$ it expects to receive in the next period will be less than $S(1+g)$. This is so because to receive $S(1+g)$ in one year's time is tantamount to receiving $S(1+g)/(1+r)$ now and saving it at the bank at an interest rate of r. By the same token, receiving $S(1+g)^i$ in i years' time is equivalent to getting $S[(1+g)/(1+r)]^i$ right away. Consequently, the present value of the stream of future sales revenues over the period $t = 0, 1, 2, \ldots, n$ is

$$V = \sum_{i=0}^{n} S \left(\frac{1+g}{1+r} \right)^i \tag{16.1}$$

The task is therefore to maximize V with respect to g and S.

This may sound easy enough, but the problem is complicated by the fact that g is itself partly dependent on S, and that the relationship between these two variables is non-linear. To sell at the point of zero marginal revenue *and* maximize the rate of growth of sales revenue is not an option for the firm. To explain this assertion it is necessary to examine the role of profits in the model.

It has already been assumed that the growth rate of sales depends on the level of profits. When current period revenue, S, is zero, profits will also be zero (at most) and no growth can take place. As S rises so profits increase up to a maximum at $S_{\pi_{max}}$. At this point g also reaches a maximum. Beyond this profit-maximizing level of sales, revenues continue to increase even though in this range costs are rising faster. When costs eventually offset revenues, g once more falls to zero; hence at this point, called for convenience S_{π_0}, total revenues might not even have peaked, but any further increase in current period sales would lead to

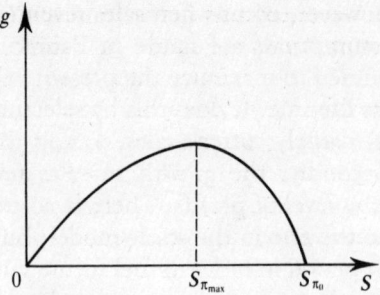

Figure 16.3 The growth function

cutbacks in the firm's size because of the losses being made. The relationship between g and S is known as the growth function and is shown in Figure 16.3. The link between growth and profits thus constrains the firm in its choice of g and S.

The curve plotted in Figure 16.3 shows the constraint; the optimand is the present value, V. To plot V in (S, g) space note that for any given present value, $\bar{V}$,

$$S = \bar{V} / \sum_{i=0}^{n} [(1+g)/(1+r)]^i \qquad (16.2)$$

which follows from Equation (16.1). Therefore S and g are inversely related to one another for a given V. A series of isopresent-value curves can therefore be drawn which are in general convex to the origin. As the present value of the stream of future sales, $\bar{V}$, rises, so the isopresent-value curves move further away from the origin, towards the north-east. A map of such curves is illustrated in Figure 16.4.

The point of tangency of the growth function and the highest

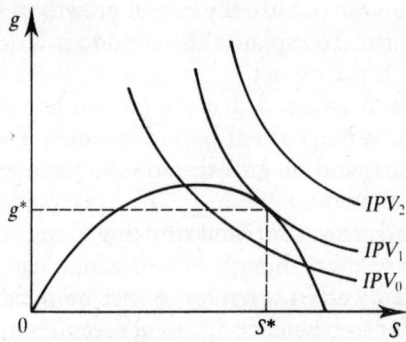

Figure 16.4 The dynamic sales revenue maximization model

attainable isopresent-value curve is the optimum point for the firm. No greater present discounted value of future sales can be achieved given the fact that profits must be made in order to secure future growth. The optimal rate of growth for the firm is g^* and the optimal level of sales in the current period is S^*. These are the values which guarantee the highest possible present value of the stream of future sales revenues.

The growth rate, g^*, is associated with some unique level of profits, π^*, through the growth function. The minimum profit constraint, π^*, is thus endogenously determined in Baumol's dynamic model. Once this has been found, instantaneous sales revenue is maximized subject to the requirement that profits exceed or equal π^*, in exactly the same manner as the static model of Figure 16.1.

Although rigorous as a tool for use by those firms wishing to pursue the goal of sales revenue maximization, the *descriptive* power of Baumol's model is not so impressive. It is cast in an imperfectly competitive setting (the possibilities for long run profits are not allowed to be competed away), but there is no discussion of either interdependence of firms, entry by new firms or entry deterrence tactics by established firms. In sum, the firm is viewed in isolation from the industry and no connection is established between the firm's equilibrium and that of the industry. As a result, there is no analysis of how the firm responds to changes in the market within which it operates.

Empirical evidence does not, on the whole, support the hypothesis that sales revenue maximization rules are very widely practised in business (see, for instance, Hall, 1968; Marby and Siders, 1967). This is not to suggest, however, that for certain firms - and in some industries for most firms - sales revenue is not the objective function. The model is useful in that it shows how the theory of the firm works when the optimand is something other than profits. It is also particularly interesting to see how, when this is the case, dynamic considerations affect the workings of the model.

The behavioural theory of the firm

All the theories of the firm which we consider involve optimization. Something - profits, sales or whatever - gets maximized. At the beginning of the book it was argued that any time a choice is made one option is preferred to all others. In behavioural theories of the firm the nature of the optimization problem is less obvious, but constrained optimization occurs here too. Specifically, in the theory described below the cost of changing the firm's strategy, policies and procedures is minimized in each period subject to constraints on output, inventories, sales, market share and profit. The theory might be regarded as one of 'hassle minimization' subject to minimum levels of the constraining variables. Although the model described in the next few pages may not look much like an optimization problem, it should be remembered that it is logically impossible to make a rational or consistent choice without having some objective function which acts as optimand. Certainly such optimands can change over time, but *any* meaningful theory of economic behaviour must require either rationality at one point in time or consistency over time or both. Even though the optimization problem itself is not brought out explicitly in the behavioural theory of the firm, it none the less underlies the whole model. For all the talk of conflicting goals and satisficing which is characteristic of those who espouse the behavioural model, the optimization techniques of Chapters 6 and 15 can still be used.

Like the sales revenue maximization hypothesis, the behavioural theory concerns a large firm operating under conditions of uncertainty in an imperfectly competitive market. Unlike Baumol's theory, however, the behavioural model developed by Cyert and March (1963) describes a firm in which various groups within management have their own goals. For instance, engineers may favour extensive R and D expenditure, while accountants may be more conservative and wish to pursue a profits objective. Management involved in the marketing department may regard their role as one of increasing sales while those in the public relations department seek to improve goodwill. Moreover, the multiplicity of goals is not confined to management: workers want to preserve and improve the level of their own utility subject to the constraint that the firm makes sufficient profit to keep them in employment – the utility of workers is a function of *inter alia* their wages, working conditions and hours. Shareholders in the firm want high profits and a promising prospect for improved performance in the future. Within each firm, then, there exists a large number of groups, each with its own goals. Inevitably these goals conflict with each other.

The goals set by each of the groups within the coalition known as the firm is a function of what the group thinks is attainable. Therefore the expenditure which engineers seek to secure for R and D in the next period will depend partly on precedent and partly on expectations of future performance. The target increase in sales sought by marketing personnel will be set according to what has proved possible in the past and what is known about future demand conditions. The targets set by each group are therefore a function of several variables, always including past performance. As the firm grows these targets are, in general, achieved with room to spare, because the groups tend to place more weight on past performance than on future trends in setting their goals. (Note, then, that the model is not a rational expectations model.) Growth is useful for the firm in that the conflict of demands can most likely be resolved during times of expansion when achievements exceed aspirations. During such periods the firm will be making profits which exceed the minimum required to keep its shareholders happy. The surplus of realized profits over shareholders' target profits is known as 'excess profit' and is of considerable interest in the resolution of conflict within the firm, as will be seen later.

The role of top management is to set the goals of the firm, to resolve conflict between the various groups which exist within the firm and to resolve the conflict between the goals of the firm itself and those if its constituent groups. Traditionally, five main goals are set for the firm:

(a) profits goal,

(b) sales goal,

(c) output goal,

(d) inventories goal, and

(e) market share goal.

These goals are then pursued in much the same way as one knocks down coconuts in a shy: once one goal has been achieved (one coconut knocked down), the firm concentrates on the achievement of the other goals (knocking down the other coconuts). None of the goals is itself a maximand; the firm aims at nothing more than 'satisfactory' performance in terms of profit, sales, output, market share and stock accumulation. Rather than maximize a single objective, the firm aims to 'satisfice', that is, achieve 'acceptable results in several measures of performance'. Put simply, then, the first job of top management is to define the words 'satisfactory' and 'acceptable' in quantitative terms.

The goals of the firm, defined by top management, represent an attempt realistically to satisfy as nearly as possible the goals of each group within the organization. They are set as a result of a bargaining process between top management and the individual groups. The profits target must be set high enough to satisfy shareholders but not so high as to constrain sales to levels below those needed to satisfy the marketing department, for instance. To the greatest possible extent, top managers must seek to please all of the people all of the time. When, as is usual, the conflicts of objectives within the firm cannot all be resolved by setting appropriate goals, the managers must use special means to placate the groups which feel aggrieved by the goals which have been set.

There are several means by which conflicts can be resolved. First, money payments can be used as an attempt to meet the targets of certain groups if such targets are of a pecuniary nature, or otherwise as compensation for the fact that these goals have not been met. In particular, 'slack' payments made out of the firm's excess profits are made to various groups within the firm even when those groups are satisfied with their lot. Slack payments are particularly useful in that by varying the magnitude of slack payments from year to year the firm can report a roughly unchanged level of profits every year; this in turn stabilizes the aspiration levels of groups within the firm. Slack therefore dampens the impact on the firm of changes in its environment and thus enables the firm to operate smoothly without forcing sudden and unacceptable changes on any particular group in the firm. Conflicts can also be resolved by making policy decisions regarding the future direction of the firm; for instance, a policy commitment to expand R and D activity will likely satisfy the engineers' demands, or pacify them in the event that their goals over the last period have not been met.

Sensitivity of management to the needs of the various departments of the firm is also an important factor in minimizing the severity of intra-firm conflict. In particular, top management must be seen to respond fairly to each group's demands, by giving priority to the most pressing concerns in each period; during a strike, then, firm–union relations should be given priority, while the demands of the production department for new investment should receive top priority by the management when the existing machinery falls to pieces or when a new technology becomes available. The rule of thumb for management, therefore, is: 'given the fact that there are only twenty-four hours in a day, always concern yourselves first with your worst headache. Once that's cured, move on to the next worst problem.' The way in which the efficiency of the firm is improved is 'problematic'. That is, only when a particular problem becomes especially apparent is a solution sought. Moreover, rather than consider all alternative remedies for a problem, top management examines only a handful of possible solutions and then implements any one of them which is affordable and which promises to improve the existing situation; the time constraint on managers often prevents them from adopting what might be the 'best' solution simply because they do not have the time to analyse the whole situation sufficiently thoroughly.

So much for the basic framework of the behavioural theory. Let us now consider how a firm which operates according to the behavioural theory might work. To simplify matters assume that the top management sets only two goals: a sales revenue goal and a profits goal. The process by which decisions are made is illustrated in Figure 16.5.

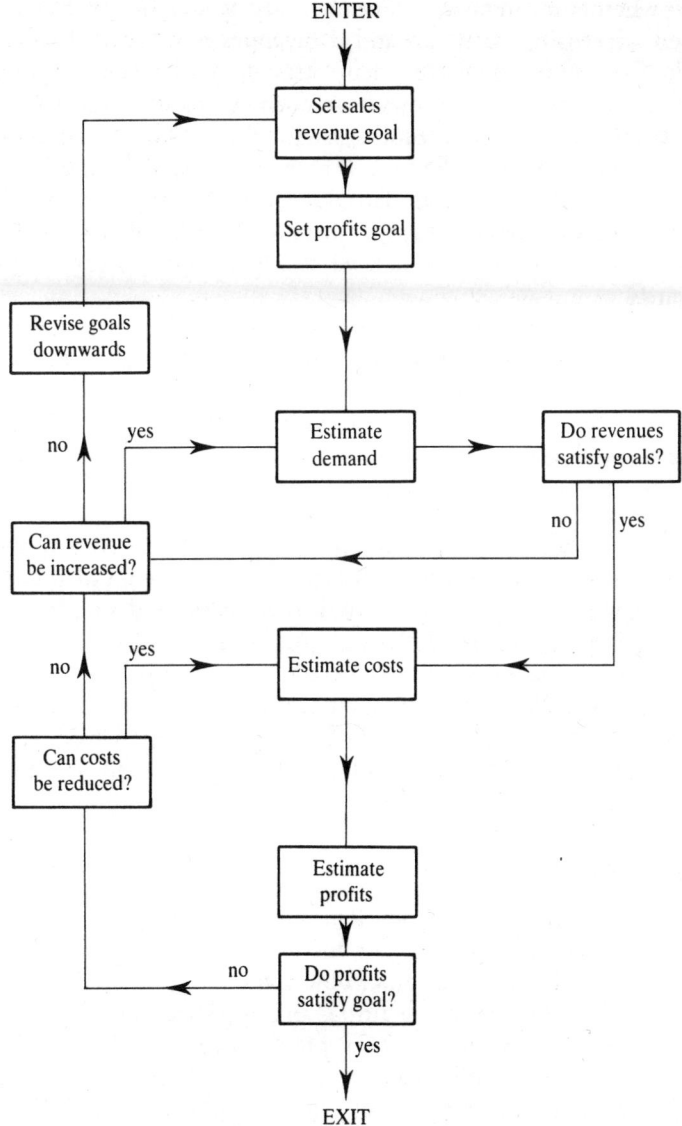

Figure 16.5 A behavioural model of the firm

The first step is that of goal formation. Once top management has decided on its targeted levels of sales and profits (and whatever else) it forms an estimate of the demand for its output in the coming period. If, based on this estimate, the firm expects to make sufficient revenue to reach its revenue target it proceeds to estimate costs. Otherwise it must find out whether it can raise its revenue – say by way of a price change or increased advertising. If it can and if revenues now reach the targeted level, the firm can move on to estimate costs; if not, the revenue goal must be revised downward. Once costs have been estimated, expected profits can be calculated. If these profits satisfy the profits goal no further decisions need be made by the firm. If they do not, on the other hand, the firm must try to reduce its costs. This done, if profits still do not reach the target an attempt must be made to increase revenue. If this too fails to bring profits up to the desired level, the profit goal must be revised downwards.

This process continues until all goals are satisfied. At no stage is any economic variable maximized; all management does is to enable the attainment of a whole variety of goals. Maybe some of the goals can only just be achieved, or maybe they can all be achieved with room to spare. As Cyert and March claim:

> Each goal enters as a simple constraint. All of the goals taken together define a space of acceptable solutions.... Where the firm has discretion we think it forms what we have called decision strategies or rules.... If alternatives are generated strictly sequentially, the choice phase is quite simple: choose the first alternative that satisfies the objectives.... Search [for satisfactory alternatives], like decision making, is problem-directed [and occurs] in the neighbourhood of the current alternative.... The neighbourhood of existing policy rule inhibits the movement of the organization to radically new alternatives [because] of the problems of conceiving the adjustments required by radical shifts. (Cyert and March, 1963, pp. 10, 20, 86, 121, 122)

In sum, then, the firm is a problem minimizer which satisfies a set of constraints concerning profits, production, sales, inventories, market share and, possibly, a host of other objectives.

The behavioural theory of the firm is an impressive contribution to the body of microeconomic theory. It has provided considerable insight into the manner in which complex firms set their goals. It also explains the role of slack payments, a feat which lies beyond the capabilities of conventional theory. The realism of the behavioural theory is particularly impressive.

However, from the point of view of the manager, the behavioural theory suffers a number of serious shortcomings. First, managers whose aim is hassle minimization could not use a formal economic model to help them minimize their administrative problems simply because the magnitude of 'problems' cannot be measured in numerical terms. Secondly, even if the severity of 'problems' could be evaluated on a cardinal scale, the results of a behavioural model depend critically on the starting point. Two firms which had different output levels in the last period but which are otherwise identical should, if the theory were to be used prescriptively, behave differently from one another also in the current period. Thirdly, it seems absurd to suggest – as this theory might sometimes do – that a firm would forgo a massive increase in profits for the sake of a marginal increase in the amount of hassle involved.

Both the sales revenue maximization hypothesis and Cyert and March's behavioural theory, plus other alternatives to profit maximization (for instance, Marris, 1963; Williamson, 1963) represent important extensions to the theory of the firm. However much they might differ from the standard 'neoclassical' model presented earlier in the book – and the differences are indeed considerable – the technique of constrained optimization remains fundamental to all these theories. The tools of analysis developed in earlier chapters therefore remain applicable, although the economist must, at the beginning of any study of a particular firm, determine the nature of that firm's objective function and its constraints. Economic studies designed to prescribe the 'best' strategy for a firm must always start by defining 'best' in very specific and unambiguous language.

That economic analysis, and in particular the methodology of constrained optimization, can so easily handle theories as diverse as the neoclassical and behavioural models, is strong testament to its power. At the same time, the power of the method and its catholic applicability in the study of choice serves as a warning: the 'best' means different things to different individuals and firms. There is nothing more crucial to good economic analysis than a precise statement of the objective function and the attendant constraints.

Exercise: Behavioural approaches to the electricity industry

Using the data provided at the end of Chapter 8, examine the hypothesis that the monopolist supplier of electricity in the United Kingdom was, in 1970, a sales revenue maximizer.

Chapter 17
Concluding comments

While much of this book has been cast in the context of single product, profit-maximizing firms, it should be clear that the techniques and methods of analysis are equally applicable in the context of any multi-product firm with any clear objective. Even in the firm which behaves as suggested by the behavioural theory – where satisficing rules replace optimization – information about macroeconomic trends, demand and costs is needed in order to guarantee satisfactory performance.

Before prescribing policy an economist must know the objectives of a firm. It is true that different groups of managers have different goals – that while engineers tend to favour aggressive R and D, accountants are more cautious – but an economist interested in prescribing (as opposed to describing) the actions of a firm must be concerned with a single goal, possibly subject to a number of constraints. The behavioural theory as it stands is interesting and plausible as a descriptive theory, but as a tool of normative analysis it lacks power. If the purpose of applied managerial economics is to advise management about the best of several alternatives, then a single objective function must exist; if the purpose is to advise management of which of the alternative strategies provide 'satisfactory' performance, then an applied economist can do that too, but whenever this is done the power of economic analysis is underutilized.

The versatility of the techniques described in the foregoing chapters is considerable. By using some measure of the 'cost of change' as minimand and by adding minimum profit, sales and market share constraints to the problem of Chapter 15 the model can easily be adapted to suit the behavioural theory. By maximizing total revenue subject to a profits constraint it could become a sales revenue maximizing model. Since *all* economic decisions involve choice, and since the best choice is always one which optimizes the objective function subject to a number of constraints, the techniques used will vary little even if the objectives pursued change.

Hopefully, the reader is by now convinced of the value of economic analysis to business. Although the mathematical techniques involved cannot always be applied with the same degree of confidence and accuracy to business problems as to engineering problems, they enable full use of the information available and so enable an increased rationality in decision-making. While the cost of employing decision rules of this type was once prohibitive for many companies, the microprocessor revolution and the increased availability of relatively cheap computer software has made the use of this type of analysis almost universally accessible to firms of all sizes.

Certain subjects of interest to managers and which properly fall under the canopy of economics have not been discussed at length in this book. Capital budgeting, the role of advertising, the problems of multi-product firms, and labour relations have been mentioned only briefly. Dynamic optimization and dynamic games are potentially useful techniques which have not been covered at all in this book. All these subjects require analysis which goes beyond the scope of the present text, and which – because of the time constraints which operate on the typical introductory conversion course – must await the student's attention at a future time.

Appendix 1
Elementary methods of differential calculus

Given that a variable y depends on another variable x, how much would y change as a result of a change of one unit in x? The answer to this question clearly depends on the nature of the relationship between y and x. If a linear function is envisaged, such as

$$y = 5 + 3x \tag{A1.1}$$

then as x rises by 1 unit, y must rise by 3 units. In general, if

$$y = c + mx \tag{A1.2}$$

where c and m are parameters (constants), then as x rises by 1 unit, y must rise by m units. In this example, m represents the slope or the gradient of the function. In general, the slope is denoted by dy/dx, so in the above example

$$\frac{dy}{dx} = m \tag{A1.3}$$

Things get a little more complicated if the function is not linear. For instance, if

$$y = x^2 \tag{A1.4}$$

the function is negatively sloped when x is negative, positively sloped when x is positive, and is absolutely flat when $x = 0$ (see Figure A1.1). Accurately to evaluate the slope of the Function (A1.4) requires a solution which proceeds as follows.

Consider a small change in x, namely an increase of Δx. This raises the left-hand side of Equation (A1.4) by Δy. Hence

$$y + \Delta y = (x + \Delta x)^2 = x^2 + 2x\Delta x + (\Delta x)^2 \tag{A1.5}$$

Subtracting Equation (A1.4) from Equation (A2.5) gives

$$\Delta y = 2x\Delta x + (\Delta x)^2 \tag{A1.6}$$

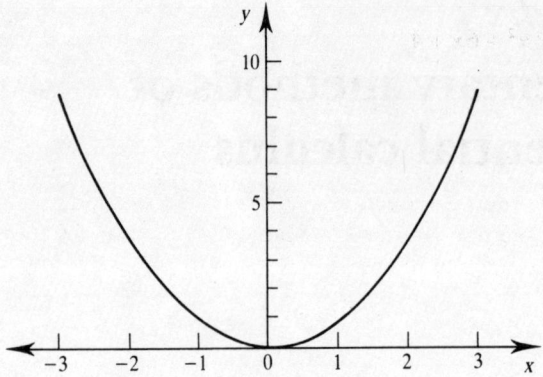

Figure A1.1 The function $y = x^2$

Dividing throughout by Δx yields

$$\frac{\Delta y}{\Delta x} = 2x + \Delta x \tag{A1.7}$$

As Δx becomes smaller and smaller, Equation (A1.7) approaches

$$\frac{dy}{dx} = 2x \tag{A1.8}$$

So the slope of Function (A1.4) equals $2x$. This clearly satisfies the requirement that the slope should be negative when x is negative, positive when x is positive, and zero when x is zero.

Consider now a somewhat more complicated function.

$$y = x^3 + 3x^2 + 4x + 2 \tag{A1.9}$$

Proceeding as before,

$$\begin{aligned} y + \Delta y &= (x + \Delta x)^3 + 3(x + \Delta x)^2 + 4(x + \Delta x) + 2 \\ &= x^3 + 3x^2\Delta x + 3x(\Delta x)^2 + (\Delta x)^3 + 3x^2 + 6x\Delta x + 3(\Delta x)^2 \\ &\quad + 4x + 4\Delta x + 2 \end{aligned} \tag{A1.10}$$

Subtracting Equation (A1.9) from Equation (A1.10) gives

$$\Delta y = 3x^2\Delta x + 3x(\Delta x)^2 + (\Delta x)^3 + 6x\Delta x + 3(\Delta x)^2 + 4\Delta x \tag{A1.11}$$

Dividing through by Δx,

$$\frac{\Delta y}{\Delta x} = 3x^2 + 3x\Delta x + (\Delta x)^2 + 6x + 3x\Delta x + 4 \tag{A1.12}$$

As Δx tends towards zero, Equation (A1.12) tends to

$$\frac{dy}{dx} = 3x^2 + 6x + 4 \tag{A1.13}$$

So the slope of Function (A1.9) equals

$$3x^2 + 6x + 4 \tag{A1.14}$$

From the examples given above, a very general rule can be deduced which can make the solution of these problems considerably easier. That rule can be stated as follows:

If $\quad y = \alpha_1 x^{\beta_1} + \alpha_2 x^{\beta_2} + \alpha_3 x^{\beta_3} + \ldots$

then

$$\frac{dy}{dx} = \alpha_1 \beta_1 x^{\beta_1 - 1} + \alpha_2 \beta_2 x^{\beta_2 - 1} + \alpha_3 \beta_3 x^{\beta_3 - 1} + \ldots$$

Hence in the first non-linear example above, where

$$y = x^2 \tag{A1.4}$$

$\alpha_1 = 1$ and $\beta_1 = 2$, with $\alpha_i = \beta_i = 0$, $i \neq 1$. So

$$\frac{dy}{dx} = \alpha_1 \beta_1 x^{\beta_1 - 1} = 2x \tag{A1.8}$$

In the second example, where

$$y = x^3 + 3x^2 + 4x + 2 \tag{A1.9}$$

$\alpha_1 = 1$, $\beta_1 = 3$, $\alpha_2 = 3$, $\beta_2 = 2$, $\alpha_3 = 4$, $\beta_3 = 1$, $\alpha_4 = 2$ and $\beta_4 = 0$. Hence

$$\frac{dy}{dx} = \alpha_1 \beta_1 x^{\beta_1 - 1} + \alpha_2 \beta_2 x^{\beta_2 - 1} + \alpha_3 \beta_3 x^{\beta_3 - 1} + \alpha_4 \beta_4 x^{\beta_4 - 1}$$

$$= 3x^2 + 6x + 4 \tag{A1.13}$$

Further examples are given below:

$y = x^3 \quad \Rightarrow \quad \dfrac{dy}{dx} = 3x^2$

$y = 2x^2 + 5x + 2 \Rightarrow \dfrac{dy}{dx} = 4x + 5$

$y = 6x + 3 + x^{-1} \Rightarrow \dfrac{dy}{dx} = 6 - x^{-2}$

It is often the case that the left-hand variable, y, depends on more than one right-hand variable, say x and z. Suppose, for instance, that

$$y = 5 + 3x^2 - 4z \tag{A1.15}$$

In such cases it is possible to find the slope of y with respect to each of the right-hand side variables separately, under the assumption that when one right-hand variable changes the other remains constant. Hence

$$\frac{\partial y}{\partial x} = 6x \quad \text{and} \quad \frac{\partial y}{\partial z} = -4 \tag{A1.16}$$

The most common use of the above techniques in economics involves the search for an optimum. A firm may need to know at what level of output it optimizes (maximizes) its profits. Clearly that level must be characterized by a situation where any increase or fall in output results in a fall in profits. It must be at a turning point on the profit–output function where the slope of the function is zero.

To illustrate the above argument, consider the function

$$y = -x^3 + 9x^2 - 15x - 10 \tag{A1.17}$$

where y denotes profits and x is output.

$$\frac{dy}{dx} = -3x^2 + 18x - 15 \tag{A1.18}$$

If profits are to be maximized, Equation (A1.18) must be set equal to zero. In other words, the profits–output function must be flat. Hence

$$-3x^2 + 18x - 15 = 0 \tag{A1.19}$$

This implies that

$$(-3x + 3)(x - 5) = 0 \tag{A1.20}$$

and so $x = 1$ or $x = 5$. Substituting back into Equation (A1.17) it is easily seen that when $x = 1$, $y = -17$, and when $x = 5$, $y = 15$. Profits are therefore maximized when $x = 5$. (They are minimized when $x = 1$.)

The act of finding the slope of a function is known as *differentiation*. The slope itself is called the *first derivative* of the function. If there exists more than one right-hand side variable in the function the method of *partial differentiation* is employed. In this instance the slopes are called *partial derivatives*.

All the methods discussed above belong to the differential calculus. A more comprehensive introduction to these methods may be found in Archibald and Lipsey (1967) or in Glass (1980).

Appendix 2
Elementary methods of matrix algebra

A matrix is an array of numbers set out in rectangular form. In general, a matrix has m rows and n columns and is therefore said to be a matrix of order m by n. If $m = n$, the matrix is a square matrix. If $m = 1$, the matrix may be known as a row vector of order n. If $n = 1$ then the matrix is said to be a column vector of order m.

Suppose that we are interested in a consumer's expenditure on beer and wine in two stores. The information may be summarized in a table thus:

	Cans of beer bought	Bottles of wine bought
Store 1	4	2
Store 2	8	1

This information could also be represented by the square matrix **A**, where

$$\mathbf{A} = \begin{bmatrix} 4 & 2 \\ 8 & 1 \end{bmatrix} \quad (A2.1)$$

A second consumer may have his purchases of wine and beer summarized by matrix **B**, where

$$\mathbf{B} = \begin{bmatrix} 3 & 4 \\ 2 & 7 \end{bmatrix} \quad (A2.2)$$

This indicates that the second consumer buys three cans of beer in store 1 and two cans in store 2. Furthermore, he buys four bottles of wine in store 1 and seven bottles in store 2.

The store-specific consumption of beer and wine by both individuals is given by matrix **C**, where

$$\mathbf{C} = \mathbf{A} + \mathbf{B} = \begin{bmatrix} 4 & 2 \\ 8 & 1 \end{bmatrix} + \begin{bmatrix} 3 & 4 \\ 2 & 7 \end{bmatrix} = \begin{bmatrix} 7 & 6 \\ 10 & 8 \end{bmatrix} \quad (A2.3)$$

This is an example of the addition of matrices. It is essential that the two matrices being added together should be of the same order. That is, they should both have the same number of rows, m, and the same number of columns, n.

Suppose now that the price of beer and the price of wine in both stores is given by the table below:

	Price (£)
Beer	0.6
Wine	2

This information could also be represented by the column vector, **D**, where

$$\mathbf{D} = \begin{bmatrix} 0.6 \\ 2 \end{bmatrix} \quad \text{(A2.4)}$$

The total revenue earned by each store from sales to the two customers in the example can be found by calculating the product **CD**. The product of two matrices, the first of which has order $m \times n$, and the second of which has order $n \times p$, is a matrix of order $m \times p$, defined so that

$$e_{ij} = \sum_k c_{ik} d_{kj} \quad \text{(A2.5)}$$

where x_{ij} is the element in the ith row and jth column of matrix **X**. Hence

$$\mathbf{E} = \mathbf{CD} = \begin{bmatrix} 7 & 6 \\ 10 & 8 \end{bmatrix} \begin{bmatrix} 0.6 \\ 2 \end{bmatrix} = \begin{bmatrix} 7 \times 0.6 + 6 \times 2 \\ 10 \times 0.6 + 8 \times 2 \end{bmatrix} = \begin{bmatrix} 16.2 \\ 22 \end{bmatrix} \quad \text{(A2.6)}$$

Therefore £16.20 is spent in Store 1 and £22 is spent in Store 2.

A matrix of particular interest to the practitioner of matrix algebra is one known as the identity matrix, which consists of ones all along the main diagonal and zeros elsewhere. The identity matrix is usually denoted by **I**, and it is unusual because any square matrix remains unchanged when post-multiplied by **I**.

For example, **CI** = **C** since

$$\begin{bmatrix} 7 & 6 \\ 10 & 8 \end{bmatrix} \begin{bmatrix} 1 & 0 \\ 0 & 1 \end{bmatrix} = \begin{bmatrix} 7 & 6 \\ 10 & 8 \end{bmatrix} \quad \text{(A2.7)}$$

For this reason, the identity matrix, **I**, is rather similar to the number one in scalar algebra (the product of any scalar, x, and one must be x itself).

While multiplication using matrices is fairly straightforward, division is not. Suppose we want to divide **B** by **C**. To do this it is necessary to multiply **B** by a matrix which is known as the inverse of **C** (in much the same way as $a/b = a \times (1/b)$ in scalar algebra). It turns out that the inverse of **C** is given by

$$\mathbf{C}^{-1} = \begin{bmatrix} -2 & 1.5 \\ 2.5 & -1.75 \end{bmatrix} \tag{A2.8}$$

We know that this is so because $\mathbf{C}^{-1}\mathbf{C} = \mathbf{I}$ since

$$\begin{bmatrix} -2 & 1.5 \\ 2.5 & -1.75 \end{bmatrix} \begin{bmatrix} 7 & 6 \\ 10 & 8 \end{bmatrix} = \begin{bmatrix} 1 & 0 \\ 0 & 1 \end{bmatrix} \tag{A2.9}$$

(A method for calculating the inverse of a 2 × 2 order matrix is given at the end of this appendix.)

To divide **B** by **C**, we must therefore 'pre-multiply' **B** by the inverse of **C**. The result is given by **F** where

$$\mathbf{F} = \mathbf{C}^{-1}\mathbf{B} = \begin{bmatrix} -2 & 1.5 \\ 2.5 & -1.75 \end{bmatrix} \begin{bmatrix} 3 & 4 \\ 2 & 7 \end{bmatrix} = \begin{bmatrix} -3 & 2.5 \\ 4 & -2.25 \end{bmatrix} \tag{A2.10}$$

It is worth noting at this stage that it is only square matrices that are capable of being inverted.

Just as the practitioner of scalar algebra is concerned with addition, multiplication, division and exponentiation, so is the practitioner of matrix algebra. The latter of these procedures involves – in scalar quantities – raising a number, x, to the power y (by multiplying x by itself y times). When working with matrices, something analogous to the square of a scalar can be computed by pre-multiplying a matrix (of any order) by its own transpose. (The transpose of a matrix is obtained by interchanging its columns and rows; consequently $a_{ij} = a'_{ji}$ where a_{ij} is the element in the ith row and jth column of Matrix **A**, and a'_{ji} is the element in the jth row and ith column of the transpose of Matrix **A**. Note that the transpose of **A** is commonly denoted **A**′.) So we may write:

$$\mathbf{G} = \mathbf{A}'\mathbf{A} = \begin{bmatrix} 4 & 8 \\ 2 & 1 \end{bmatrix} \begin{bmatrix} 4 & 2 \\ 8 & 1 \end{bmatrix} = \begin{bmatrix} 80 & 16 \\ 16 & 5 \end{bmatrix} \tag{A2.11}$$

The product of a matrix and its own transpose must be a square matrix.

Matrices can be used in problems involving the differential calculus. The method is remarkably similar to that used in scalar algebra. For instance, if $\mathbf{H} = \mathbf{G} - \mathbf{F}'\mathbf{F}$ then

$$\frac{d\mathbf{H}}{d\mathbf{F}} = 2\mathbf{F} \tag{A2.12}$$

in exactly the same way as

$$y = 6 + x^2 \Rightarrow \frac{dy}{dx} = 2x \qquad (A2.13)$$

A method for the computation of the inverse of a 2×2 order matrix was promised earlier. If

$$\mathbf{X} = \begin{bmatrix} a & b \\ c & d \end{bmatrix} \qquad (A2.14)$$

then

$$\mathbf{X}^{-1} = \begin{bmatrix} d/(ad-bc) & -b/(ad-bc) \\ -c/(ad-bc) & a/(ad-bc) \end{bmatrix} \qquad (A2.15)$$

This introduction to matrix algebra is necessarily brief. More comprehensive introductions may be found in Bradley and Meek (1986), Jeffrey (1979) and Johnston (1972).

Appendix 3
Ordinary least squares regression

In what follows the line of best fit is estimated for the general linear function:

$$Y_i = b_1 + b_2 x_{2i} + b_3 x_{3i} + \ldots + b_n x_{ni} + u_i \qquad (A3.1)$$

where the subscript i refers to the ith observation, or the ith point on the scatter diagram. The variable Y is the variable to be explained; it is known as the dependent variable or the regressand. The variables $x_2, x_3, \ldots, x_n$ are those variables which influence Y. They will be called explanatory variables, independent variables or regressors. There are n regressors including the constant (intercept) term, b_1. The constants $b_1, b_2, b_3, \ldots, b_n$, are known as coefficients. One coefficient accompanies each explanatory variable, and a further coefficient, b_1, represents the autonomous level of Y (that is, the expected level of Y if $x_2 = x_3 = \ldots = x_n = 0$). The whole point of regression analysis is to estimate the values of the coefficients $b_1, b_2, \ldots, b_n$, using known observations of the Y and x variables. It is the b coefficients that define the slope and position of the line of best fit. The term u_i represents random disturbance associated with the ith observation. Put another way, it represents the amount by which the line of best fit underestimates or overestimates the actual value of Y, given observed values of the regressors. The sum (over all observations) of the u_i terms must be zero if the estimated line truly is the line of best fit, since only thus can the expected (or mean) deviation of actual values from the estimated line be zero. It is a fundamental assumption of the ordinary least squares method that the distribution of u_i be random and normal with a zero mean. Such a distribution is known to electrical engineers, musicians and (by now) economists as 'white noise'.

Equation (A3.1) can conveniently be rewritten in matrix form. Readers unfamiliar with elementary matrix algebra may find it useful to refer to Appendix 2 at this stage. Hence

$$Y = Xb + u \qquad (A3.2)$$

where **X** is the matrix,

$$X = \begin{bmatrix} 1, & x_{12}, & x_{13}, & \ldots, & x_{1n} \\ \vdots & \vdots & \vdots & & \vdots \\ 1, & x_{i2}, & x_{i3}, & \ldots, & x_{in} \\ \vdots & \vdots & \vdots & & \vdots \\ 1, & x_{m2}, & x_{m3}, & \ldots, & x_{mn} \end{bmatrix} \tag{A3.3}$$

and where Y, b and u denote the vectors

$$Y = \begin{bmatrix} Y_1 \\ \vdots \\ Y_i \\ \vdots \\ Y_m \end{bmatrix} \qquad b = \begin{bmatrix} b_1 \\ \vdots \\ b_j \\ \vdots \\ b_n \end{bmatrix} \qquad u = \begin{bmatrix} u_1 \\ \vdots \\ u_i \\ \vdots \\ u_m \end{bmatrix} \tag{A3.4}$$

It should be noted at this stage that there must be more observations than there are explanatory variables (that is $m > n$) for regression to be possible.

Since it is usual for the statistician to work with a sample of observations taken from a larger population of obtainable data, the coefficients estimated by the regression method will, in general, be merely *estimates* of the true coefficients, and the random disturbances implied by the regression results will be merely estimates of the true extent of random disturbance. While the true relationship between Y and X is given by Equation (A3.2), then, the estimated relationship is more accurately given by

$$Y = Xb + e \tag{A3.5}$$

where b represents the vector of estimated coefficients and e is the vector of estimated random disturbances.

In order to estimate the line of best fit we must minimize the sum of the absolute value of disturbances. That is, we must minimize

$$\sum_{k=1}^{m} |e_k| \tag{A3.6}$$

In this way as much as possible of the responsibility for explaining the vector on the left-hand side is shifted away from the vector e and towards the vector b.

The problem of minimizing the sum of absolute deviations is formally equivalent to that of minimizing the sum of squared deviations,

$$\sum_{k=1}^{m} e_k^2 \qquad (A3.7)$$

and so this is what we shall proceed to do. It is for this reason that the method of regression being described here is known as ordinary least squares (OLS).

The square of the vector e is given by $e'e$, and it is this which, by means of some fairly simple matrix calculus, must be minimized. Note that, from Equation (A3.5),

$$e = Y - Xb \qquad (A3.8)$$

$$\Rightarrow e'e = (Y - Xb)'(Y - Xb) \qquad (A3.9)$$

$$= Y'Y - 2b'X'Y + b'X'Xb \qquad (A3.10)$$

The problem now becomes one of choosing the vector of b so that $e'e$ is minimized. This is done by differentiating Equation (A3.10) with respect to b and setting the result equal to zero. The first-order condition is therefore given by

$$\frac{d(e'e)}{db} = -2X'Y + 2X'Xb = 0 \qquad (A3.11)$$

(The second-order condition is satisfied since $2X'X > 0$.) Hence

$$X'Xb = X'Y \qquad (A3.12)$$

and

$$b = (X'X)^{-1}X'Y \qquad (A3.13)$$

Equation (A3.13) is fundamental. It shows that, given m observations of the dependent and explanatory variables, a fairly simple calculation yields the OLS estimates of the regression coefficients. Once the coefficients have been estimated (as in Equation (A3.13)), inferences can be made about the influence of the explanatory variables on the dependent variable, and (when there is only one variable regressor) the estimated line can be plotted on a graph. In practice, of course, the tedious manipulation of data is nowadays typically undertaken by computer. Numerous software packages exist which can perform even complicated regressions quickly – sometimes even in less than a second. Such software is easy to use and is cheap and readily available.

The above discussion has provided no more than the briefest of introductions to regression analysis. The interested student who wishes to learn more is referred to Johnston (1972), Theil (1971) or Judge et al. (1985).

Appendix 4
Profit maximization under monopoly in a two-period model

Consider the following two-period model. The monopolist wishes to maximize the net present value of its stream of profits with respect to output in each period and its first period investment decision. Hence it wishes to

$$\max J = \pi_1 + \pi_2/(1 + r) \tag{A4.1}$$

where π_i is profit in the ith period and r is the (exogenous) rate of interest. Denote by q_i and p, respectively, ith period output and price, and let $c(.)$ be the cost function. Then

$$\pi_1 = p(q_1)q_1 - c(q_1) - I \tag{A4.2}$$

where I is investment undertaken in the first period with a view to raising second period profits. Profits in the latter period are given by

$$\pi_2 = p(q_2)q_2 - c(q_2) + f(I) \tag{A4.3}$$

J is maximized with respect to q_1, q_2 and I, subject to the demand function

$$p = p(q_i) \tag{A4.4}$$

Hence,

$$J = p(q_1)q_1 - c(q_1) - I + [p(q_2)q_2 - c(q_2) + f(I)]/(1 + r) \tag{A4.5}$$

The first-order conditions are:

$$\frac{\partial J}{\partial q_1} = 0 \Rightarrow p(q_1) + q_1 p'(q_1) = c'(q_1) \tag{A4.6}$$

$$\frac{\partial J}{\partial q_2} = 0 \Rightarrow p(q_2) + q_2 p'(q_2) = c'(q_2) \tag{A4.7}$$

where a prime denotes the first derivative. There is also a condition on the level of investment, I, which requires that $J'(I) = 0$.

The key result, however, is that both Equations (A4.6) and (A4.7) imply that marginal revenue (given by the left-hand side of the equations) should *in each period* equal marginal cost (right-hand side).

References

Archibald, G. C. and Lipsey, R. G. (1967) *An Introduction to a Mathematical Treatment of Economics*, London: Weidenfeld and Nicolson.
Arize, A. (1987) 'The supply and demand for imports and exports in a simultaneous model', *Applied Economics*, 19, pp. 1233–47.
Baumol, W. (1959) *Business Behaviour, Value and Growth*, New York: Macmillan.
Baumol, W. (1977) *Economic Theory and Operations Analysis*, Englewood Cliffs, New Jersey: Prentice-Hall.
Bays, C. W. (1986) 'The determinants of hospital size: a survivor analysis', *Applied Economics*, 18, pp. 359–77.
Becker, G. S. (1976) *The Economic Approach to Human Behavior*, Chicago: University of Chicago Press.
Bradley, I. and Meek, R. L. (1986) *Matrices and Society*, Harmondsworth: Penguin.
Branson, W. H., Halttunen, H. and Masson, P. (1977) 'Exchange rates in the short run', *European Economic Review*, 10, pp. 303–24.
Corden, W. M. (1984) 'Booming sector and Dutch disease economics: survey and consolidation', *Oxford Economic Papers*, 36, pp. 359–80.
Corden, W. M. and Neary, J. P. (1982) 'Booming sector and deindustrialisation in a small open economy', *Economic Journal*, 92, pp. 825–48.
Coutts, K. J. and Cripps, T. F. (1982) *The CEPG model of the UK Economy*, Cambridge: Department of Applied Economics, University of Cambridge.
Cyert, R. M. and March, J. (1963) *A Behavioural Theory of the Firm*, Englewood Cliffs, New Jersey: Prentice-Hall.
Dantzig, G. B. (1951) 'Maximization of a linear function of variables subject to linear inequalities', in Koopmans, T. C. (ed.) *Activity Analysis in Production and Allocation*, New York: Wiley.
Deaton, A. S. (1975) 'The measurement of income and price elasticities', *European Economic Review*, 6, pp. 261–73.
Deppler, M. C. and Ripley D. M. (1978) 'The world trade model', *International Monetary Fund Staff Papers*, 25, pp. 147–206.
Economist (1975) 'Aluminium: Short slump and longer shortage', *The Economist*, 1 March, p. 64.
Economist (1987) 'Payment by lottery', *The Economist*, 4 April, pp. 83–5.

Farris, P. L. (1971) 'Export supply and demand for US cattle hides', *American Journal of Agricultural Economics*, **53**, pp. 643-6.
Frankel, M. (1973) 'Pricing decisions under unknown demand', *Kyklos*, **26**, pp. 1-24.
Friedman, M. (1957) *A Theory of the Consumption Function*, Princeton: Princeton University Press.
Fuss, M. and McFadden, D. (1978) *Production Economics: a Dual Approach to Theory and Applications*, vol. 1 and 2, Amsterdam: North-Holland.
Glass, J. C. (1980) *An Introduction to Mathematical Methods in Economics*, Maidenhead: McGraw-Hill.
Gudgin, G. (ed.) (1988) *Regional Economic Prospects*, Cambridge: Cambridge Econometrics and Northern Ireland Economic Research Centre.
Hall, M. (1968) 'Sales revenue maximisation: a reply', *Journal of Industrial Economics*, **17**, pp. 78-81.
Halter, A. N. and Dean, G. W. (1971) *Decisions Under Uncertainty*, Cincinnati: South-Western Publishing Co.
Hayes, K. (1987) 'Cost structure of the water utility industry', *Applied Economics*, **19**, pp. 417-25.
Heathfield, D. and Wibe, S. (1987) *An Introduction to Cost and Production Functions*, Basingstoke: Macmillan.
Houthakker, H. S. and Magee, S. P. (1969) 'Income and price elasticities in world trade', *Review of Economics and Statistics*, **51**, pp. 111-25.
Houthakker, H. S. and Taylor, L. D. (1966) *Consumer Demand in the United States, 1929-1970: Analyses and Projections*, Cambridge, Mass.: Harvard University Press.
Jeffrey, A. (1979) *Mathematics for Engineers and Scientists*, Walton-on-Thames: Nelson.
Johnes, G. and Haycox, A. (1986) 'Cost structures in a large hospital for the mentally handicapped', *Social Science and Medicine*, **22**, pp. 605-10.
Johnston, J. (1960) *Statistical Cost Analysis*, New York: McGraw-Hill.
Johnston, J. (1972) *Econometric Methods*, Tokyo: McGraw-Hill.
Jorgenson, D. W. and Stephenson, J. A. (1969) 'Anticipation and investment behavior in US manufacturing, 1947-60', *Journal of the American Statistical Association*, **64**, pp. 67-89.
Judge, G. G., Griffiths, W. E., Hill, R. C., Lutkepohl, H. and Lee, T. (1985) *The Theory and Practice of Econometrics*, New York: Wiley.
Kagel, J. H., Battalio, R. C., Rachlin, H., Green, L., Basmann, R. L. and Klemm, W. R. (1975) 'Experimental studies of consumer demand behavior using laboratory animals', *Economic Inquiry*, **13**, pp. 22-38.
Kossentos, K. (1973) *Production Functions for UK Manufacturing Industry*, unpublished MA dissertation, University of Lancaster.
Kuznets, S. (1946) *National Product Since 1945*, New York: National Bureau of Economic Research.
Lancaster, K. (1966) 'Change and innovation in the technology of consumption', *American Economic Review*, **56**, pp. 14-23.
Laver, M. (1980) 'The great British wage game', *New Society*, **51**, pp.495-6.

Layard, P. R. G. and Nickell, S. J. (1986) 'Unemployment in Britain', in Bean, C., Layard, P. R. G. and Nickell, S. J. (eds.) *The Rise in Unemployment*, Oxford: Blackwell.

Levich, R. M. (1985) 'Empirical studies of exchange rates', in Jones, R. W. and Kenen, P. B. (eds.) *Handbook of International Economics*, vol. 2, Amsterdam: North-Holland, pp. 979–1040.

Luce, R. D. and Raiffa, H. (1957) *Games and Decisions*, New York: Wiley.

Marby, B. D. and Siders, D. L. (1967) 'An empirical test of the sales maximisation hypothesis', *Southern Economic Journal*, 33, pp. 37–8.

Marris, R. (1963) 'A model of the managerial enterprise', *Quarterly Journal of Economics*, 77, pp. 185–209.

McCallum, J. (1986) 'Unemployment in OECD countries in the 1980s', *Economic Journal*, 96, pp. 942–60.

Ministry of Agriculture Fisheries and Food (1974) *Report of the National Food Survey Committee*, London: HMSO.

Mizon, G. E. (1977) 'Inferential procedures in non-linear models: an application in a UK industrial cross-section study of factor substitution and returns to scale', *Econometrica*, 45, pp. 1221–42.

National Economic Development Office (1974) *The increased cost of energy – implications for UK industry*, London: NEDO.

Parkin, M. (1970) 'Incomes policy: some further results on the determination of the rate of change of money wages', *Economica*, 37, pp. 386–401.

Peston, M. (1959) 'On the sales maximisation hypothesis', *Economica*, 26, pp. 128–36.

Peston, M. and Coddington, A. (1967) *The Elementary Ideas of Game Theory*, London: HMSO, reprinted in Townsend, H. (ed.) (1980) *Price Theory*, Harmondsworth: Penguin.

Phillips, A. W. (1958) 'The relation between unemployment and the rate of change of money wage rates in the UK 1861–1957', *Economica*, 25, pp. 283–99.

Radford, R. A. (1945) 'The economic organization of a POW camp', *Economica*, 12, pp. 189–201.

Renton, G. A. (ed.) (1975) *Modelling the Economy*, London: Heinemann.

Sachs, J. D. (1981) 'The current account and macroeconomic adjustment in the 1970s', *Brookings Papers on Economic Activity*, 12, pp. 201–68.

Scott, D. (1987) 'UK economic forecasts: a comparative survey', *Business Information Review*, 4, pp. 3–23.

Shipley, D. D. (1981) 'Pricing objectives in British manufacturing industry', *Journal of Industrial Economics*, 29, pp. 429–44.

Sinclair, M. T. and Sutcliffe, C. M. S. (1982) 'Keynesian income multipliers with first and second round effects: an application to tourist expenditure', *Oxford Bulletin of Economics and Statistics*, 44, pp. 321–38.

Smith D. (1978) 'The demand for alternative monies in the UK 1924–77', *National Westminster Bank Review*, pp. 34–49.

Theil, H. (1971) *Principles of Econometrics*, New York: Wiley.

Tobin, J. (1950) 'A statistical demand function for food in the USA', *Journal of*

the *Royal Statistical Society A*, **113**, pp. 113–41.
Wallis, K. (ed.) (1985) *Models of the UK Economy*, 2nd edn, Oxford: Oxford University Press.
Wallis, K. (1989) 'Macroeconomic forecasting: a survey', *Economic Journal*, **99**, pp. 28–61.
Wetmore, J. M. (1959) 'Policies for expanding the demand for farm food products in the United States', *University of Minnesota Technical Bulletin 231*, Minneapolis.
Williamson, O. (1963) 'Managerial discretion and business behaviour', *American Economic Review*, **53**, pp. 1032–57.

Index

accelerator, 146, 196, 219
adaptive expectations, 192–4
advertising, 2, 31, 40, 44–5, 47, 118–20, 137
aggregate demand, 153–4, 181–2, 188–9
aggregate supply, 184–6, 189
aluminium, 23–4
average cost, 87, 90–2, 109–15
average product of labour, 95–6
average revenue, 101–3, 104–17

balance of payments, 203–15
barriers to entry, 106–14
Bayes–Laplace criterion, 134, 226–7
beer, demand for, 51–2
behavioural theory, 231, 237–43
Blackburn Rovers, 31
bliss point, 68–9, 75, 77–8
bonds, 162
Bretton Woods, 201, 206, 209
budget constraint, 48, 50, 62–4, 68, 70–1, 75–7, 80
budget deficit, 172

calculus, 11, 247–50
capital, 87, 96–9, 146
cattle, 15, 17–18, 28, 138
Channel tunnel, 97
characteristics of goods, 47–51
Cobb–Douglas, 55–8, 64–5, 67, 73, 222–3
collusion, 128, 135–7
Common Agricultural Policy, 19–20
complements, 14, 31, 32, 56–7
computers, 6, 8, 39, 62, 66, 81, 82, 86, 217, 245, 257
consumption, 145–52
consumption technology, 36, 47–51
corner solution, 76
cross price demand curve, 32
cross price elasticity of demand, 30–2, 140
cross section data, 37

decision analysis, 6, 131–7, 226–7
demand, 2, 4, 10–15, 33–4, 63–4, 107–17, 224–5
dependent variable, 38, 39, 255
dirty float, 212
disposable income, 145
dual, 96, 182
duopoly, 127–31
Dutch disease, 202–3
dynamic games, 216
dynamic multiplier, 159–60

economies of scale, 88
elasticity, 25–35, 116–18, 135, 162, 178, 200, 209, 212–13
electricity price, 120–1
Engel curve, 32, 213
environment of the firm, 2, 127, 131–7
equilibrium, 19, 147, 150, 152, 164, 168–9, 174–5, 211
European Community, 19
exchange rate, 3, 143, 200–15
explanatory variable, 39, 255
exports, 148–9, 199–215
external effects, 20–1

fixed cost, 88, 92–4
foodstuffs, demand for, 34–5
forecasting, 140, 217–30
foreign trade, 199–215
full information maximum likelihood, 41
futures market, 201–2

Gabor–Granger test, 36, 45–6
game theory, 5, 126–31
general equilibrium, 4
Giffen good, 5, 26, 60–1
government expenditure, 148–53

hospitals, costs in, 99–100
hot money, 214
Hurwicz criterion, 133

265

identification problem, 41–2
imports, 148–9, 199–215
income elasticity of demand, 30–1, 140, 209, 212–13
indifference curve, 62–4, 67, 70–1, 73, 75, 82
inferior good, 13–14, 31, 32, 60–1, 63, 145
inflation, 2, 4, 97, 140, 162–3, 187–98
information, 20, 21, 105, 180
injections, 147–50, 152, 155, 168, 173–4
inputs, 5, 56–62, 66, 87, 110
interest rates, 3, 4, 97–9, 142, 143, 162–77
internal rate of return, 98–9
International Monetary Fund, 201
investment, 6, 123, 141, 145–52
IS curve, 167–77, 181–2
isocost line, 58–60, 66, 68, 71, 88–90, 141
isopresent-value curve, 236–7
isoprobability subjective sales curve, 124–6
isoprofit rate curve, 123–6
isoquant, 56–62, 66, 67, 71, 73, 82, 88–90, 141

Kuhn–Tucker conditions, 79–81, 85
Kuznets puzzle, 155–8

labour, 87, 180–98
Lagrangian function, 66–81, 223
Lagrangian multiplier, 69–81, 85
law of diminishing marginal utility, 12, 57, 62
law of diminishing productivity, 57, 88, 139, 182
line of best fit, 37–8, 213, 255
linear programming, 66, 81–6
liquidity preference, 162–77
listeria, 14
LM curve, 167–77, 181–2, 214
long run, 65, 87, 88–92

M0, 161
M3, 161
Manx kippers, 10
marginal analysis, 11, 103–4
marginal cost, 76, 89–92, 108–17, 233–4
marginal cost pricing, 112, 114
marginal product of labour, 95–6, 182
marginal propensity to consume, 145, 148, 155, 156, 158
marginal revenue, 101–5, 108–17, 234
marginal utility, 11–13, 70, 76
market demand curve, 14–15
market failure, 20
market share, 1, 232, 239
market supply curve, 17
mark-up pricing, 196, 219
marriage, 1
Marshall–Lerner condition, 200, 207, 213
matrix algebra, 251–7

maximin, 129, 132–3
maximax, 133
maximum principle, 216
minimax regret, 134–5
misspecification, 39–40, 42
money illusion, 191–2, 211
money-market, 161–79, 181
money stock, 143, 162–77, 207, 214
Monopolies and Mergers Commission, 71, 107, 114
monopoly, 106, 113–20
monopsony, 115, 117–18
multicollinearity, 40–1
multiplier, 148, 150–1, 154, 156, 159, 165, 170, 179

national income, 3, 140, 144–55, 162–3, 188, 205
natural rate of unemployment, 192
noise, 4, 255
non-co-operation, 128
nonlinear programming, 5, 66, 75–81
normal good, 32, 63
normal profit, 103

objective function, 1, 16, 17, 53, 54, 82, 103, 237–8, 243, 244
oil price, 3, 135–7, 140, 203
oligopoly, 2, 5, 107
opportunity cost, 16–17, 134
optimization, 53–86
options, 202
ordinary least squares, 38, 43, 220–4, 255–7
own price elasticity of demand, 26–30, 116–18, 135, 209, 212–13, 225
overheads, 92–4

payoff matrix, 126–35, 225–6
perfect competition, 2, 105–6, 107–13
permanent income hypothesis, 157–8, 219
Phillips curve, 186–98, 219
present value analysis, 96–9, 234–7
price, 1, 10, 18–22, 101, 108–18, 140, 143
price discrimination, 116–18
principal components, 41
product differentiation, 107, 113
product market, 143–60, 167–75, 181
production function, 5, 54–6, 64–5, 67, 73, 80, 184, 222–3
productivity, 5, 88, 94–6, 186, 208
profit, 2, 53, 93–4, 225–6
profit maximization, 2, 53, 103, 107–20, 216
purchasing power parity, 208–9, 211

rational expectations, 192–4, 219, 239
rationing, 71–3
rats, 1

regression analysis, 5, 15, 33, 36–44, 176, 215, 216, 220–4, 255–7
regret table, 134
research and development, 88, 238, 240, 244
returns to scale, 88, 223
ridge estimator, 41
risk, 5, 97, 122–31

sales revenue maximization, 1, 29–30, 103, 231–7
salmonella, 14
satisficing, 238–9, 244
saving, 7, 145–52
scatter diagram, 37–8
shadow price, 69
short run, 65, 87, 88–92
shortage, 19
simplex, algorithm, 82–5
simultaneous equations, bias, 41, 42
slack payment, 240, 242
spot market, 202
stagflation, 190–3
statistical demand function, 4, 36–52
stock-market crash, 4, 162–3
stocks, 18, 147, 153
subsidies, 19, 209
substitutes, 14, 31, 32, 56–7, 118
supernormal profit, 103, 109–11, 114, 128, 208, 232–4

supply, 10, 15–18, 107–12
surplus, 19

tariff, 209, 211
tax, 19, 148–52
test market, 36, 44–5
three stage least squares, 41
time series data, 37
total cost, 87, 96, 223–4, 232–3
total product of labour, 94–6
total revenue, 29–30, 93–4, 101–4, 225, 232–3
total utility, 11–13
trade-off model of demand, 36, 47–51
two stage least squares, 41

uncertainty, 5, 122, 131–7
unemployment, 3, 140, 187–98
user cost of capital, 73
utility, 10, 11–13, 49, 62, 67, 82

variable cost, 92–4
velocity of circulation, 164

wage, 2, 73, 143, 180–98
welfare economics, 4, 21, 112–13
withdrawals, 147–50, 152, 155, 168, 174

Consultancy Considerations

Objectives:
1. Market share / profit?   Diverse
   Max profit
2. Competition / Specialist market
3. Dependence / self reliance — Certainty — develop ratio
4. Structure for variable macro economy
   - National income
   - Price levels — optimal
   - Unemployment mature
   - Gov. Policies — Taxes

5. Market buoyancy